Phototherapy and Therapeutic Photography in a Digital Age

The digital age has brought about a worldwide evolution of phototherapy and therapeutic photography. This book provides a foundation in both phototherapy and therapeutic photography and describes recent developments.

Phototherapy and Therapeutic Photography in a Digital Age is divided into three parts: in the first, an introduction and overviews from different perspectives; in the second, approaches and contexts, including phototherapy, re-enactment phototherapy, community phototherapy, self-portraiture and family photography. This is followed by a conclusion looking at the future of phototherapy and therapeutic photography in terms of theory, practice and research.

The book is for anyone interested in the therapeutic use of photographs. It will be of particular interest to psychological therapists and especially psychotherapists, counsellors, psychologists and art therapists, as well as photographers and others wishing to explore further the use of photographs therapeutically within their existing practices.

Del Loewenthal is Director of the Research Centre for Therapeutic Education, Department of Psychology, Roehampton University. He is also in private practice as a psychotherapist, photographer and counselling psychologist in Wimbledon and Brighton. He is founding editor of the *European Journal of Psychotherapy and Counselling* and former Chair of the United Kingdom Council for Psychotherapy Research Committee.

Phototherapy and Therapeutic Photography in a Digital Age

Edited by
Del Loewenthal

LONDON AND NEW YORK

First published 2013
by Routledge
27 Church Road, Hove, East Sussex BN3 2FA

Simultaneously published in the USA and Canada
by Routledge
711 Third Avenue, New York, NY 10017

Routledge is an imprint of the Taylor & Francis Group, an informa business

British Library Cataloguing in Publication Data
A catalogue record for this book is available from the British Library

Library of Congress Cataloging in Publication Data
Phototherapy and therapeutic photography in a digital age/edited by
Del Loewenthal.
   p.cm.
   Includes bibliographical references and index.
   I. Loewenthal, Del, 1947–.
   [DNLM: 1. Photography. 2. Psychotherapy – methods.
   3. Mental Disorders – therapy.   WM 450.5.P5]
   615.8'31 – dc23
   2012029448

ISBN: 978-0-415-66735-7 (hbk)
ISBN: 978-0-415-66736-4 (pbk)
ISBN: 978-0-203-07069-7 (ebk)

Typeset in Times New Roman and Gill Sans
by Florence Production Ltd, Stoodleigh, Devon

Printed and bound in Great Britain by
TJ International Ltd, Padstow, Cornwall

This book is dedicated to
Roberto Brunini (1954–2011)

Contents

Illustrations

Contributors

Brigitte Anor, Jerusalem, Israel is an expressive art therapist and the Founder of the Photo Therapy Institute in Jerusalem, which is a three-year programme that is built upon Brigitte's belief that both the use of the camera and the photographic image itself have the power to generate an emotional experience that itself can foster personal, inter-personal and professional growth. Brigitte teaches in the Institute in Jerusalem and at the Tel-Aviv University. She has also taught workshops in other locations in Israel and in Europe. The theme of her doctoral thesis was 'The different roles of photographic images in the narration of our lives: From submission to rebellion.' As an expressive art therapist, Brigitte stresses the significance of the potential of photography as a springboard for a dialogue with the different art therapies and trains professionals who wish to transform photography into a therapeutic tool in various applications.

Rodolfo de Bernart, Florence, Italy is a Professor of Family Therapy in Psychiatry Specialization at the University of Siena. He founded the Instituto di Terapia Familiare di Firenze ('Institute of Family Therapy of Florence') in 1981 and has since then used – and trained other psychotherapists to use – visual arts (especially photos and cinema) in therapy in his Institute and in its network of thirty-four Institutes all over Italy, as well as during many international conferences. He has written more than 200 papers and some books in Italian, English, French and Spanish. He is editor of *Mediazione Familiare Sistemica*, and member of the board of the most important *Journal of Family Therapy* and *Journal of Family Psychotherapy*. He served as treasurer of EFTA–TIC (European Family Therapy Association,Training Institute Chamber) as President of EAP, SITF, AIMS and FIAP, and is currently Member of the EFTA Board and Vice President Past President of EAP (European Association for Psychotherapies).

Terry Dennett has curated the Jo Spence Memorial Archive London for sixteen years. In another life he is a Fellow of the Royal Anthropological Institute with a special interest in urban crisis and social exclusion. Currently he is also President of the Association for Historical and Fine Art Photography. In his curatorial role, Dennett continues to assist students worldwide who are interested in Jo Spence and her therapeutic concerns.

Ulla Halkola is a psychotherapist and an organisation developer. She has worked as an Education Coordinator for the Training and Developing Centre Brahea at the University of Turku for twenty two years, organising courses in the fields of psychotherapy, mental health, health-promoting and organisational development. She has trained in phototherapy since the year 2000 in Finland and other countries and been a chairperson for two organising committees for International congresses on Phototherapy and Therapeutic Photography. She is one of the founding members and the first Chairperson (2004–06) of the Finnish Phototherapy Association and a member of the Finnish Art Photographers' Union. In January 2009 *The Therapeutic Power of Photography* was published by Duodecim Medical Publications Ltd of which she is one of the editors. www.spectrovisio.net.

Hasse Karlsson is a Professor of Integrative Neuroscience and Psychiatry at the University of Turku and Chief Physician at the Turku University Central Hospital, Department of Psychiatry. He is the Director of Turku Brain and Mind Centre. In the field of psychotherapy, he has specialised in brief dynamic psychotherapy and in interpersonal psychotherapy, and conducted functional neuroimaging studies of the brain on emotion regulation and on changes induced by psychotherapy. Hasse is also Editor-in-Chief of the *Nordic Journal of Psychiatry* and has written about 120 scientific articles, of which around seventy are in international peer-reviewed journals, and has contributed and co-authored several books on philosophy of medicine, psychotherapy and other topics. One of the books he has edited is a book on philosophy of psychiatry: *Mielen malleja. Psykiatrian tieteenteorian uusia kysymyksiä*, Yliopistopaino, Helsinki 1994 (*Models of Mind – Emerging problems in the theory of science in psychiatry*).

Keith Kennedy taught for five years in secondary schools in Enfield Wash and Tottenham before breaking out and working as a paid helpmate in a range of educational establishments. His interest in play-ways of learning stood him in good stead for doing this, as all ages need to play, and even learn from time to time. Though he trained to be a drama teacher, his preference for the school film rather than school play soon developed into a commitment to using film in all of his varied practices. Working out of the Hornsey College of Art's teacher-training department, he and his students conducted full-scale projects in a number of London hospitals, including the Middlesex and the Henderson. The latter he considers to have been the finest teaching unit of the many in which he worked. In our present 'dumbed-down' days we go sadly in want of such institutions.

Alexander Kopytin obtained a degree in Psychiatry in 1984 and worked in various psychiatric institutions in St Petersburg. He obtained a certificate in Psychotherapy and introduced art psychotherapy in his work with patients from 1995, primarily using group interactive art therapy. He has been teaching psychotherapy and art psychotherapy since 1996. In 2002 he developed the first post-graduate diploma course in art therapy in Russia, which has been taught ever since in St Petersburg. He has been Chair of the Russian Art Therapy Association (established in 1997) and Chief Editor of *Healing Art: International Art Therapy Journal* (published in Russian) since 1997, and Vice-Chair of the Section of Art and Psychiatry, World Psychiatric Association since 2006. He has written and edited over twenty-five books on various aspects of the theory and practice of art therapy, phototherapy/photo-art therapy including *Techniques of Phototherapy* (St Petersburg: Rech, 2010) and *Art Therapy of Mental Disorders* (St Petersburg: Rech, 2011).

Del Loewenthal is Professor of Psychotherapy and Counselling and Director of the Research Centre for Therapeutic Education at the University of Roehampton where he also convenes doctoral programmes. He is an analytic psychotherapist, chartered psychologist and photographer. Del is founding editor of the *European Journal of Psychotherapy and Counselling* (Routledge). His publications include *Post-Existentialism and the Psychological Therapies: Towards a Therapy without Foundations* (Karnac, 2011) and, co-edited with Richard House, *Critically Engaging CBT* (Open University Press, 2010), *Childhood, Wellbeing and a Therapeutic Ethos* Karnac, Books, 2009) and *Against and For CBT* (PCCS Books, 2008). He is also the author of *Case Studies in Relational Research* (Palgrave Macmillan, 2007), *What is Psychotherapeutic Research?* with David Winter (Karnac, 2006) and *Postmodernism for Psychotherapists* co-edited with Robert Snell (Routledge, 2003). Del has a small private practice in Brighton and Wimbledon. www.delloewenthal.com.

Rosy Martin is an artist–photographer, psychological therapist, workshop leader, lecturer and writer. She works both as an artist–photographer using self-portraiture, still life photography, digital imaging and video, and as a psychological therapist exploring the relationships between photography, memory, identities and unconscious processes. From 1983, with Jo Spence, she pioneered re-enactment phototherapy. She has published widely and exhibited internationally since 1985; her books include *Ageing Femininities: Troubling representations* (2012) and *Stilled* (2005). She has run intensive experiential workshops and lectured in universities and galleries throughout Britain, Canada, Eire, Finland and the USA. She has held lecturer positions in photographic theory, art history and visual culture at universities in the UK. She was a consultant researcher in a multidisciplinary team on 'Representing self, representing ageing' at Sheffield University. Rosy is a psychological therapist in private practice.

Cristina Nuñez is a Spanish artist–photographer and, as she calls herself, a 'therapeutic self-portrait facilitator': since 2005 she has taught her method *The Self-Portrait Experience®* in Italy, Spain, Finland, Germany, Luxemburg, Canada and the US, in prisons, mental health institutions, museums, art and photography schools and companies. Her artwork has been published and shown around the world since 1995, at the Mois de la Photo in Montreal 2011, Rencontres de la Photographie d'Arles, Palazzo Reale in Milan, Casino of Luxemburg, Palazzo Vecchio in Florence, Festival FotoGrafia in Rome and the Museum of Contemporary Photography in Cinisello, Milan. Her book *Someone to Love*, her autobiography in self-portraits and her complete self-portrait method, has been published by Private Space Books in Barcelona, Spain. www.self-portrait.eu.

Carmine Parrella is a psychologist and a psychotherapist. Since 1992, he has used creative visual approaches through photo and video for rehabilitation, prevention and therapy in the Public Centre for Mental Health, ASL2 Piana di Lucca, Italy. Here, he uses photo and video as potential mediators of socio-therapeutic processes where the focus is on the personal growth process and the empowerment of the creative skills of the community.

Mike Simmons is a photographic artist and educator, with research interests in developing new approaches to exploring issues of social concern through the application of creative photography, with particular emphasis on the themes of loss, memory and identity. He has contributed to numerous exhibitions, conferences and symposia in the UK, Europe, Australia and the USA. IIe is leader of the taught Masters programme in Photography and part of the Photographic Studies and Creative Imaging research group at De Montfort University, Leicester.

Mark Wheeler is an art psychotherapist and systemic practitioner working in the NHS and private practice. Mark engages families and individuals in conversations with photographs (prints, mobile phone images, or substitute). He teaches trainees and qualified practitioners as well as undergraduates. Mark was the first British photography graduate to undertake postgraduate Art Therapy training. His dissertation (1992) was 'Phototherapy: The use of photographs in art therapy', for which he interviewed Judy Weiser and plundered her library. Mark continues to make and exhibit photographs. In 2004 he was made a Fellow of the Royal Photographic Society. www.phototherapy.org.uk

Julia Winckler is a Senior Lecturer in Photography at the University of Brighton, School of Art in Media. Her research interests bring together knowledge gained from degrees in African Studies and Anthropology (University of Toronto); social work (University of Toronto) and photography (University of Brighton). Much of her work is concerned with archives of memory: projects include *Retracing Heinrich Barth*; *Two Sisters*; *Leaving Atlantis* and *Traces*. Julia has written about her long-standing use of participatory photography as a tool for social change in the book chapter 'Connecting self and the world: "image-ing" the community' for *Through Our Eyes: My light* (2008, Robert H.N. Ho Foundation, Hong Kong); her collaborative phototherapy practice is discussed in 'Acts of embodiment: explorations of collaborative phototherapy', co-authored with Stephanie Conway, for *Wild Fire: Art as activism*, Deborah Barndt (ed.) 2006, Sumach Press.

Acknowledgements

Many thanks to so many people for enabling me to develop this book on *Phototherapy and Therapeutic Photography in a Digital Age*, furthering my interests in psychotherapy and photography.

First, my thanks to all the contributors of this book whom I have the fortune to know personally and from whom I have learned so much. Also, my thanks to previous pioneers of phototherapy and therapeutic photography, in particular Jo Spence and Linda Bergman from the UK and also, from North America, all of whom I have been privileged to meet, Judy Weiser, David Krauss and Joel Walker.

I would particularly like to acknowledge the European Union's Leonardo da Vinci Lifelong Learning Partnership Programme, funding our PHOTOTHERAPYEUROPE project, which led to this book's focus on European developments. Special thanks to the leaders of the various European organisations that made up this project team: Ulla Halkola and Tarja Koffert from the University of Turku, Finland; Leena Koulu and Pirkko Pehunen from the Finnish Phototherapy Association; and Carmine Parrella from the Mental Health Centre in Lucca, Italy. My thanks to all those people too numerous to mention with whom I had such important meetings in these different countries.

I would like, however, to mention one of them, Roberto Brunini, photographer of the Mental Health Centre in Lucca, to whom this book is dedicated in recognition of his part, and thereby potentially all our parts, in developing individual and community health through phototherapy.

My further thanks to the team I led from the Research Centre for Therapeutic Education (RCTE) at Roehampton University, London, UK, namely, Christine Wells, Di Thomas, Michael Chanan, Sophie Hamilton, Tom Cotton and in particular the technical help received throughout from Martin Evans.

Further thanks to all those at Routledge and in particular Kate Hawes, Joanne Forshaw and Camilla Barnard for their encouragement and patience. Also, last but not least my thanks to Betty Bertrand-Godfrey and Joanna Gee from the RCTE and Jane Loewenthal for their help in getting this book together.

Permissions

Extracts from the following are reproduced with the kind permission of the publishers, Taylor & Francis, UK:

1: Del Loewenthal (2009). Editorial. *European Journal of Psychotherapy & Counselling*, 11(1), 1–6.
    Del Loewenthal (2010). Picture book. *Every Child Journal*, 1(3), 10–12.
2: Ulla Halkola (2009). A photograph as a therapeutic experience. *European Journal of Psychotherapy and Counselling*, 11(1), 21–33.
3: Terry Dennett (2009). Jo Spence's camera therapy: Personal therapeutic photography as a response to adversity. *European Journal of Psychotherapy and Counselling*, 11(1), 7–19.
4: Mark Wheeler (2009). Photo-psycho-praxis. *European Journal of Psychotherapy and Counselling*, 11(1), 63–76.
6: Rosy Martin (2009). Inhabiting the image: Photography, therapy and re-enactment phototherapy. *European Journal of Psychotherapy and Counselling*, 11(1), 35–49.
8: Cristina Nuñez (2009) The self-portrait, a powerful tool for self-therapy. *European Journal of Psychotherapy and Counselling*, 11(1), 51–61.
Epilogue: Brigitte Anor (2001) Hands up: Surrendering to subjectivity. *Poiesis: A Journal of the Arts and Communication*, 3, 89–92.

Photograph credits

Cover: Del Loewenthal
Prologue: The photograph – Keith Kennedy
1: Alice's warts – Del Loewenthal; Jani's photo – Mervi Rutanen
2: Ulla Halkola
3: Terry Dennett
4: Mark Wheeler
5: Mike Simmons
6: Rosy Martin/S
7: Ulla Halkola
8: Cristina Nuñez
9: Del Loewenthal
11: Daniel and Amber – Holly Oliver; Back to a time – Richard Clayton
12: Alexander Kopytin
Epilogue: Hands up! – Brigitte Anor; Warsaw ghetto – courtesy of the United States Holocaust Memorial Museum Photo Archives

Photo 0.1 The photograph (Kennedy).

See: www.horvatland.com/images/entrevues/mccullin-03.jpg.

Prologue

'The photograph'[1]

Keith Kennedy

See me, looking at you. Sitting here in my window, trying to catch your eye.

A man just stopped in front of me, looked, and spoke to a woman behind him: 'There's a smack in the eye for you.' But, she sailed by with hardly a glance. Probably, she was looking for truth in beauty, and I can only be one of those things. But he took in every inch of me, I'm pleased to say.

I am a photograph. I am here to be stared at.

Once, I was just a frame in a roll of film and might have become a happier image. But, no luck there, given where I was taken. Biafra, 1971. Most of all, given whose camera did the taking. A great, white hunter of sorts. I was dedicated, one fine day – CLICK! – I was born. Mother and child! I suppose it was luck of sorts. We were waiting for him. He didn't have to say 'Cheese'.

Am I a work of art? Really, I hope not. Art's for easy-going times, yes? So, ignore my fancy surroundings. *Moi, je suis la guerre.*

'Obscene!' said a little old lady, earlier. Maybe, because *I feel that*, too, and it's a bad feeling – so, what's the point of my being here?

I am a photograph on a wall, looking at you looking at me and – why? There can be only one question that really counts: Have you a space for us in your family album? Paste us in, please.

Note

1 Don McCullin told me that this image is one he would always keep. See my sketch of his photograph of a stricken mother and child where she is offering her withered breast to her emaciated offspring (Photo 0.1).

Part I

Introduction

Theories and approaches

Chapter 1

Introducing phototherapy and therapeutic photography in a digital age

Del Loewenthal

Phototherapy and therapeutic photography

'What is photography for? Can it change our minds?' So starts a review (Dalley, 2008) applauding the power of photography in a Parisian exhibition on sustainable developments and environmental issues (The International Prix Pictet Exhibition – Palais de Tokyo, Paris, Oct./Nov., 2008). This book considers whether the therapeutic use of photographs could also be powerful in facilitating sustainable personal developments through various professional practices.

Certainly, the cultural importance of photographs has been well located elsewhere (for example Barthes, 1980; Sontag, 1990). Freud used photographs in psychoanalysis in order to caution his over-enthusiastic disciples and to remind them of their task. It is said that he had two photographs on his desk: one, of a patient looking 'well, hopeful and healthy' at the commencement of therapy, and the other at the end of therapy looking 'dejected, depressed and beaten by life' (Symington, 1986: 25). Freud also encouraged his patients to bring him their dreams. So would it be helpful for them to bring us their photographs?

Importantly, we are now in the digital era where the growth of digital photography, including mini movies and mobile phone cameras, together with the rapid use of photography on social networking sites such as Facebook, Flickr, YouTube and Twitter, ensure that phototherapy and its related practices now present a potentially major opportunity, not just for the older person, who still may have a family album, but as a vital way of engaging with the preferred technology of younger generations.

One impetus for this book was the first International Conference on Phototherapy and Therapeutic Photography to be held outside North America, which took place in Finland (June 2008). Following European Pioneers (see Spence, 1986 and Berman, 1993), much of the subsequent development of phototherapy has taken place in North America (e.g. Judy Weiser, David Krauss and Joel Walker). More recently, however, there have been developments in Europe, particularly the United Kingdom, and there have been further innovations, particularly in Finland, as well as in such countries as Italy, Israel, Germany, Lithuania, Spain, Russia and the Netherlands.

The First International Phototherapy Symposium was held in the United States of America in 1979. Psychologist Judy Weiser, who was involved then, suggests in her book *PhotoTherapy Techniques* (1999), that photographs can be used as therapeutic tools. She delineates five main techniques:

- the projective process, which is about 'using photographic images to explore clients' perceptions, values and expectations' (Weiser, 1999: ix);
- working with self-portraits in order to enable clients to understand the images they make of themselves;
- seeing other perspectives, which enable clients to examine photographs taken of them by others;
- metaphors of self-construction, which is looking at ways of reflecting on photographs taken or collected by the client;
- photo systems, which are ways of reviewing family albums and photo-biographical collections.

Finally, to take her last chapter heading, she argues for phototherapy as promoting healing and personal growth. Indeed, many of the chapters in this book suggest a more humanistic location for many involved with this work, even though an initial primacy is given to projective techniques. However, an important more psychoanalytic rendering is provided by the pioneering work of Linda Berman in *Beyond the Smile* (1993), whose influence will also be found in these pages.

For readers not familiar with phototherapy and therapeutic photography, I am going to take the unusual step for me of briefly describing my experiences of undertaking some phototherapy workshops at that conference in 2008. I am an academic, analytic psychotherapist and counselling psychologist with an interest in continental philosophy, who previously trained as a humanistic counsellor and subsequently completed a degree in photography. I had also previously turned down the opportunity to use photographs to work on myself as I had felt it to be somewhat unsafe. However, through my interest in continental philosophy, the work of Merleau-Ponty, who gave primacy to perception, comes to mind when discussing phototherapy. He states, 'our perception ends in objects, and the object once constituted, appears as the reason for all the experiences of it which we have had or could have' (Merleau-Ponty, 1962: 67). He may provide an explanation of how phototherapy works in stating that 'The present still holds on to the immediate past without positing it as an object, and since the immediate past similarly holds its immediate predecessor, past time is wholly collected up and grasped in the present' (Merleau-Ponty, 1962: 69).

The first workshop I attended was by Judy Weiser. The photograph I chose, which called to me, was of a wall falling down. Working in our triads, I was amazed how quickly this related to my life at that moment in time. Similarly, other people soon got in touch with what was troubling them in their lives. Judy defined what she originally termed 'phototherapy' as the use of photographs within what we would take to be a more traditional counselling/psychotherapy session. (Other approaches seem to be more centred around taking photographs of the client. However, it does get more complicated in that there are those, particularly in North America, although rare, who do 'phototherapy' who take photographs of their clients, and there are those who start with 'therapeutic photography' and subsequently carry out traditional psychotherapy.) I also found helpful her description of personal snapshots as 'footprints of the mind', with any photo potentially continuing stories beyond words. Judy also suggested that we take photos of what is important in our lives, often at an unconscious level, and that in many ways all photographs we take are to some extent also self-portraits.

Family photographs were indeed the topic of another workshop, facilitated by David Krauss, another of the key founders of phototherapy (Krauss and Fryrear, 1983). In this workshop we were asked to bring five family photographs. Once again new thoughts came to me: Why had I not brought in a photo of my father? Why was there not a photo of the whole family? Why was the photo with nobody in it so much more about my relationships with people? Again, participants found this approach very powerful – so many people seemed to be working through horrendous life events through photography. Here, one could see how it was possible to now speak of what could be seen on the faces of a participant's child but could not be spoken of before. Or what it might mean to somebody to really not be in the (family) picture. I was also reminded that I had found it helpful getting family photos and putting them in chronological order and taking them to my own personal therapy – though, importantly for me, this had not been suggested by my therapist.

The third workshop I attended was facilitated by Joel Walker, another of the North American innovators. The title of his paper, 'The use of ambiguous artistic images for enhancing self-awareness in psychotherapy' (1986), describes well my experience of the workshop, which usefully encouraged me to project onto a chosen image through my description of what I thought it was saying. A further workshop I attended was on developments in Finland attempting to use phototherapy within psychotherapy. It was co-led by the experienced Finnish trainer and psychotherapist Tarja Koffert. Here one was asked to choose a photograph that dealt with trauma in the attachment relationship. The idea was that one first chose a photo that spoke about attachment and then another that dealt with the experience of trauma with that attachment. I chose a photo of two men and a woman on a park bench with the photographer taking the picture from behind, with the man in the middle putting his arm around the woman on the right, but she, unbeknown to him, was holding the hand of the man on his left. The photograph I chose for trauma was one of a jagged piece of glass. I again entered surprisingly quickly into aspects of my life that I had previously found very problematic, although I was not conscious of these aspects being around for me at the time. However, I did then find it difficult to switch off and move to the next technique. I also found that there was a tendency for participants to talk of themselves as victims, but that our responsibility for the pain and suffering that we may have caused, albeit perhaps as a consequence, and may still be causing others, was not very much in evidence.

This primacy given to autonomy rather than heteronomy and the problematics for our culture of doing this, was the subject of my own paper presented at what was to be the first of three conferences (which have particularly influenced this book): 'Exploring and developing the personal and the professional as the practice of ethics through photography.' This is based on an exploration of the French philosopher Emmanuel Levinas' ideas about what it might mean to put the other first, as opposed to oneself, which is again in contrast to Buber's I/It, I/Thou concept of ethics (Loewenthal, 2011). From these ideas, I have made an examination of well-known photographs as to whether the photographers have put themselves or the photographed first. (I have made use of this matrix in training psychotherapists, photographers and other professional groups in terms of their ethical practice (Loewenthal, 2006, 2008).)

In this conference I and other participants were able to learn of the work done, for example, by Jo Spence who used therapeutic photography in working through her successful fight with breast cancer and her unsuccessful fight with leukaemia (see Chapter 4). Also, the work presented by Rosy Martin appears to have very much influenced developments in Finland (see Chapter 6). This re-enactment phototherapy with its performative aspects is, so Rosy suggested, to enable people to break out of the story of the family album, which is seen as being usually edited by others so that it does not challenge their notions of the ideal.

There were over forty papers presented in this first conference and many more at the subsequent conferences at Roehampton, London and again in Turku, Finland (see Appendix for examples of these further developments carried out in phototherapy and therapeutic photography), together with various associated exhibitions in Turku, London and Brighton. This has meant that what is presented in this book has been the result of difficult decisions on what to include.

At the initial workshops I attended it became immediately apparent to me from the way the participants worked with each other both how photographs could be used within the therapeutic hour and also that there were concerns as to the appropriateness of people's motivations for facilitating photography in this way. Indeed, throughout the workshops and actual conferences, the question of what was the appropriate training was never really resolved (and to the best of my knowledge has still not been); and in fact conflicts between those working together were at least as poor an advertisement for how this approach can heal as conflicts in other therapeutic modalities. I also found the attempt at apparent humanistic closure of therapeutic sessions through trying to switch clients' attentions to aspects less anxiety provoking was something with which I no longer felt at home.

One question that was very much in evidence at the initial conference was who should be allowed to practice what, and with whom? For example, as this work involves working in a relationship, to what extent is there a case for having one's own therapy and seeing a supervisor who has also had personal therapy, in order to be clearer as to when one is saying something for oneself, rather than for another? It has been said in analytic psychotherapy that one spends the first ten years paying for one's therapy and the next ten years with the client/patient paying for it. But if one hasn't had the equivalent of the first ten years, then is there an increased danger that we are unknowingly getting others to explore our own unexplored mine/mind fields? Certainly, my experience of the workshops opened up new areas for me and on my return I was able to hear in a different way from patients about photographs (and paintings) – hence, the following selection of chapters primarily developed from these three conferences for readers to assess the usefulness of these approaches for their practices. While I, of course, hope that the selection of authors will provide a contribution towards the development of phototherapy and therapeutic photography, I am also aware, owing to space limitations, I have not been able to include other papers that may well be of interest to readers – hence the Appendix where references to these papers can be found.

Regardless of whether one thinks one can only experience through language, I was convinced of the potential usefulness of photographs to bring to the surface repressed thoughts and feelings that might not emerge so easily, if at all, in psychotherapy and counselling alone. Although I found that I personally, probably because of my training, prefer a more traditional therapeutic process of working this through and therefore favour, as a practitioner, being more open to photographs within traditional psychotherapy.

However, phototherapy and therapeutic photography workshops appear a popular means through which many people have useful therapeutic experiences and, indeed, not only may at least some people prefer this to individual brief, increasingly cognitive behavioural therapy, but it may also be more economical to provide.

This book, however, is about the therapeutic use of photographs within existing professional practices and for the editor and many of the contributors, phototherapy and therapeutic photography are not seen as professions in their own right.

Illustration: three brief case studies

Particularly for those who are new to phototherapy and therapeutic photography, what follows are three case studies illustrating different approaches in England, Finland and Italy in the therapeutic use of photographs with young people.

As has been mentioned, and will be explored in more depth, phototherapy uses photographs to help people discuss difficult subjects. It can be used with anyone – but I and others have found it particularly effective with children who struggle to articulate themselves emotionally but respond powerfully to visual images.

Again, in brief and to be discussed in more depth later, phototherapy can help people 'verbalise' feelings about which they were previously unable to speak. This can be done in traditional therapy – either by using the client's photos or by the therapist and the client taking photographs as part of the session. Phototherapy can be used on an individual basis in therapy, or as a group project where a school class or community group use pictures to discuss relationships.

Phototherapy isn't always easy. It helps children to explore good and bad aspects of life – as in Alice's case, below, one of three case studies that hopefully illustrate how phototherapy can work with different young people.

Case study 1: Alice, UK (see Chapter 7)

Alice had warts on her hands and was being bullied at school; I used photography therapeutically by taking photographs of Alice's warts (see Photo 1.1) and discussing them with her, resulting in Alice being able to look at them and talk about them as part of her.

Later, Alice said:

> I had warts and when the therapist photographed them up close they looked grotesque. Making myself confront my warts gave me a new confidence to look at good and bad things about myself. The warts might have been connected to my anxiety although it's difficult to admit – it's a vicious circle having warts. You get them because you're anxious and then you get more anxious because you have them. Taking photographs of the warts breaks this cycle in

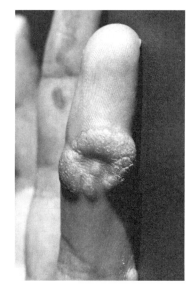

Photo 1.1
Alice's warts (Loewenthal).

the same way. Having to look at your fears helps release them. It's like you're confiding in the camera – sharing the weight of your problems with someone else.

Alice's warts disappeared soon after her phototherapy.

Case study 2: Community phototherapy, Italy (see Chapter 9)

Carmine Parrella, a visual psychologist at the Centre for Mental Health in Lucca, near Florence, holds community phototherapy sessions with children from four years old.

One method he uses is to ask for one of the children to be the photographer for a day. They are excused from their work to take pictures of their day at school – and their teacher must not interfere. They can even stand on a table and take as many or as few photographs as they want – just like a professional photographer.

Some children take photographs only of objects – others of emotions. The children can go between the classroom and the computer room where they can get advice on taking better photos from the psychologist. If they keep 'cutting heads off', they might be advised to stand back a little. (However, if a 'mistake' is stylistic expression – perhaps they are 'cutting heads' because they are feeling aggressive – the psychologist says nothing.) Carmine says 'children are more instinctive photographers than adults' – they are confident about the images they want to capture.

These pictures can help the teacher get to know the student better. The teacher explores what the world looks like to students – which can be surprising. For example, the teacher may assume a child is popular and happy – until they see photos of them alone and sad.

Another use of community phototherapy (see Chapter 9) is making a book with photos of each child in a class. Choosing photographs can be a class activity – everyone can discuss the photo the child would choose and the photo other children think best represents them.

Yet another example was when Carmine provided a digital photographic course for fathers and their children. One activity would involve fathers and children making a photo diary on a day in the life of the other. Teachers, children and fathers could then select photos to exhibit – digital cameras made this relatively easy.

Case study 3: Jani, Finland (see Chapter 2)

Mervi Rutanen is a counsellor who studied phototherapy at the University of Turku. She used phototherapy to help Jani and his mother create a bond.

Jani's mother was asked to bring her favourite photo of her child. The therapist made a big copy of the photo to work with in the session. Jani's mother was asked to frame this photo using materials that appealed to her. Mervi gave Jani a disposable camera. His task was to take photos of his mother framing the photo of him.

Mervi took photos of Jani photographing his mother framing his photo. Initially, Jani and his mother worked separately with a lot of space between them. As they continued, Jani moved nearer his mother and began to take photos more spontaneously. The frame his mother made was in the shape of a heart (see Photo 1.2). At the end of the session, Jani asked the therapist for a pen. He wrote on the heart frame 'To My Mum'. In a later session, Jani's mum said she treasured that photo.

Photo 1.2 Jani's photo (Rutanen).

Photographs can be used in otherwise traditional approaches to psychotherapy and counselling explored in this book. Clients can also bring in and discuss photographs that evoke meaning in their lives, like family albums. Phototherapy can be used as a therapeutic tool for particularly disadvantaged people. It is suggested that phototherapy should only be used in a way that is client-led and is not recommended to be used by someone who has a specific agenda, however well intentioned. Children (or anyone else) should not be led to believe they are following their own agenda while, in fact, being manoeuvred into the goal of the person introducing them in the therapeutic use of the photograph. Phototherapy often relies on a 'projective' technique, where the child describes what's on his or her mind by thinking they see it in the photograph. It is a powerful technique and I think should be used by someone who has had a 'sufficient' training and with appropriate supervision.

This is surely also true of when projective devices are intentionally used, for example, when teaching English literature, rather than allowing learning to just emerge through the teacher–student relationship. So phototherapy can help children and others to develop emotional capacity but only if they don't feel their trust is betrayed.

It would seem good practice that the teacher/psychological therapist should learn to let the child/young person speak while staying relatively quiet, and try and ensure that their own anxieties do not get in the way. Indeed, one way in which the therapist/facilitator appears most helpful is when (according to Rogers, 1951) they can:

- reflect back what the person is saying;
- occasionally offer (tentatively) what the child/young person appears to be feeling;
- sometimes say how the child/young person makes them feel.

In schools, phototherapy is not a replacement for teaching but it can help children to express themselves and explore emotional thinking. Having introduced phototherapy and therapeutic photography as the most prominent approaches used in exploring the therapeutic use of photographs, together with some introductory case studies, I will now provide a more detailed outline of the book.

Overview of the book

In summary, this international book is for those interested in the recent worldwide evolution of phototherapy and therapeutic photography in our digital age. As has been said, while key developments can be seen to have originally taken place in phototherapy and therapeutic photography in the 1980s and early 1990s, there have been significant recent advances – particularly in Europe, namely, in the UK, Finland and Italy – that take advantage of the digitalisation of photography, making it a medium that is increasingly accessible. The intention of this book is both to provide a foundation in phototherapy and therapeutic photography and to describe these recent developments.

As for potential readers, this book is for anyone interested in the therapeutic use of photographs. It is hoped it will be of particular interest to psychological therapists, especially psychotherapists, counsellors, psychologists; creative therapists including art therapists, as well as photographers, their teachers, trainers/coaches; those involved with reminiscence, social change, organisational and management development consultants and others wishing to explore further the use of photographs therapeutically within their existing practices. For such professionals, it is intended that what is presented here addresses the need of the practitioner to come alongside and work with clients in a digital era where, for example, digital photography has become such a prevalent part of our culture. In general, this book is designed to enable practitioners to keep abreast of changes in our cultural practices in a way that clients can see what is being offered as therapeutically relevant.

There was inevitably a question as to how to present this book. It is primarily written for those who are new to what has been termed phototherapy and therapeutic photography as well as those who wish to be updated, particularly in relation to the explosive arrival of our digital age. The book is divided into three parts: in the first, an overall introduction and overview from different perspectives; in the second, approaches and contexts, including phototherapy, re-enactment phototherapy, community phototherapy, self-portraiture, family photography. This is followed by a conclusion looking at the future of phototherapy and therapeutic photography in terms of theory, practice and research.

More specifically, the Prologue chosen for this book is 'The photograph' by Keith Kennedy. The reasons for this are twofold: first, as a good example of the power of the photograph from the photograph's perspective (based on Donald McCullin's image of a stricken mother and child). The second reason is to hopefully give pride of place to Keith Kennedy as one of the most important unsung pioneers of phototherapy who led an important photographic group at the Henderson Hospital in the UK that included Jo Spence (see Chapter 3).

The chapters in this book are loosely based in three parts. The early chapters are more an introduction to the theories of and approaches to phototherapy and therapeutic photography. The book then moves on to look at more detailed use of photographs in various practices. The emphasis of the final chapters in the book is more on research and looking to the future of phototherapy and therapeutic photography. However, while chapters are placed under the heading of their main focus, their authors generally make significant contributions to all three parts of this book.

The first chapters in this book focus more on 'Introduction: theories and approaches', and this, Chapter 1, is entitled 'Introducing phototherapy and therapeutic photography in a digital age'. Here I provide an overview of the book. This is followed by a brief illustration of different methods of working therapeutically with photographs with three brief case histories from the UK, Finland and Italy. I then follow this with a more comprehensive introduction to phototherapy and therapeutic photography in a digital age and the growing importance of the use of photographs for self-representation and expression. I am now concluding this introduction with a brief overview of the other chapters.

Chapter 2 is Ulla Halkola's 'A photograph as a therapeutic experience'. Here this Finnish pioneer examines the psychotherapeutic significance of a photograph. The background here for the observation of the theoretical basis of phototherapy is the classification of the methods of phototherapy into three categories: Looking at biographical photographs, taking new photographs, and looking at both symbolic and associative photographs. The classification is the one used in Finland and is regarded as similar to semiotician Roland Barthes' thoughts on the special nature of photographs. The author argues that both internal and external pictures give a richness to the therapy process and also to the development of phototherapy.

Having started to provide a grounding in phototherapy, the next chapter focuses on the evolution of therapeutic photography. Here, in Chapter 3, Terry Dennett writes about 'Jo Spence's camera therapy: personal therapeutic photography as a response to adversity'. Terry comments that a complete formal history of the early development of the field of therapeutic photography in the UK has yet to be written, but in this chapter Terry attempts to provide a review of at least some of the work of his late former partner and collaborator, Jo Spence (1934–92).

Chapter 4, 'Fotos, fones & fantasies', is written by the art therapist and systemic practitioner, Mark Wheeler, who emphasises the importance of our digital era. In this chapter Mark widens the phototherapy field to include the interconnected actions of the phone camera, other mobile image making and viewing devices, social networking websites, online galleries and outsider art; Mark states that he considers these activities as much from an art-historical perspective as from neurobiological and psychoanalytic perspectives. 'Fotos, fones & fantasies' draws on familiar domestic photography, fine-art photography, art history, art therapy, neuroscience and psychological aesthetics.

In Chapter 5 Mike Simmons explores what he terms a 'Creative photographic approach: interpretation and healing through creative practice'. Mike contests that our lives are negotiated through our relationship to others, and understanding our position within that social setting is informed by lived experience. Employing 'a creative photographic approach' utilises photography's unique ability to both describe and express, providing an alternative vocabulary to connect with, describe and evaluate our lives, bringing insights that might otherwise remain hidden through more traditional, non-visual modes of enquiry.

The previous chapters were more concerned with theories and approaches. The next chapters have a greater focus on 'The use of photographs in various practices'. However in just the same way as the chapters on theories and approaches refer to their use in 'various practices' so do the following chapters also describe in part 'theories and approaches'. They have been chosen for this part as it is considered that their main focus is the context of phototherapy and therapeutic photography.

This new part starts with Chapter 6, 'Inhabiting the image: photography, therapy and re-enactment phototherapy'. This outlines the most recognised contemporary exponent of therapeutic photography, which Rosy Martin, the author of this chapter helped create with Jo Spence. Rosy argues that photography, which she regards as 'this ubiquitous medium that most people use and that has the potential to be democratic', too often ends up as a repetition of conventional iconic images. However, photographs offer up the possibilities of a slippery surface of meanings and potential narratives for the viewer, which are the rich veins that phototherapy explores. Rosy discusses therapeutic work with found images and alternative visual diaries. A case study is included to illustrate the methodology. Rosy concludes by questioning what happens when this work moves from process to product.

Chapter 7, '*Talking pictures therapy*: the therapeutic use of photographs in counselling and psychotherapy', is where the use of phototherapy in psychotherapy, counselling and counselling psychology is explored. Here I describe a case study where photographs are used therapeutically in a school setting individually with four children who have up to six sessions of what I term *talking pictures therapy*.

In Chapter 8, 'The self-portrait as self-therapy', the multilingual Cristina Nuñez explores this approach that is growing in importance and with which she is internationally identified. Here Cristina argues that, in the digital era, self-portraiture enables anyone to produce a work of art instinctively, without knowing anything about photography, and more and more people today feel a strong urge towards self-representation. The decision to represent oneself can provide what is termed here a 'state of grace': the feeling of centredness that occurs in moments of creative work in which the emotions are naturally retained because our 'higher self' is in command.

Chapter 9 is where Carmine Parrella and Del Loewenthal consider the notion of community phototherapy and the way in which it has been developed by Carmine at the Mental Health Centre in Lucca. They describe, as a case study, how the project evolved, the different therapy groups that were developed and their interrelationships. Examples are given of the community at work and how it has influenced people there who are mental health patients. The idea of community phototherapy is to create a space of integration of symptomatic and non-symptomatic people in the community, so the relationship between the two sectors of the community is developed on the basis of creativity and subjectivity.

Chapter 10 on the use of photographs in family therapy is by one of the most experienced phototherapists, Rodolfo de Bernart, Director of the Instituto Di Terapia Familiare in Florence, Italy. In his chapter, Rodolfo explores the important consequences concerning the development of audio-visual based therapeutic techniques, with particular reference to the photographic genogram used in training and in therapeutic settings.

Next, Chapter 11 also examines some implications of phototherapy and therapeutic photography but this time the emphasis is even more on the student of photography. Here, Julia Winckler writes on therapeutic uses of photography by photography degree students. Julia focuses on a small number of student projects, describing the students' working methods and therapeutic and aesthetic outcomes. Working with Derrida's notion of the 'archive of the present' and Freud's work on excavation of memory traces, students have developed imaginative responses that frequently address loss, mourning, absence and longing. Over time, Julia considers she has come to understand that some of these projects represented major turning points for the students: affecting their sense of self, their relationship to the past ('I had never thought about the time before I was born') and providing them with tools to tackle painful or complex issues in visual ways.

Chapter 12, 'Photography and art therapy', comes from Alexander Kopytin whose extraordinary work in Russia is of international interest. The chapter aims to stimulate thinking about photography from an art-therapeutic perspective and considers the nature and the role of the so-called 'technical images' from a cultural–anthropological viewpoint, so as to better understand their influence on modern people's life. The chapter also provides a review of art-therapeutic publications to demonstrate the increasing role of photography as an expressive tool for clients. Finally, it presents findings from an intercultural Russian–British study, in which art therapists' experience of using photography in their artistic and clinical practice was investigated.

Again, while the concluding chapters of this book explore 'Research and the future' of phototherapy and therapeutic photography, previous authors have also alluded to this; for example, Chapter 8.

Chapter 13 is by Hasse Karlsson, Editor-in-Chief of the *Nordic Journal of Psychiatry* and Professor of Psychiatry at the University of Helsinki in Finland. Hasse's chapter is of vital importance in showing us what is known about neuroscience and what we can and cannot currently claim with regard to phototherapy and therapeutic photography. It explores, on the assumption that mental processes derive from operations of the brain (Kandel, 1988), the neurobiological effects of phototherapy or, more importantly, the little evidence there is available on this.

Chapter 14, Del Loewenthal's 'The future of phototherapy and therapeutic photography', provides a conclusion for this book. The future development of practice, theory and research in phototherapy and therapeutic photography in our digital era is considered with particular reference to training, professionalisation, changing views of theory and the growing field of visual research.

The Epilogue is provided by Brigitte Anor, where the theme of the power of the photograph that started this book is returned to, in this case regarding an iconic photograph of the Warsaw Ghetto and exploring its therapeutic possibilities.

Whatever the technological future, it would appear that many of those who have contributed to this book have been helped in finding their voice through the use of photography and are now helping others. Hopefully, this book is making a contribution to phototherapy and therapeutic photography finding their own voice(s) within our cultural practices. This chapter, in introducing phototherapy and therapeutic photography in a digital age, and the contents of the book, provides, it is hoped, a basis for exploring these, particularly European, developments in the field.

Appendix

Examples of further developments carried out in phototherapy and therapeutic photography[1]

Brigitte Anor (Israel) – *The emotional impact of newspaper photographs on the narration of our life-story* (Turku, June 2008)

Brigitte Anor (Israel) – *Shooting back: reflections on phototherapy in times of war* (Turku, February 2011)

Francisco Aviles-Gutiérrez (Mexico) – *Working with phototherapy techniques in a hospital environment* (Turku, June 2008)

Rodolfo de Bernart (Italy) – *The image of the family: with special attention to the photographic genogram* (Turku, February 2011)

Anat Botzer (Israel) – *Business, phototherapy in cancer patients, and contribution to the community* (Turku, June 2008)

Kate Broom (UK) – *Pictures in a context and the communication of needs* (Turku, February 2011)

Elina Brotherus (Finland) – *Decisive days: use of self in my photographic practice* (Turku, June 2008)

Teresa Cabruja Ubach (Spain) – *Narratives/portraits, performance and collective/ individual de-subjectivational practices* (Turku, February 2011)

Annette Cahn (Holland) – *Look at you* (Turku, June 2008)

Maria Grazia Cantoni (Italy) – *Phototherapy as a therapeutic tool to change one's distorted script and perception of the self* (Turku, June 2008)

Maria Grazia Cantoni (Italy) – *Receptive photo therapy* (Turku, February 2011)

Julia Cayne (UK) – *From Phenomenology to Reverie* (London, October 2010)

Tom Cotton (UK) – *There is a fault in reality: a film project exploring experiences of schizophrenia, and its implications for phototherapy* (Turku, February 2011)

Terry Dennett (UK) – *An overview of the work of Jo Spence 1974–92* (London, October 2010)

Kitty Enbom (Finland) – *Art therapy – phototherapy* (Turku, February 2011)

Kimberly Faulkner (USA) – *Phototherapy: the use of Photoshop and digital media in an urban hospital setting* (Turku, June 2008)

Ellen Fisher-Turk (USA) – *Fisher-Turk method of photo therapy* (Turku, June 2008)

Jonathan M. Friesem (Israel) – *Youth filmmaking as a social and psychological therapeutic method for youth at risk: experience in Israel since 2006* (Turku, February 2011)

Hanna Hakomäki (Finland) – *Storycomposing(r) with photos – music therapy meets phototherapy* (Turku, June 2008)

Ulla Halkola and Tarja Koffert (Finland) – *The Many Stories of Being – how to use photos in mental health promotions with children and adolescents with phototherapy techniques* (London, October 2010)

Ulla Halkola (Finland) – *The many stories of being* (Turku, February 2011)

Virpi Harju (Finland) – *Doors – picture series – looking for a well working picture series* (Turku, February 2011)

Liisa Heimo-Vuorimaa (Finland) – *Learning coping skills for chronic pain* (Turku, June 2008)

Liisa Heimo-Vuorimaa (Finland) – *The use of photographs to interpret and recreate body image when rehabilitating chronic pain* (London, October 2010)

Marika Heinäaho (Finland) – *Digital storytelling experiences during Bachelor's thesis, 2010* (Turku, February 2011)

Hanna Hentinen (Finland) – *ETC as a tool for an image-oriented therapist – offering insights to the therapeutic factors of photography* (Turku, June 2008)

Mervi and Juha Herranen (Finland) – *Photographs as tools of counselling and coaching* (Turku, February 2011)

Patrik Ikäläinen, Hannele Jasu, Meira Leimu, Tuuli Mäkinen, K. Syrjä, Miina Savolainen, Mika Venhola (Finland) – *Processing gender identity – the interactive process of empowering photography* (Turku, June 2011)

Kristian Jalava (Finland) – *A lifestyle – Magazine as a method to 'get things done'* (Turku, June 2008)

Pirita Juppi (Finland) – *Digital storytelling* (Turku, February 2011)

Minna Juutilainen (Finland) – *Healing from interpersonal trauma with phototherapy* (Turku, February 2011)

Hasse Karlsson (Finland) – *Functional brain imaging (PET, fMRI) in the study of emotions evoked by pictures and films* (Turku, June 2008)

Hasse Karlsson (Finland) – *Phototherapy & neuroscience* (Turku, February 2011)

Tarja Koffert (Finland) – *Photos in depressive patient's psychotherapy* (Turku, June 2008)

Tarja Koffert (Finland) – *Self-portraits, family albums and emotional processing in therapy* (London, October 2010)

Tarja Koffert (Finland) – *Self-portraits and family albums and emotional processing in therapy sessions* (Turku, February 2011)

Alexander Kopytin (Russia) – *Photography and art therapy: possibilities for partnership* (Turku, February 2011)

Leena Koulu, Pirkko Pehunen and Erkka Valovirta (Finland) – *Learning coping skills for atopy* (Turku, June 2008)

Leena Koulu, Pirkko Pehunen (Finland) – *An experiential journey to atopic symptoms – work with children during a rehabilitation course for atopic families* (London, October 2010)

Mari Krappala, Maria Nurmela, Eeva Hannula, Hertta Kiiski and Tiina Palmu (Finland) – *Phototherapeutic methods as part of interartistical processes* (Turku, February 2011)

David Krauss (USA) – *Photo-reminiscence with elderly clients* (Turku, June 2008)

Nirit Lavy Kucik (Israel) – *The power of the current moment – enjoying the unknown as a key element in doing and teaching phototherapy* (Turku, June 2008)

Bodil Lindfors (Finland) – *Written in the body? Unlocking preverbal memories by means of re-enactment phototherapy and body oriented psychotherapy* (Turku, June 2008)

Marita Liulia (Finland) – *Something ancient – Something new: tarot photos as symbols for understanding human life* (Turku, June 2008)

Del Loewenthal (UK) – *Exploring and developing the personal and the professional as the practice of ethics through photography* (Turku, June 2008)

Del Loewenthal (UK) – *Researching phototherapy and therapeutic photography* (London, October 2010)

Del Loewenthal (UK) – *'Talking pictures therapy' as brief counselling in a school setting: a collective case study* (London, October 2010)

Del Loewenthal (UK) – *Researching phototherapy: comparing the use of photographs with standard measures in 'talking pictures therapy'* (Turku, February 2011)

Maarit Mäkelä and Pirkko Pehunen, Psychoterapist (Finland) – *Gaze, gender and performing body: experiences of play and re-enactment in therapeutic photography* (Turku, June 2008)

Teemu Mäki and Arja Elovirta (Finland) – *Testing your identity and ideals – artist's/pedagogue's/curator's thoughts on the be your enemy project* (Turku, June 2008)

Edward Mamary (USA) – *Our lives photovoice: using photography to explore sexual health of non-gay identified African American men who have sex with men* (Turku, June 2008)

Mira Mamon (Israel) – *Photographer as photo-therapist, photo-therapist as a photographer* (Turku, February 2011)

Rosy Martin (UK) – *Re-enactment phototherapy – memory, identities and unconscious processes* (Turku, June 2008)

Rosy Martin (UK) – *'Look at me!' Representing self: representing ageing. Using phototherapy techniques within a multi-disciplinary research project* (London, October 2010)

Rosy Martin (UK) – *From 'Outrageous Agers' to 'Look at me': Using phototherapy techniques within a multi-disciplinary research project* (Turku, February 2011)

Lyndsey Moon (UK) – *The use of grounded theory in researching photographic responses* (London, October 2010)

Cristina Nuñez (Spain) – *Self-portrait, a powerful tool for self-therapy* (Turku, June 2008)

Cristina Nuñez (Spain) – *The self portrait experience* (Turku, February 2011)

Satu Nurmela (Finland) – *Learning and/or healing with digital storytelling* (Turku, February 2011)

Netta Norro (Slovenia) – *Reflections on the creative process through self-photography – portraits on overcoming fear of photography* (Turku, February 2011)

Carmine Parrella (Italy) – *Photography as a medium to create innovative sociotherapeutic settings in mental health programs* (Turku, June 2008)

Carmine Parrella (Italy) – *Researching community phototherapy* (London, October 2010)

Carmine Parrella (Italy) – *Phototherapy with mental health clients* (Turku, February 2011)

Olga Perevezentseva (Russia) – *Perevezentseva's "PSYrole" method: a psychological treatment using "planned photographic role-images" for increasing self-understanding and psychological growth* (Turku, February 2011)

Maija Perho (Finland) – *Art and culture for well-being* (Turku, February 2011)

José Ramos and Natasha Oliveira (Portugal) – *Phototherapy in a psychiatric day hospital* (Turku, February 2011)

Mimmu Rankanen (Finland) – *Imagine reality – document imagination, photos in expressive arts therapy* (Turku, February 2011)

Rosie Rizq (UK) – *The development of interpretive phenomenological analysis in exploring 'borderline personality disorder' – a case study* (London, October 2010)

Liisa Salmenperä (Finland) – *The use of photo cards* (Turku, February 2011)

Miina Savolainen (Finland) – *Empowering photography* (Turku, June 2008)

Miina Savolainen and Mika Venhola (Finland) – *Processing gender identity – the interactive process of empowering photography* (London, October 2010)

Marja Seppälä (Finland) – *Mun Juttu / My Tale* (Turku, February 2011)

Liisa Seppänen and Ulla Halkola (Finland) – *Just about a woman? – Role of photographs when encountering with a breast-cancer* (Turku, June 2008)

Jan Sitvast (The Netherlands) – *The Photo-instrument: an intervention that mediates the expression of patient experiences in mental health care* (Turku, June 2008)

Jan Sitvast and I. Bogert (The Netherlands) – *Just look at me! An evaluation of an innovative intervention in a psychiatric rehabilitation setting – from recent experiences* (Turku, February 2011)

Mike Simmons (UK) – *Beyond words: creative photographic practice and the interpretation of grief* (Turku, June 2008)

Mike Simmons (UK) – *Pictures from life: an alternate model in bereavement care for children, young people and their families* (Turku, June 2008)

Mike Simmons (UK) – *The creative photographic approach* (London, October 2010)

Jurate Sucylaite (Lithuania) – *A photograph as a visualization of new inner insight in the end of poetry therapy session* (Turku, June 2008)

Astrid Ståhlberg (Sweden) – *PHOTOLANGAGE® A technique of group animation* (Turku, June 2008)

Else-Maj Suolinna (Finland) – *Photographs as an aid in writing your life story – a personal story* (Turku, June 2008)

Josef Timar (Germany) – *'Camera poetica' – evolution of a self-expression photography project into an interactive multiple media art project – Modified applications for phototherapy and therapeutic photography?* (Turku, June 2008)

Josef Timar and Philipp Martius (Germany) – *Camera poetica* (Turku, February 2011)

Seija Ulkuniemi, Tanja Holmberg (Finland) – *Breaking the frames – histories and other stories about family photography* (Turku, June 2008)

Seija Ulkuniemi and Tanja Holmberg (Finland) – *Getting connected with the past, oneself, and distant peers (classroom teacher education) – creating and sharing photographs in virtual reality* (Turku, February 2011)

Maria Uzoni (The Netherlands) – *TimeLine involving clients' photos changing personal history, processed in a creative art act* (Turku, February 2011)

Andréa Vannucchi and Tarja Lapila (Finland) – *How would i know what is in your mind? Photography as part of interactive communication with elderly people when promoting active and healthy everyday life* (Turku, June 2008)

Andréa Vannucchi and Tarja Lapila (Finland) – *How to know what is in your mind?* (Turku, February 2011)

David Viñuales (Spain) – *Considering the implications of photography in phototherapy* (Turku, February 2011)

Joel Walker (Canada) – *The use of photographic imagery in psychotherapy – a 30 year personal retrospective* (Turku, June 2008)

Lynn Weddle (UK) – *Photography and self-reflection: the being dyslexic project* (Turku, February 2011)

Judy Weiser (Canada) – *Introducing phototherapy and therapeutic photography – An overview to their development during the past three decades* (Turku, June 2008)

Judy Weiser (Canada) – *Who is doing what, where: a review of phototherapy-related practices, people, projects, research and websites around the world* (Turku, February 2011)

Mark Wheeler (UK) – *Photo-psycho-praxis – the psychological aesthetics of making, viewing and talking about photographs* (Turku, June 2008)

Mark Wheeler (UK) – *The smartphone and psychotherapy: paradigm shift in systemic and psychodynamic attachment theory or just an irritating buzz in the pocket* (London, October 2010)

Julia Winckler (UK) – *I had never thought about the time before I was born: working within and beyond the photographic archive with BA Photography students at the University of Brighton* (London, October 2010)

Note

1   These papers were presented at the following conferences:

> International Conference on Phototherapy and Therapeutic Photography – Turku, Finland, 16–18 Jun 2008.
> PHOTOTHERAPYEUROPE: European Phototherapy Symposium: Researching Phototherapy and Therapeutic Photography – London, UK, 19–21 October 2010.
> PHOTOTHERAPYEUROPE: European Phototherapy Symposium: Learning and Healing with Phototherapy Symposium – Turku, Finland, 2–4 February 2011.

References

Barthes, R. (1980). *Camera Lucida: Reflections on photography*. New York: Hill & Wang.

Berman, L. (1993). *Beyond the Smile: The therapeutic use of the photograph*. London: Routledge.

Dalley, J. (2008, 1 November). The first prix pictet. *Financial Times*.

Kandel, E. (1998). A new intellectual framework for psychiatry. *American Journal of Psychiatry*, 155, 457–469.

Krauss, D. and Fryrear, J. (eds). (1983). *Phototherapy in Mental Health*. Springfield, IL: Charles Thomas.

Loewenthal, D. (2006). Counselling as a practice of ethics: Some implications for therapeutic education. *Philosophical Practice*, 2(3), 1–9.

Loewenthal, D. (2008). Introducing post-existential practice. *Philosophical Practice*, 3(3), 316–321.

Loewenthal, D. (ed.) (2011). *Post-existentialism and the Psychological Therapies: Towards a therapy without foundations*. London: Karnac.

Merleau-Ponty, M. (1962). *Phenomenology of Perception*. London: Routledge.

Rogers, Carl (1951). *Client-centered Therapy: Its current practice, implications and theory*. London: Constable.

Sontag, S. (1990). *On Photography*. New York: Anchor.

Spence, J. (1986). *Putting Myself in the Picture: A political, personal and photographic autobiography*. London: Camden Press.

Symington, N. (1986). *The Analytic Experience: Lectures from the Tavistock*. London: Free Association Books.

Walker, J. (1986). The use of ambiguous artistic images for enhancing self-awareness in psychotherapy. *Arts in Psychotherapy*, 13(3), 241–248.

Weiser, J. (1999). *Phototherapy Techniques: Exploring the secrets of personal snapshots and family albums* (2nd edn). Vancouver: Photo Therapy Centre.

See also the comprehensive website Judy initiated: www.phototherapy-centre.com/home.htm.

Chapter 2

A photograph as a therapeutic experience

Ulla Halkola

The psychotherapeutic significance of photographs

In this chapter the psychotherapeutic significance of a photograph will be explored. The Finnish word for photograph '*valokuva*' (composed of two words 'light' and 'image') provides insights for exploring the theme. 'Light' presents the light of life, but also shadows and darkness, while the 'image' carries meanings for people preceding verbal expression and interaction. In early childhood and already in the foetal stage, according to present knowledge, people have different mental images, body images and sensory images through which they perceive their existence.

In psychotherapy, the principal aim in using photographs is to reach a point where, in confidential interaction, photographs and photographing function as impulses to memory and to recognising and expressing emotions, thus promoting the self-understanding of the client. It is a question of a comprehensive process where the photos used in therapy are connected to client's mental images, beliefs and memories of self. The event of viewing or taking photos evokes sensations, emotions and memories, which can be of a very early, painful or surprising nature. The role of photographs in psychotherapy is functional; the actual therapy is based on the professional skills of the psychotherapist, acquired within his/her specific frame of reference.

We can define phototherapy in many ways and I think it is important to do this in every country or culture in the way that suits our professional work best. There are many definitions of phototherapy, emanating from phototherapy pioneers such as Stewart, Krauss and Weiser. For example, Stewart (1979: 42) defines phototherapy as, 'the use of photography or photographic materials, under the guidance of a trained therapist, to reduce or relieve painful psychological symptoms and to facilitate psychological growth and therapeutic change'.

Furthermore, in my opinion phototherapy and therapeutic photography are very similar and both need to be carried out by professional, trained people. The targets of therapeutic photography might be health promotion, healing, rehabilitation, empowering work or learning to express yourself, but in any case it needs to be facilitated by someone who has professional skills in health – social or educational professionals – and understands the power of photos and photography.

This chapter is also based on semiotician, social theorist Roland Barthes' (1980) thoughts on the special nature of photographs, and on psychotherapeutic theories, such as psychodynamic psychotherapy and cognitive constructivist psychotherapy theories, which draw the basis of their knowledge from modern brain research. Barthes contemplates all the basic elements, exploring the empirical world of the human mind through emotions, thoughts, actions and their interconnections. Consequently, it is important to face *what has been*, it is important to know what touches and disturbs the mind, where the '*punctums*' (private meanings – as discussed later in this chapter) are. In turn, it is interesting to observe how people function as *operators*, *spectators* and *spectrum* (the object photographed). The functional classification by Barthes can also be applied to the classification of methods of phototherapy.

Over the last few years, many new studies, applicable to the *visual field* in psychotherapy, have been published in the fields of psychiatry, cognitive neurology, neurobiology, as well as in photographic research, leading to the role of images and photographs being viewed in a fascinating light.

The therapeutic exploration of crisis and trauma are, in my opinion, central in psychotherapeutic work in that they attempt to understand the source and core of the psychological disorder in the person's mind. The aim is to get to the origin of the disorder and to gain knowledge of the events, emotions and experiences involved, so that the person's emotional life and behaviour can become comprehensible to him/herself, and through this comprehension, positive life changes can become possible. In some situations the client can be helped and treated chronologically close to the psychological crisis, but usually, in psychotherapy, we deal with traumas that originate from early childhood, youth or other past experiences. Therapy can therefore be considered as a journey or exploration of the unknown, a darkness of the mind. How can a photograph bring to light through this exploration the structure of a traumatised mind and, in turn, function as a therapeutic experience?

It is in my opinion that this journey begins with exploring early childhood experiences.

Early interaction – to be seen and accepted

The history of psychotherapy, which dates back over a hundred years, provides an interesting background for the studies of the human mind. Sigmund Freud revolution-ised psychiatry at the beginning of the twentieth century by emphasising psychological depth concepts such as the possibility of instincts influencing the human mind and emotions. Freud disengaged from the neurologic–physiological research tradition of the times and attempted to create a new 'psychodynamic' theory in which the instincts of life and death were central to human development, as well as the multilevel and complex mother–child relationship. In the twenty-first century, the importance of early childhood relationships and interactions are still seen, in most of the psychotherapies, as the essential basis for life and for succeeding in life. Attachment theories, originating from the work of Bowlby, are psychological and evolutionary theories that provide a descriptive and explanatory framework for understanding interpersonal relationships between human beings. Attachment theorists consider the human infant to have a need for secure relationships with adult caregivers, without which normal social and emotional development will not occur. And what is most impressive is that new brain imaging techniques allow us to see concrete glimpses of how the brain functions and develops in early childhood interactions, as well as in emotional states of later life.

Schore (2003), a Californian neurobiology researcher and psychoanalyst, has been involved with several research groups, studying the development of the human brain and emotional development, and through this work he draws a parallel between early interaction and the therapy relationship regarding brain function. Schore (2003) states that emphatic interaction can develop the ego in childhood and in psychotherapy. From this viewpoint, the effectiveness of phototherapy is based on the following hypotheses:

- Phototherapy stresses the importance of non-verbal communication in the therapeutic relationship and during the therapy sessions.
- Memories and emotions related to childhood relationships can be evoked through childhood photographs in a significant way.
- Through using photographs and photography in psychotherapy, it is possible to facilitate an empowering experience for those clients who have suffered from a lack of acceptance and care; for example, through eye contact.

Phototherapy and social interaction

The mirror neuron system brings yet another reason for the importance of interaction and observation of action. In the 1990s, Italian brain researchers Gallese *et al.* (1996) found, using functional magnetic resonance imaging (fMRI), 'mirror properties' of the human brain – thus, the name mirror neuron system. The mirror neurons were first found in monkeys, but it was later discovered that human brains have similar neurons. The function of mirror neurons is to understand the goals, intentions and emotions of other people, and subsequently to make it possible to react to their actions and emotional state. Assessing the feelings and intentions of others is achieved through observation. We obtain information about other people's attitudes, intentions and feelings by examining their facial gestures, postures, movements and eyes.

According to Rizzolatti *et al.* (2006) the mirror neuron system is also the basis for moral feelings. Our brain leads us to adjust our feelings with the feelings of other people: 'When someone else suffers, our brain causes us to suffer.' Studies have shown that empathic persons mimic other people's facial expressions and gestures more frequently than non-empathic persons. Researchers affirm that the link between the mirror neurons and empathy is clear; it is after all a question of simulating another person's movements of mind and emotions in one's own mind (Hari, 2006). The mirror neuron theory originally developed in Italy by Rizzolatti and further in Finland by Heitanen *et al.* (2008) offers a theoretical basis for using photographs in therapy to help social interaction and to identify feelings, as attentiveness to and interest in recognising faces and interpreting feelings that happen when looking at photographs. Viewers appear particularly sensitive to facial expressions and hand gestures. Viewing photos awakens feelings and incites empathy and can be used as a learning process in therapy.

From the point of view of phototherapy, facial expressions are important indicators of feelings. According to studies, people recognise universally the basic emotions of joy, hatred, disgust, fear and sadness from each other's facial expressions (Saarela *et al.*, 2007). A connection exists between emotions and expression of feelings, as it is important to inform others of the nature of one's emotions. Studies of facial expressions show evidence not only of the universal nature of emotions, but also of how the spectator's emotions and state of mind impact the observations and recollection of the observations (Phelps, 2006). Studies also show potentially how people suffering from depression make observations and interpretations that focus on the negative, viewing dejection and gloominess in people and the world around them (Furey *et al.*, 2006).

These spectators' experiences of facial expressions and factors affecting their interpretation are of particular interest from the point of view of therapeutic work, requiring attention in the therapy sessions.

Heitanen *et al.* (2008) were able to measure the impact of the gaze and demonstrate how it is involved in human motivational reactions. Their study shows that eye contact between two people, including averted gaze, affect the functions of the neural system, which regulates approach and avoidance behaviour. A person's direct gaze prepares the subject for an approach; similarly an averted gaze generates avoidance.

Finnish psychotherapist and trainer Tarja Koffert, who is one of the Finnish pioneers using photography in psychotherapy, suggests that from her experience, autobiographical photos and the taking of self-portraits has a powerful therapeutic effect. Photographs of faces are, in her opinion, an important tool in our learning about how we understand our lives and relationships with significant others.

The action of viewing – biographical photos

From a psychotherapeutic point of view, the biographical photographs are the most interesting and significant source when working with photographs. Family albums and snapshots are important material in understanding a person's life. As one of the pioneers of phototherapy, Judy Weiser (1999) says that biographic collections are visual diaries of life.

In the late 1970s Roland Barthes, French researcher on culture and literature, studied the special nature of photographs in a rather illuminating way. His book, *Camera Lucida*, is a classic on the theoretical study of photographs. What makes photographs special compared to other images is, according to Barthes, the fact that a photograph is the concrete evidence of a moment that has been (Barthes, 1980).

For nearly thirty years, through his essays describing the special nature of photographs, Barthes has motivated other researchers to study the intrinsic characteristics of photographs. Inspired by Barthes, and aware that a number of creditable studies and theses have already been written on the theme, I shall engage myself in the challenge and explore, as if the topic was new, the therapeutic use of photographs from the following points of view:

*   the relation between photographs and reality;
*   the relation between photographs and memories;
*   the relation between photographs and biographical meanings.

The relation between photographs and reality

The reality value of photographs, which has been discussed at length, is beginning to waver given the onset of a digital age. The reality value of photographs encourages criticism; for example, as visual culture researcher Seppänen (2001: 73) claims:

> An image can be a reflection of reality, an image can veil and distort reality, an image can hide the lack of reality and an image can carry absolutely no reference to reality.

However, despite criticisms, we cannot deny the possibility that photographs reflect something of reality. Family album and biographical photographs, for example, have an appeal still in the fact that a photograph can preserve moments of the life we have lived (Barthes, 1980). Further, death is also present, as that moment in time no longer exists and, as a result, photographs can bring about a longing and a feeling of nostalgia. Barthes (1980) located both an emotional level and functional level in photographs. He examined photographs through his own experiences and bodily feelings and noticed that a photograph can be the object of three actions: to do, to look and to be the object. The photographer is the *operator*, the person who looks at the photographs is the *spectator* and the person or thing being photographed is the object, the *spectrum*. Barthes' tri-partition has proved useful also in the classification of the methods of phototherapy.

Another of Barthes' concepts, his definition of photographs on grounds of the feelings and emotions they provoke, has proved immensely popular. He classifies photographs into *studium* and *punctum* photographs, describing *studium* photographs as ordinary photographs, photographs of general interest, intended to provoke only average effect. The photographer's intention, whether it is to inform, to represent, to surprise, to cause, to communicate, or to provoke desire, is visible to the spectator. However, importantly, the photograph does not touch the spectator at a deep emotional level. With *punctum* photographs, on the other hand, the spectator forms a personal emotional relationship with the photographs. The *punctum*, according to Barthes, rises from the photograph with such strength that it can shoot out like an arrow. As Barthes (1980: 47) states, 'the *punctum* is like a sting, hole, speck or a cast of the dice . . . A photograph's *punctum* is that accident which pricks me.'

In my opinion, from a phototherapeutic viewpoint, Barthes' definition of *punctum* images is well in line with the current brain and memory research. Looking at a *punctum* image provokes a significant combination of emotions and memories that can further cause anguish and pain, bringing to mind difficult past events and associated feelings that disrupt the balance of the mind. A *punctum* image can be a biographical, newspaper image, art or any other image and is often intimate and emotive in a way that, through the emotions triggered, becomes of special importance.

Roland Barthes wrote *Camera Lucida* around the time his mother died, a turning point where he was about to lose a loved one. In his grief he sought a connection to his mother by looking at his family photo albums:

> There I was, alone in the apartment where she had died, looking at these pictures of my mother, one by one, under the lamp, gradually moving back in time with her, looking for the truth of the face I had loved. And I found it. The photograph was very old. The corners were blunted from having been pasted into an album, the sepia print had faded, and the picture just managed to show two children standing together at the end of a little wooden bridge in a glassed-in conservatory, what was called a Winter Garden in those days. My mother was five at the time, her brother seven. I studied the little girl and at last rediscovered my mother.
>
> (Barthes, 1980: 63)

Barthes found a photograph of his mother that in his eyes showed the kindness and goodness that he experienced from her. The winter garden photo helped him in his grief to remember his mother the way she was, the true person, not just her photo. In the photo, however, the mother does not appear as his mother, but shows his mother as a child. In his book Barthes says that looking at the photograph was his way of conquering his experience of, and feelings of, her death.

Barthes' experiences of the value of the photograph, as the witness of a moment and a source of nostalgia and emotional observation, illustrates the value of photographs as tools in psychotherapy. He suggests that, through photographs, we can find emotional connection with significant people and events of our lives.

The relation between photographs, memories and biographical meanings

Through his own self-observation, Barthes (1980) found how the emotionally significant picture rises from the flood of images and pierces consciousness like an arrow. The concept of *punctum* receives theoretical support from the field of psychology research and in particular observational psychology, which suggests that biologically and socially significant stimuli automatically direct human attention. Attention-orientating mechanisms allow us to select meaningful information from our environment by increasing efficiency at the expense of other information processes. Nummenmaa (2006) bases his studies on the development of species and assumes that biologically significant objects important from the point of view of well-being would be given priority in the knowledge systems of our mind, and that attention would be focused on this type of object without conscious effort.

The basic idea of phototherapy is that from the abundance of photos there are significant photographs that arouse interest as if they were magnets and, subsequently, once chosen, their contents will be discussed and studied from multiple aspects. The essential point is that working with photographs is not restricted to verbal descriptions; with photographs, associative work is also possible, almost promoting time travel led by emotions. Biographical time travel involves remembering one's own life. Biographical photographs are therefore a logical source of knowledge of one's life events, in addition to verbal reminiscing. Barthes' (1980: 77) previously mentioned insights into the photograph – 'That has been' and 'It [the *punctum*] shoots out of [the photograph] like an arrow and pierces me' – provide a challenge that should not be overlooked in psychotherapy.

From the viewpoint of phototherapy it is interesting to note the connection between perception and previous experiences as a special characteristic related to memory: memory encoding and memory retrieval. The concept was created by Tulving (1989), where the idea is that the principle of the specificity of encoding, according to that unique way in which an event is structured in one's mind and how it is encoded into the mind, also determines how the event will be retrieved. It is beneficial for the process of remembering if the circumstances during encoding and retrieving are similar.

Schacter (1996) describes this phenomenon in his book *Searching for Memory: The brain, the mind and the past*. According to Schacter, it is confusing that the successful retrieval of memories is highly dependent on the availability of memory clues, because self-perception is so strongly connected to remembering the past. He states how we are not aware of all the events in our past, because we do not come across memory clues that would evoke memories. In order for us to improve our understanding of ourselves we must one way or another find or create clues that help us to remember forgotten events. Without memory clues these events would disappear.

Feelings, memory and flashbacks after threatening situations

In a severe crisis, emotions become activated and control human feelings and activities for survival. Further, it is important to note that an efficient body alarm system is an advantage in terms of the ability to react to a crisis, but in the long term it can be fatal to the human psyche. The foundations for experiencing feelings are formed at an early stage in emotional interaction through being emotionally close to people (Damasio, 1999).

It is characteristic of a difficult traumatic event to remain in the memory for a long time, to remain unchanged, and to be susceptible to uncontrollable sensory effects; for example, visual recalling. The extremes of remembering a trauma may change from detailed recalling of sense perceptions to the diversity and fragmentation of memories or even to a total forgetting of the event. Trauma researcher Van der Kolk (1989) even mentions *on–off experiences* characteristic of a trauma memory wherein traumatic memories are no longer conscious. The problem is that in a traumatic experience, the different parts of the memory, which are connected to the event, are not integrated. It is also typical that there are difficulties in describing a trauma by verbal means. The experience in this case is, to some extent, an encapsulated experience and a piece of unconscious information that cannot be understood and verbalised into memory or con-nected to one's own life story. The difficulty in reaching events is the central problem in post-traumatic stress reactions and disorders.

Just like memory, emotions are also a part of the puzzle. The memory of a traumatic experience can stay with a person as an undefined somatic experience or, for example, as a feeling of fear or disgust with which a person cannot form an understandable contact. In the more severe cases this can lead to psychiatric disorder. In psychiatry, the unconnected and unattainable nature of a traumatic event is called dissociation. Dissociation can be described as the inability to piece together thoughts, feelings and memories into a meaningful entity to form a part of one's own life story. Dissociated memories can be like emotional roller coasters or black holes that are safe when kept separate from one's own world of experience.

In terms of psychotherapeutic work, it is important to be aware of the importance and nature of the black holes and scars during the client's trauma experience as well as the effects of the experience on the present. Phototherapy provides a means of successful processing of a traumatic experience, whereby a situation is reached where the memories of the trauma become an integral part of the person's life story and he/she can then trust in surviving the trauma (Berntsen and Rubin, 2007).

The photograph as a tool in psychotherapy

The use of photographs in psychotherapy gives people new tools to understand their situation. I have devised a collection of photographs that I call Spectro Cards (Halkola and Koffert, 2011) for phototherapy. Two examples of these are given in this chapter (see Photos 2.1 and 2.2, chosen by a client named Charlotte) which Del Loewenthal

Photo 2.1
Charlotte's first choice of photograph
(Halkola).

Photo 2.2
Charlotte's second choice of photograph
(Halkola).

refers to when describing their use in counselling and psychotherapy in Chapter 7 and
14. Photographs and taking photographs help people to perceive events and to realise
their importance at a non-verbal level. Second, it is easy to talk and to reminisce when
looking at photographs, even about difficult events in life. Photographs are a part of
the reality, but they also leave room for reinterpretations. Photographs are children of
the moment that detach you from the 'here and now'. And, within therapy, photographs
are viewed, taken and experienced together.

In the process of psychotherapy, the role of the therapist stands to treat the client
and to support his/her psychological process. A reflective approach is important in the
therapeutic relationship and requires the therapist to be involved in the client's situation.
It also requires constant self-observation, thorough self-knowledge and the ability to
acknowledge transference and counter-transference.

Schore (2003) compares the nature of the psychotherapeutic relationship with the
attachment relationship in early childhood. Both involve an emotional relationship,
regulation of feelings, becoming understood and an element of growth. Schore's (2003)
thesis is that the essence of the change mechanism is a face-to-face interaction, and
that change takes place at an unconscious level. Expressing feelings and regulating
feelings in a safe environment furthers the development of the client's self-understanding.
The additional value of a photograph compared to a traditional conversational therapy
is the fact that photographs bring to the interactive therapy sessions a concrete object,
a symbol – a photograph that can be perceived and worked with together by the client

and the therapist. It is of great importance that the majority of photographs used in therapy are biographically meaningful pictures. Photographs give the therapist a realistic picture of the external reality of the client outside the therapy and the causes of confusion he/she encounters in that reality: the *punctums*. In this respect, phototherapy differs from art therapy, where the client paints or produces mental landscapes and a reflection of his/her internal world. Phototherapy involves the presence of pictures that are representations of the external reality brought to existence by using a camera. One must bear in mind, however, that taking a photograph is always the photographer's expression of mind, his/her choice and thus a personal, individual product. Photographs themselves do not tell truths; however, they offer symbolic material and open doors to a world of possibilities that can be discussed together.

References

Barthes, R. (1980). *Camera Lucida: Reflections on photography*. New York: Hill & Wang.

Berntsen, D. and Rubin, D.C. (2007). When a trauma becomes a key to identity: Enhanced integration of trauma memories predicts posttraumatic stress disorder symptoms. *Applied Cognitive Psychology*, 431, 417–431.

Damasio, A.R. (1999). *The Feeling of What Happens*. New York: Harcourt.

Furey, M.L., Tanskanen, T., Beauchamp, M., Avikainen, S., Uutela, K., Hari, R. and Haxby, J.V. (2006). Modulation of early and late neural responses to faces and houses by selective attention. *Proceedings of the National Academy of Sciences of the United States of America*, 103, 1065–1070.

Gallese, V., Fadiga, L., Fogassi, L. and Rizzolatti, G. (1996). Action recognition in the premotor cortex. *Brain*, 119, 593–609.

Halkola, U. and Koffert, T. (2011). The many stories of being. In *PHOTOTHERAPYEUROPE: Learning and Healing with Phototherapy – A handbook*, University of Turku: Publications of the Brahea Centre for Training and Development.

Also available at http://phototherapyeurope.utu.fi/photoeurope_handbook.pdf.

Hari, R. (2006). Sosiaalisen vuorovaikutuksen aivoperustasta. Kirjassa Mieli ja Aivot. Kognitiivisen neurotieteen oppikirja (eds H. Hämäläinen, M. Laine, O. Aaltonen and A. Revonsuo). *Gummerus*, Luku (8)2, 399–405.

Hietanen, J.K., Leppänen, J.M., Nummenmaa, L. and Astikainen, P. (2008). Visuospatial attention shifts by gaze and arrow cues: An ERP study. *Brain Research*, 1215, 123–136.

Nummenmaa, L. (2006). Orienting of social attention. Doctoral thesis. University of Turku, Turun yliopiston julkaisuja, sarja B, osa 292, Turku, Finland.

Phelps, E.A. (2006). Emotion and cognition: Insights from studies of the human amygdala. *Annual Review of Psychology*, 57, 27–53.

Rizzolatti, G., Fogassi, L. and Gallese, V. (2006). Mirrors in the mind. *Scientific American*, 295(5), 54–61.

Saarela, M.V., Hlushchuk, Y., Williams, A.C. de C., Schürmann, M., Kalso, E. and Hari, R. (2007). The compassionate brain: Humans detect intensity of pain from another's face. *Cerebral Cortex*, 17, 230–237.

Schacter, D.L. (1996). *Searching for Memory: The brain, the mind, and the past*. New York: Basic Books.

Schore, A. (2003). *Affect Dysregulation and Disorders of the Self*. London: W.W. Norton & Company.

Seppänen, J. (2001). *Katseen voima. Kohti visuaalista lukutaitoa*. Tampere: Vastapaino.

Stewart, D. (1979). Photo therapy: Theory & practice. *Art Psychotherapy*, 6(1), 41–46.

Tulving, E. (1989). Memory: Performance, knowledge and experience. *European Journal of Cognitive Psychology*, 1, 3–26.

Weiser, J. (1999). *PhotoTherapy Techniques: Exploring the secrets of personal snapshots and family albums*. Vancouver: Phototherapy Centre.

Van der Kolk, B.A. (1989). The compulsion to repeat the trauma: Revictimization, attachment and masochism. *Psychiatric Clinics of North America*, 12, 389–411.

Chapter 3

Jo Spence's camera therapy
Personal therapeutic photography as a response to adversity

Terry Dennett

Introduction: group camera and Jo Spence

One of the pioneers of contemporary therapeutic photography in the UK, who has not received due recognition, is the Art and Drama teacher Keith Kennedy. Working at the Henderson Psychiatric Hospital in the 1970s, Kennedy formulated what he called 'Group Camera' to use with patients in the psychiatric community there. He then taught these techniques to professional photographer Jo Spence, who he called in to assist. Their meeting can be seen as the key event for setting the scene for the subsequent later development in the UK of 'Therapeutic Photography', by Jo Spence and her various later collaborators.

The Henderson hospital and its antecedence

The Henderson Hospital established in 1947 quickly gained an international reputation as a pioneer in the democratic community non drug treatment of mental illness. It carried forward and extended earlier work formulated at the Social Psychotherapy Centre, Hampstead, in 1946 by Joseph Bierer, the first psychotherapist in a public mental hospital, noted especially for his pioneering of community and group therapies, and the creation of social clubs for recovering patients. Maxwell Jones (1949–55) further developed the concept of the 'therapeutic community' at the predecessor to the Henderson Hospital, the Social Rehabilitation Unit, Belmont Hospital, in Sutton. Belmont eventually encouraged the development of other units, making it possible in 1972 for Drs Whiteley, Hinshelwood and Manning to found the Association of Therapeutic Communities.

About Jo Spence

Jo Spence was a photographer, writer and workshop organiser – and eventually a cancer activist – who in a short but busy life made numerous major contributions to many areas of contemporary photography. A diagnosis of breast cancer in 1982 caused her to decide to use her photography therapeutically, as an integral part of her broader alternative and complementary cancer treatment programme.

Spence never deliberately set out to be an innovator but she was one of those individuals who come along from time to time with fresh ideas gained through the experience of solving their own problems, who then feel driven to communicate these ideas, and in so doing shake up a complacent status quo – thus making some lasting changes to contemporary practice.

She was not a trained therapist (and never tried to misrepresent herself as such), but was more fortunate than most non-professionals in being able to bring to her illness experience a pre-existing background in both professional photography and a knowledge of alternative medicine, as well as a broad understanding of film and theatre acquired in the course of her work at the British Film Institute. Spence was able to see many rare films during her employment at the British Film Institute in London, including work by the great Russian directors Sergei Eisenstein, Lev Kulasov and Dziga Vertov – whose methods of collision linkage and factography influenced the later development of the photo theatre method. Sergei Eisenstein's notion of film as process underlies a lot of Spence's thinking, and his view that the task of the director/photographer is to process the spectator through a series of 'collisions' or shocks. This can also be seen as a natural process that takes place outside art/films.

Therefore, unlike most non-medical people suddenly struck down by illness, she had no need to spend valuable time acquiring any extra skills but could instead quickly apply her already existing knowledge base to the task of organising her own health survival programme.

As an experienced photographer, Spence immediately saw the value of this medium as a natural part of her preferred alternative and complementary cancer treatments. A committed album maker, she soon set about creating the first of her 'visual illness diaries', and from the beginning created photographs not only for her own immediate use as self-therapy and personal documentation, but also consciously constructed for future use as critical campaign material for the women's and disability movements as well. After her recovery from her breast cancer surgery treatment, this work was indeed used in various publications and also became an important touring photo exhibition: 'The Picture of Health'(1986).

Therapeutic staging

Spence's 'therapeutic staging', developed quite by accident out of her previous 'photo theatre' work, led to the Massachusetts Institute of Technology's exhibition 'Remodelling Photo History'. After her return from hospital she noticed that one of the staged pictures taken of her breast the night before her operation (see the photograph in Spence, 1986: 157), showed unintended therapeutic effects: this image was not a re-enactment of an existing situation, but was instead a projection into the future and a visual statement of ownership directed towards the hospital who would the next day carry out the breast-removal cancer surgery. Thereafter, therapeutic staging photo-activities were routinely done in parallel with the straight photo-documentation for her visual illness diary, as a necessary and complementary addition to the simple statement of what was in front of the camera. In this way, she found she could integrate what she saw with what she felt internally. From the start Spence was considered a slightly unusual patient, especially when a nurse saw Spence's staged breast picture in her case. Because of her insistence (after much research) that she wanted only a lumpectomy rather than the conventional full mastectomy, Spence was seen by the hospital staff as a nuisance and a time waster. This opinion was reinforced when she rejected anti-depressant drugs in favour of meditation and music therapy (and later camera therapy). It is worth noting

Photo 3.1 Jo Spence's mirror therapy (Dennett).

that ten years later it was recognised that in the case of small tumours like hers, a lumpectomy is as effective as mastectomy for breast cancer treatment (Gottlieb, 2002).

Mirror therapy

Spence seems to have been one of the few to adopt the mirror as a phototherapeutic tool. Her reasons were diverse: not only did the mirror enable her eye to see itself without the intervention of the camera or having to wait for prints to be processed, it was also an inexpensive way of staging and rehearsing scenarios for later photography and subsequent photographic projects. Additionally, it was seen as a tool for a 'reflective participation' with herself – a means whereby she could be both patient and imaginary therapist, both self and other (an example of which can be seen in Photo 3.1).

Once again her studies prior to her illness had provided a valuable collection of material to call upon in her time of need. And in fact, since her death, it seems to be increasingly recognised that those who can bring previous knowledge and life experience to bear on their illness do far better than those with no such prior background experiences.

In the 1970s, Spence investigated the mythology of the mirror as part of her college degree studies of magical realism and the Cinderella myth. During that work she had been intrigued by the various ancient notions of the mirror as the gateway to another world and by the Greek story in which Perseus can only slay the Medusa by looking at her reflected in a mirror (a metaphor she found resonant with her own initial fear of looking directly at her cancerous breast when she first realised she had a tumour inside it). Her college studies also included work on the story of Amaterasu (the Japanese sun goddess lured out of her cave by a mirror to relight the world), as well as the many references to the mirror in Lewis Caroll's *Alice Through the Looking Glass* (2003).

Scripting

Scripting is a semi-ritualistic method for mapping out the basic elements of a therapeutic photo drama prior to it being photographed. It was inspired by the methods of Carl Happich (www.themystica.com/mystica/articles/v/visualization_training.html) and Robert Desoille (Desoille, 1961; Honeycutt, 2003, 2008), both of whom advocated the use of predetermined scenes and symbolic archetypal images in therapy. Spence modified these ideas by suggesting the use of dialectical concepts rather than specific scenes. Working in this focused way the photographer could then generate images based upon their own culture and life experience. Scripting in Spence's reworking not only employs a preliminary diagramming to help structure the scripted photo play but also 'mind mapping' for post session analysis.

It will also be seen that Spence's scripting system also includes a physical therapy (the act of practising facial expressions) that materially enhances the basic photo play.

Scripting was also influenced by the writings of Kenneth Burke (1969) – especially his 'Pentad' (used by playwrights, authors and journalists to examine the form and structure of their work and consisting of a five-element analysis of a situation, broken down into the act, scene, agent, agency and purpose) and his concept of 'Dramatis' (if action, then drama; if drama, then conflict; if conflict, then victimage).

Scripting was only intended to help Spence with her solo therapy work and was not used with the later collaborative phototherapy but Spence did successfully practise this method in two group sessions with other cancer sufferers in Nottingham (Spence, personal communication).

Additionally, in 1991, at the suggestion of her partner David Roberts, she adapted the work of Eric Eriksson so therapeutic photodrama could be used in her work on their personal relationship. This work apparently included a physical facial expression element (David Roberts personal communication).

Collaborative photo therapy

As named and developed in 1983 by Jo Spence together with Rosy Martin, 'collaborative photo therapy' combined some of Jo Spence's earlier Nottingham cancer camerawork, such as therapeutic staging with the co-counselling system (also known as 'relational counselling' (or 'RC'), that was formulated in the early 1950s by Harvey Jackin (1970). Unlike more traditional counselling done as psychotherapy by trained/licensed mental health therapists, co-counselling is not a formal therapy field and instead uses reciprocal peer-to-peer counselling where each participant takes turns being counsellor and client. Spence and Martin reworked the co-counselling system to introduce an important re-evaluation of the usual photographer–sitter/client relationship: the sitter becomes creative director while the photographer's role is elevated to that of therapist; the camera operation is then seen as a simple technical process. After each session the roles are reversed and the previous photographer becomes the new creative director. Each then

---

Box 3:1 Spence's notes re: mirror practice in self-portraiture therapy

Desensitization---- release emotions-- change tight body language-- re model old image into something else-- say Yes when my face and body says No ------ To look -----when my mind says don't look---- at that mutilated Breast

To change the visual concept from --- dependant self-pitying victim--- to a positive A survivor---- Cancer War Hero--put on some medals-- a soldiers hat ???-- people used to look up to War heroes didn't they--- not any more though!!!!!!

 Qualities to think about:
The Mirror is dumb non evaluative and non-human -- whatever I do in front of it -- It can't be critical like a person- It is not my Mummy or Daddy -- mirror pictures are a private self-activated show -- just for me until I want to invite others in.

Mirror images cannot be saved for others to see later --- so it is safe to be uninhibited and show /release my most exposed self--? important when I'm vulnerable to work alone for a session ??? but needs courage--do/will I always have the courage to face reality alone ?? Mirror image is a reflection of the living image in real time ----but as ephemeral as real time--- it is not automatically preserved- except-imperfectly-in memory

The Photographer as a Resurrectionist--- not a body snatcher --- not TAKING pictures but reconstituting events

The Camera process can encapsulation real-time aspects-- but only as a dead embalmed cultural artifact------- photographs are pieces of paper-- why do people forget that ----So our task as photographers is to resurrect these dead things- to use our Art to get the shapes encoded in the paper to express something of the realities of the former living essence we confronted with our camera---

Thank God for a shared process of communication----- What would we do without it--and who will truly read our images and our intent when we do not share the same cultural codes?

Mirror image -- a part self -- a shadow self-- looks real -- moves in time and space but only a reflected illusion -- therefore some of my pretend situations and constructed image rehearsals will be no less real than others I can choose my visual reality-- dress up ---makeup --all appear real -- but all are illusion in the mirror

The Mirror and the Camera -- Set up Camera with bulb release to click any useful images -- first start with mirror rehearsal -- No Photos --- only looking -- then more photos less [looking--------

'Surviving Mirror Therapy' Script: Script influenced by the work of Elisabeth Kübler-Ross -- Combines mirror expression exercises followed by mirror photo play:

Script sequence
Disbelief Denial: Anger Resentment: Bargaining Depression Acceptance:
Facial Expressions: Disbelief Denial Anger Resentment
Photo Play: Bargaining Depression Acceptance
Spend at least 5 minutes rehearsing each script element before photography

has full creative management of their own sessions and ownership of their session films afterwards.

In order to acknowledge this collaborative relationship in published pictures produced during such work, Spence and Martin created a double 'credit byline' (for example, 'Jo Spence in collaboration with Rosy Martin') and therefore their therapeutic photography work (though originally called 'photo therapy') moved much closer to film in its multiple accreditation recognition.

The publication of Jo Spence's (1986) book *Putting Myself in the Picture: A political, personal and photographic autobiography* discussing these methods has been largely responsible for much interest in this kind of work by photography and media students in the UK. However, not many students seem to have taken up the challenge of working collaboratively or in groups, presumably because of the individualistic grading and examination system that still operates in UK colleges.

Acknowledgements

I would like to express my thanks to the late Nelson Wilbey of the Well Spring Book Shop in London for his advice and assistance during the preparation of this chapter.

References

Burke, K. (1969). *A Grammar of Motives*. Berkeley, CA: University of California Press.

Carroll, L. (2003). *Through the Looking Glass and What Alice Found There*. London: Puffin Classics.

Desoille, R. (1961). *Théorie et pratique du rêve-éveillé dirigé*. Geneva: Le Mont-Blanc.

Gottlieb, S. (2002). Lumpectomy is as effective as mastectomy for breast cancer. *BMJ*, 325, 921.

Happich, Carl. Available from: www.themystica.com/mystica/articles/v/visualization_training. html (accessed 30 December 2011).

Honeycutt, J.M. (2003). *Imagined Interactions: Daydreaming about communication*. Cresskill, NJ: Hampton Press.

Honeycutt, J.M. (ed.) (2008). *Imagine That: Studies in imagined interaction*. Cresskill, NJ: Hampton Press.

Spence, J. (1986). *Putting Myself in the Picture: A political personal and photographic autobiography*. London: Camden Press.

Bibliography

Regarding Jo Spence and her work

Dennett, T. (1983). *Re-modelling Photo History* (exhibition catalogue). Massachusetts: Massachusetts Institute of Technology.

Dennett, T. (1992). *Real Stories: The 'Crisis Project: Scenes of the Crime'* (exhibition catalogue). Odense, Denmark: Museet for Fotokunst.

Dennett, T. (1994). Notes of 'The Final Project: A photofantasy and phototherapeutic exploration of life and death' (unpublished manuscript). London: Jo Spence Memorial Archive.

Dennett, T. (1995). Jo Spence 1934–1992: An afterword and a warning (unpublished manuscript). London: Jo Spence Memorial Archive.

Dennett, T. (2001). The wounded photographer: The genesis of Jo Spence's 'camera therapy'. *Afterimage*, 29(3), 26–27.

Dennett, T. (2005). *Jo Spence: 'Beyond the Family Album' and other projects* (exhibition catalogue). Belfast: Exposed Photography.

Evans, J. (ed.) (1997). *The Camerawork Essays. Context and meaning in photography.* London: Rivers Oram Press.

Hagiwara, H. (ed.) (2005). *Jo Spence Autobiographical Photography.* Osaka: Shinsuisha Press.

Hevey, D. (1989). Liberty, equality, disability. *Ten*: 8(35), 2–15.

Hirsch, M. (1997). *Family Frames: Photography, narrative, and postmemory.* Cambridge: Harvard University Press.

Martin, R. (1990). Dirty linen: Photo therapy, memory, and identity. *Ten*, 8(37), 1–10.

Salomon-Godeau, A. (1987). Review of *Putting Myself in the Picture. Art in America*, July, 25.

Spence, J. (1976). *The Politics of Photography.* London: Camerawork.

Spence, J. (1978–79). What do people do all day? Class and gender in images of women. *Screen Education*, 29, Winter, 9–45.

Spence, J. (1980). Beyond the family album. *Ten*, 8(4), 21–23.

Spence, J. (1980). Self-portraits. *Ten*, 8(4) Spring.

Spence, J. (1981). Cultural sniper. *Ten*, 8(2), 9–25.

Spence, J. (1981). The sign as a site of class struggle: Reflections on works by John Heartfield. *Block*, 5, 2–13.

Spence, J. (1983). Confronting cancer. *City Limits*, 22 July, 4.

Spence, J. (1983). War photos: The home front (unpublished lecture for Polytechnic of Central London). London. Date unknown – collection Jo Spence Memorial Archive.

Spence, J. (1984). Public images/private functions: Reflections on high street practice. *Ten*, 8(13), 7–17.

Spence, J. (1986). Body beautiful or body in crisis? *OpenMind*, 21, 10–14.

Spence, J. (1986). Photo therapy. *Venue*, 14(101), 48–49.

Spence, J. (1986). *Putting Myself in the Picture: A political, personal and photographic autobiography.* London: Camden Press.

Spence, J. (1986). The picture of health. *Spare Rib*, 163, 19–24.

Spence, J. (1986). The picture of health: Part 2. *Spare Rib*, 165, 20–25.

Spence, J. (1987). Putting yourself in the picture. *Women Live*, 2, 12–16.

Spence, J. (1987). Things my father never taught me. *Ten*, 8(25), 24–25.

Spence, J. (1988). Notes on photo therapy sessions between Valerie Walkerdine and myself (unpublished manuscript). London: Jo Spence Memorial Archive.

Spence, J. (1989). Disrupting the silence: The daughter's story. *Women Artists Slide Library Journal*, 29, 14–17.

Spence, J. (1989). Notes after photo therapy session with Tim (unpublished manuscript). London: Jo Spence Memorial Archive, April.

Spence, J. (1990). 'No, I can't do that, my Consultant wouldn't like it'. In *Silent Health: Women, health, and representation* (pp. 75–90). London: Camerawork.

Spence, J. (1990). Could do better . . . *Variant*, 8, 27–32.

Spence, J. (1990). Identity and cultural production: Or, on deciding to become the subject of our own histories rather than the object of somebody else's. *Views: The Journal of Photography in New England*, 11(3), Summer, 8–11.

Spence, J. (1991). Soap, family album work, and hope. In: Spence, J. and Holland, P. (eds), *Family Snaps: The meanings of domestic photography* (pp. 200–207). London: Virago Press.

Spence, J. (1991). *Unbecoming Mothers: A daughter's view* (exhibition catalogue curated by Sue Isherwood and John Solomon). Bristol: Watershed Media, 25–28.

Spence, J. (1995). *Cultural Sniping: The art of transgression.* London: Routledge.

Spence, J. and Dennett, T. (1976). Photography, ideology and education. *Screen Education*, 21, 85–96.

Spence, J. and Dennett, T. (1977). Remodelling photo-history: An afterword on a recent exhibition. *Screen Education*, 23(1), May/June, 85–86.

Spence, J. and Dennett, T. (1982). Remodelling photo history. *Ten*, 8(9), 34–38.

Spence, J. and Dennett, T. (1992). The crisis project: Scenes of the crime. *Katalog*, 4, 49–51.

Spence, J. and Grover, J.Z. (1991). The artist and illness: Cultural burn-out/holistic health. *Artpaper*. In Spence (1995) *Cultural Sniping* (pp. 212–217). London: Routledge.

Spence, J. and Hevey, D. (1992). Cancer and the marks of struggle (interview with Jo Spence). In: Hevey, D. (ed.), *The Creatures That Time Forgot: Photography and disability imagery* (pp. 120–133). London: Routledge.

Spence, J. and Holland, P. (1991). *Family Snaps: Meanings of domestic photography.* London: Virago Press.

Spence, J. and Solomon, J. (1991). *What Can a Woman Do with a Camera?* London: Scarlet Press.

Spence, J., Brackx, A. and Marcolis, A. (1978). Facing up to myself. *Spare Rib*, 68, 6–9.

Spence, J., Evans, D., Dennett, T. and Gohl, S. (1980). *Photography/Politics: One.* London: Photography Workshop.

Spence, J., Holland, P. and Watney, S. (1987). *Photography/Politics: Two.* London: Comedia/Photography Workshop.

Spence, J. with Martin, R., Murray, M. and Stanjo, Y. (1985). *The Picture of Health* (Cockpit Gallery exhibition catalogue). London: Photography Workshop.

Wakakuwa, M. and Kasahara, M. (1991). *Exploring the Unknown Self: Self portraits of contemporary women* (exhibition catalogue). Tokyo: Tokyo Metropolitan Culture Foundation/ Metropolitan Museum of Photography.

Weiser, J. (1983). Using photographs in therapy with people who are 'different'. In: Krauss, D.A. and Fryrear, J.L. (eds), *Phototherapy in Mental Health* (pp. 174–199). Springfield, IL: Charles C. Thomas.

Weiser, J. (1988). PhotoTherapy: Using snapshots and photo-interactions in therapy with youth. In: Schaefer, C. (ed.), *Innovative Interventions in Child and Adolescent Therapy* (pp. 339–376). New York: Wiley.

Weiser, J. (1990). Grover wrong about 'phototherapists' Spence and Martin. *Afterimage*, 18(4), 2.

Weiser, J. (1990). 'More than meets the eye': Using ordinary snapshots as tools for therapy. In: Laidlaw, T., Malmo, C. and Associates (eds), *Healing Voices: Feminist approaches to therapy with women* (pp. 83–117). San Francisco, CA: Jossey-Bass.

Weiser, J. (1993; 1999, 2nd edition). *PhotoTherapy Techniques: Exploring the secrets of personal snapshots and family albums.* Vancouver: PhotoTherapy Centre Press.

Weiser, J. (2001). PhotoTherapy techniques: Using clients' personal snapshots and family photos as counseling and therapy tools (invited feature article in 'Special Double Issue: *Media Art as/in Therapy*'). *Afterimage: The Journal of Media Arts and Cultural Criticism*, 29(3) (Nov./Dec.), 10–15.

Weiser, J. (2005). Remembering Jo Spence: A brief personal and professional memoir. In: H. Hagiwara (ed.), *Jo Spence Autobiographical Photography* (pp. 240–248). Osaka: Shinsuisha Press.

Weiser, J. (2008). PhotoTherapy and Therapeutic Photography: Similarities and differences. Available from: www.phototherapy-centre.com/comparisons.htm#Comp2 (accessed 2 June 2008).

Wilson, S. (1996–97). White metonymy: A discussion around Jo Spence and Terry Dennett's colonization. *Third Text*, 37, Winter, 3–16.

Regarding illness narrative and visual representation

Bell, S. (1999). Narratives and lives: Women's health politics and the diagnosis of cancer for DES daughters. *Narrative Inquiry*, 9(2), 347–389.

Bell, S. (2002). Photo images: Jo Spence's narratives of living with illness. *Health*, 6(1), 5–30.

Bell, S. (2006). Living with breast cancer in text and image: Making art to make sense (special issue on 'Embodiment'). *Qualitative Research in Psychology*, 3(1), 31–44.

Bell, S. and Radley, A. (2007). Artworks, collective experience, and claims for social justice: The case of women living with breast cancer. *Sociology of Health and Illness*, 29(3), 366–390.

Einat, A. (2007). *The Invading Body: Reading illness autobiographies*. Charlottesville, VA: University of Virginia Press.

Gilman, S. (1977). *The Face of Madness: Hugh W. Diamond and the rise of psychiatric photography*. Secaucus, NJ: Citadel Press (reissue of: (1976) New York: Brunner/Mazel).

Gilman, S. (1982). *Seeing the Insane*. New York: John Wiley.

Gilman, S. (1991). *Disease and Representation: Images of illness from madness to AIDS* (2nd edn). Ithaca, NY: Cornell University Press.

Gilman, S. (1995). *Picturing Health and Illness: Images of difference*. Baltimore, MD: Johns Hopkins University Press.

Radley, A. (2009). Works of illness: Narrative, picturing and the social response to serious illness. Ganesh Nagar, India: Inkman Press.

Chapter 4

Fotos, fones & fantasies

Mark Wheeler

This chapter widens the phototherapy field by considering the interconnected actions of the phone camera, other mobile image making and viewing devices, social networking websites, online galleries and outsider art. Further, it aims to examine these activities as much from an art-historical perspective as from neurobiological and psychoanalytic perspectives.

Human interconnectedness constantly evolves to meet the demands of human existence, as human invention continues to create new technology to keep up with evolving aspirations, regardless of their utility. The psychological aesthetics of the makers, senders or uploaders and viewers of images, reflects their psychological processes in choosing these actions. This is the most widely practised outsider art on the planet and thus exemplifies in content and form the state of human interconnectedness long before observers, researchers and commentators have reached any consensus.

'Fotos, fones & fantasies' draws on familiar domestic photography, fine-art photography, art history, art therapy, neuroscience and psychological aesthetics. This chapter attempts to offer insight into the psychological dimensions of making and viewing smartphone and online gallery images and how these affect therapeutic processes whether explicitly acknowledged or not.

Phototherapy is the practice of psychotherapists, counsellors and other helping professionals who conduct conversations with clients, prompted by photographs, whether the photographs are present or not. This deceptively simple definition of contemporary phototherapy practice helps clarify the breadth and depth of practice beyond either the acts of making and viewing photographs with clients, or the passing of battered enprints (those little plastic-surfaced 6 × 4s) between client and therapist. Now that therapists are more likely to be offered a mobile phone camera gallery than prints, horizons have extended.

The phrase 'fotos, fones & fantasies' exploits text style spelling to introduce a way of thinking about the images contained within, or networked from, mobile devices such as smartphones:

> *Fotos* – refers to light, to the syntax of photography, to the individual photon striking the film, the CCD or CMOS sensor or the viewer's retina, whether direct or mediated by smartphone sensor, screen or cellular network.
> *Fones* – refers to the mobile telephone (cellphone) device itself and to sound and video recording, being both visual and auditory.

Fantasies – include the psychology of the aesthetic experience, the phenomenology of every encounter with a photographic image, the imaginal relationship with the phone and its gallery.

Art informs us more about psychology than psychology can ever inform us about art, and it does so earlier and more explicitly too. The widespread practice of smartphone photography and online display, especially on social networking sites, is the latest example.

The raw material of encounters with photographs, whether printed on paper, projected on screen, framed in galleries or shown on the screen of a handheld device (digital camera, smartphone, digital photo-frame) is not unlike raw wool newly shorn. It is a mass of fine fibres that have individually grown in apparently random directions whose interweaving makes it impossible to identify and follow any individual strand as it disappears between scores of others. Disentangling this useful material requires teasing and carding the threads before spinning a yarn. The yarns of encounters with photographs offer insights into the psychological dimensions of making and viewing all photographs, including smartphone and online gallery images. Furthermore, these yarns may be woven into patterns enabling us to identify their contribution and effect on therapeutic encounters.

Unfortunately, in teasing and separating these strands for examination, their original relationship is altered, damaging the very thing we seek to examine. The strands include, but are not limited to, speech acts; image selection; images presented; images viewed; implicit and explicit understanding; known connectivity; unknown connectivity; fantasies of connectivity; transference and countertransference (whether or not embodied in images), in addition to dimensions often present when photographs are presented outside a therapy context. In the therapy room these various strands act simultaneously, which contributes to their power as catalysts and containers. Hence, after carding, teasing and spinning our yarn, the strands need to be woven back together into a coherent material if we are to gain useful understanding.

A valuable contribution to understanding the psychology of art is equally applicable to understanding of the art of psychology. The human drive to create objects and to consume or view them has left traces over thousands of years, from cave art and fingerprints on decorated beakers to the electronic fingerprints of MySpace, Flickr and Facebook. The experience of such making and viewing might be described within the term '*psychological aesthetics*':

> Psychological Aesthetics refers to the relation between the actual (aesthetic) qualities of painting, such as line, colour, handling, composition and so on and the inner (psychological) effects that these have on the spectator.
>
> (Maclagan, 2002: 7)

The psychological aesthetics of all photographs, be they digital or wet processes, printed, projected or virtual have been described in the phrase 'Photo-Psycho-Praxis' (Wheeler, 2008, 2009) in the therapeutic contexts of photography. Whether or not these are explicitly encountered and acknowledged in the therapy room, an extra dimension becomes present when we are, inevitably, surrounded by the omnipresent webs of cellular

Photo 4.1 Twenty-first-century mobile phone user (Wheeler).

networks, 3G, the World Wide Web and social networking and online galleries. The air in the consulting room (unless we practise in a Faraday cage) is permeated by radio waves carrying all of the above, simultaneously. With only a few grams of silicon and Li-ion power source, mobile phones can decode these mysterious signals and lay them before us (see Photo 4.1).

These signals and that which is stored in any smartphone's memory almost exist as a superstructure above our practice, a superstructure that might therefore envelop practice with fantasy in the context of encounters in therapy.

Context

These cellular images now conflate the domestic context, from which much of our photographic experience emerges, with outsider and public art contexts. The sharing of domestic images can now be more widely disseminated than those in galleries and art books from the art establishment. This outsider art practice seems to reclaim from the art establishment the capacity of anyone with a minimum of equipment to make

Culture: includes society, nation, local identity, local stories, ethnicity & its stories, faith, legal systems etc, the dictates of when it is appropriate to photograph (eg weddings but not funerals), to be photographed, or to show photographs

Family scripts: include any generalising or generalised statement, habit or story that can then become a personal script or story for any family member; who takes the pictures, who controls the content and action portrayed, whether the family have a picture making tradition, where they are displayed or shown

Relationship: includes the nature and descriptions of connections, and the patterns of connections; the contextual force from the family script may operate very powerfully on who takes the photographs, to whom they are shown

Episode: includes transitions, crises, life events, and is often the overt subject of family photographs and the source of the most commonly held photographs, the activities that are photographed and the photography itself

Behaviour: includes what people do and say, and may be what the subject is performing in a photograph, the reactions of viewers to the photographs, the decision to show or not to show photographs

Individual's personal psychology: their internal world, their capacity for attachment, their internal models grown from experiences, the emotional connotation of any encounter with photographs or photographic processes may be impelled by the implicative forces that begin here.

Photo 4.2 'Photocontext' (Wheeler).

and view art in its own context. However, both that context and the aesthetic of these images now need proper consideration by psychotherapists:

> 'Aesthetic' in this sense is grounded in the material properties of painting [or photo or image on smart-phone screen in phototherapy], rather than referring to some disembodied realm of judgements about beauty or truth.
>
> (MacLagan, 2002: 7)

Just as encounters with photography in therapy or in galleries inevitably emerge from our primary experience of original photographs within domestic photography (Wheeler, 1992; 2004; 2008), our experience with digital photography begins with the domestic context. The earliest photographs of most of us are those taken by proud parents of their new infants and these are most commonly now photographed on a camera-phone and sent immediately after birth to friends and relatives. This has been common practice for over a decade but is now being supplanted by an immediate post on a social networking website to reach the widest audience as soon as possible.

From that first baby image, carefully composed, often by the proud father, in the delivery room, our lives are documented with an appropriate contextual aesthetic. The psychological processes involved in making and viewing such photographs lie in an interzone between therapeutic photography, phototherapy, fine-art photography and domestic photography.

The domestic photographic likeness (from the *cartes de visite* to the snapshots carried in purses) has an embedded cultural history predating digital media by over a century. Domestic photography was necessarily professionally conducted in the nineteenth century as the practice demanded skill with dangerous and toxic materials. The arrival in 1902 of the popular Eastman 'Kodak' camera allowed amateurs without great wealth and technical expertise to participate actively in domestic photography: a history that coincidentally runs alongside that of psychoanalysis. In the print media, new psycho-logical ideas such as psychoanalysis were disseminated simultaneously with the massive expansion of editorial and advertising photography, illustrating a hitherto unseen world. For most people who rarely had any opportunity or means to travel great distances, the world view was, then as now, mediated through the medium of photography. Thus, more of our individual knowledge of the world has for over 150 years been experienced more photographically than directly. Even today, the world outside a person's home town is usually mostly photographic. Hence generations have grown up familiarised with a connection between the external world and photographed subjects, leading to the *reality trap*. This *reality trap* arises from the fantasy that, had we been present at the photographer's shoulder, we would witness the same.

Because domestic photography is the ubiquitous context from which photographic and networking practices emerge, it offers a meta-context as the illusory reality trap, or even *reality gap*, of photographs and photography itself. To make an impromptu image on a smartphone, to view the on-screen superficial resemblance to the geometry of the scene is further to reinforce the *reality trap*. Then to upload that image immediately to a social networking site will stimulate the *reality gap* of viewing 'friends'. Their comments or 'likes' then even further reinforce the *reality trap* for the original image maker.

The *psychological aesthetics* of making and viewing digital images for online and social networking overlaps the making and viewing of photographic originals such as fine-art photography made for, and displayed, in galleries and on collectors' walls. There is a dimension (often conscious, but with unconscious contributions) of considering how the image will be seen by others on their screens. Many UK art psychotherapists trained as artists, anticipating public display of their art, before training as therapists to work with images in more private spaces. That professional history contrasts with the trend for domestic image making to be displayed online and therefore is more prone to the considerations of the self-conscious image maker.

David Lodge in *Consciousness and the Novel* (2002) argues that literature offers greater insight into psychology than psychology itself has offered. Appearing simultaneously in bookshops was Jonathan Coe's (2007) novel, *The Rain Before It Falls.* Coe's novel is inspired by a fictional narrative engagement with the Coe family album. Coe's novel informs us about our relationship with photography at least as well as any overt psychological analysis offered previously. Coe (2008) describes his personal relationship with domestic photography:

> Our entire surviving family history consists of photographs . . . it's all photographs'.

The depth and intensity of this relationship inspired the writing of *The Rain before it Falls*, and he offers this account of the writing process:

> These family pictures kick in round about the mid-1940s, so that's partly why I decided to set the early part of *The Rain Before It Falls* in that era.

Coe uses examples from *The Rain Before It Falls* to demonstrate how the photographs are essential to the verbal descriptions in the book, to the mechanisms by which the images are catalysts to the narrative, and to the words used to carry that narrative. Now, the most widely practised art form and the most widely practised domestic photography is probably the mobile telephone (cellphone) with inbuilt camera. Thus the art of cellphone photography now becomes viewed outside its original context, both in online galleries (including those in social network sites) and in the therapist's consulting room.

In the twenty-first-century clients in therapy are more likely to present photographs at child and family therapy (e.g. Child and Adolescent Mental Health Service – CAMHS) on the small screen of their mobile phone than from the old shoebox of prints that featured at the end of the twentieth century. Client and psychotherapist now have to sit side by side peering at a little screen, instead of passing a single print at a time across the therapy room, thus structurally altering the dynamic.

The comfortable familiarity of this sharing to many people now renders this a comfortable spatial relationship. It also changes the therapist's gaze and the client's experience of the therapist's gaze. Gazes may now be mediated by the image on the screen, but may also be sidelong, from which different interpretations may be inferred.

The frequent practice of the mobile phone photographer engenders in them a familiarity with the tool of their artistic expression, the cellphone camera. The journeyman experience of many professional photographers, as they practise their craft with a particular apparatus, may not imbue them with familiarity with their camera bodies and lenses equal to that of the cellphone camera operator.

That photographs contain or mediate emotional or psychological processes prompts questions demanding whether this is primarily a matter of content, whether denoted or connoted, or form itself. The denotation–connotation distinction of semiotic analysis would need rewriting thus:

Denote;
Connote;
Emote.

Max Kozloff (1978: 99) has considered the impact of encounters with photographs:

> Because still photography happens to be neither a temporal medium nor a freely created one, we remain far less physically and imaginatively omniscient as viewers when we see a photograph than when we consider a painting or look at a film.

Especially when presented with the immediacy of the small screen, viewers don't react to photographs in such a knowing way as to drawings or paintings. Viewers are caught off guard, as if their cultural filters are missing; indeed, as if responding to the very screen of memory. This lack of cultural filters is reinforced in everyday remarks such as 'This is so-and-so' rather than 'This is a photograph of so-and-so'.

Photographic truth mythologies – from fine art to Facebook

> Truth is limited and is governed by the photographer's intentions.
>
> (Blakemore, 2008)

Mythologies of 'photographic truth', and the illusion of near-perfect gestalts in photographs, emerge from the domestic context, by repeated exposure to subject then photo of subject. In newspaper or gallery images, the truth mythology prevails despite viewers having no connection to the original scene. This also sheds light on internet-based display of images. Web surfers have no a priori knowledge of the manufacture of the images; the viewer brings their own experience of previous encounters with photographs including those elsewhere on the same website. Sometimes there is a caption context, but often a webpage of other images and some search terms are the almost inverse metacontext. In other words, neighbouring images on a web page seem to contradict each other and their unconscious influence might weaken anticipated phenomenological dimensions of the encounter. For example, an image of a cake, captioned 'Nice cake' will not have the makers' anticipated viewer responses if viewed alongside images of car crashes, owing to the vagaries of search engines or those uploading to a blog. Thus, the usual fantasy of temporal continuity before and after the image, and outside the frame, are usurped by irrelevant Facebook or blog comments from other threads.

Our cultural history with photography has helped wire the underlying mechanics of our responses that enable any encounters with photographic images, of all types, to be so powerful, and therefore motivate phototherapy and therapeutic photography. The *reality trap* might be considered the underlying mechanism that makes such encounters so powerful, while a *reality gap* fuels this mechanism with fantasy to achieve photography's great strength as an expressive medium and its role in phototherapy. What, in the nature of the photographic image, allows it to bypass our personal filters, which we would routinely apply to other human made artefacts? Jo Spence (1984) suggested that the strength of viewers' responses reinforces the validity of photographs as expressive objects, whether the content is explicitly emotionally laden or perhaps ambiguous, while she was showing her work that concentrated on her experience of breast cancer, and her emotional responses and experiences of treatment.

Both the reality trap and the reality gap rely on the illusion of near perfect gestalts of the photograph appealing to the conscious intellect (Wheeler, 2004), perhaps as the latest image is viewed on the smartphone. The illusion lends itself to the notion that a photograph is less threatening than other media in the therapeutic space, yet it should be recognised by the therapist that photography can often be more powerful.

Photographs and mind-brain

Little has been published about the unconscious processes involved in photography and its consumption, but the illusion of connection between photographs and external reality implies the individual photograph's potential to stimulate responses in the limbic system. The limbic system comprises the evolutionarily earlier areas of the brain associated with emotional responses to external stimuli, and hence highly relevant to phototherapy. The desire to make and view photographs is precisely because photographs have this gamut of psychological features unique to the medium.

Krauss and Weiser (2009: 83) summarise my previous argument well:

> Wheeler notes that the image is not reality (the 'reality trap'), and he attempts to help us momentarily look away from the images and toward our physiological wiring, our enculturation, and personal phenomenology to help explain the potential power of images to convince our limbic systems that something real is happening in the 'here and now', when activated by viewing a two-dimensional representation of a three-dimensional reality presented in pixel, halide or colour dye.

Developments in neuroscience and an emerging discipline, neuro-psychoanalysis are seeking possible connections between activities of the autonomic nervous system with art and music activity. Krauss and Weiser (2009: 83) add:

> Wheeler notes that, based on people's experience of photographs made in their lifetimes and their viewing of historical photographs, they can fall prey to this 'reality trap', a belief that photographs accurately represent some aspect of physical reality that at some point in time could be viewed. This in turn leads to a 'reality gap', the belief that images, mediated through the photographer's rendition are true representations of that which could have been viewed. He suggests that 'individual knowledge of the world has for over 150 years been mediated more photographically than experienced directly'.
>
> Wheeler also points out the fallacy created when: 'Neuroscientists seem happy to use photographs unquestioningly . . . as though they are unmediated [primary] connections with the content depicted on their surface, such as the use of photographs of mothers or infants and then interpreting the results as though those mothers or infants themselves had been present with the experimental subject as they passed through the big donut of the fMRI scanner.'

Krauss also suggests another possible 'reality gap':

> The synaptic cleft (gap), the part of the nerve chain where the electro-chemical transmitters convey information from the eye and the optic nerve's paths into the limbic system, the short trip that can facilitate vision, and the aforementioned 'blind spot' can all potentiate a similar visceral response to both three-dimensional and two-dimensional representations of 'reality' (which is one explanation of why brain researchers can use these artefacts in lieu of real persons).
>
> (Krauss and Weiser, 2009: 83)

For example, Dr Helen Fisher (2002), an anthropologist at Rutgers University in New Jersey, explored the biological basis for romantic attachment: 'Fisher's group is analyzing more than 3,000 brain scans of 18 recently smitten college students, taken while they looked at a picture of their beloved' (*Los Angeles Times*, 16 December 2002). Again, Bartels and Zeki (2000; 2004), performing similar research at University College London, showed subjects a picture of their romantic partner for one study and their child for another, and observed subjects' brain activity by MRI scan. They concluded that the pattern was markedly different from when they looked at a picture of a close friend. These researchers observed repeatable and predictable differences in fMRI scans of people viewing photos of lovers to photos of other people or things, having unconsciously anticipated that photographs would serve as 100 per cent effective substitutes for real people and objects. The researchers observed that photographs excite responses from subjects that they might have anticipated had the subjects represented in those photographs been present in the scanner.

These observed neural pathways, through areas of the electro-chemical brain, bear analogous resemblance to the metaphorical traffic through metaphorical areas described by psychoanalytic models 100 years earlier. The neuroscientific model has depended on photography both as subject stimulus and measurement tool.

Documentary photographer, Eugene Smith (Smith, 2008) succinctly summarised the emotional catalyst aspect of the photograph that is so relevant to psychotherapeutic contexts:

> Photo is a small voice, at best, but sometimes – just sometimes – one photograph or a group of them can lure our senses into awareness. Much depends upon the viewer; in some, photographs can summon enough emotion to be a catalyst to thought.

The illusory veracity of the two-dimensional paper-borne photographic representation is a culturally reinforced thread. Furthermore, it repeatedly surfaces in discourse as an often-unnoticed self-reinforcing hegemony:

> A photograph is a poor thing, really. It can only capture one moment, out of millions of moments, in the life of a person, or the life of a house. As for these photographs I have in front of me now, the ones I intend to describe to you . . . they are of value, I think, insofar as they corroborate my failing memory. They are the proof that the things I remember – some of the things I remember – really happened, and are not phantom memories, or fantasies, imaginings.
>
> (Coe, 2007: 38–39)

Mobile phone images and the networks in which they appear invite convergence, not only between traditional psychoanalysis and systemic psychotherapy, but also with neuroscience. Neuroscientific descriptions of psychotherapy (e.g. Schore, 1994; Panksepp, 1999; Kaplan-Solms and Solms, 2002; Cozolino, 2002; Wilkinson, 2006; 2010) that draw on research results published about the effects of various relationships on the brain, supporting or stimulating these ideas, are actually describing the effects of images on the brain:

> All such talismanic uses of photographs express a feeling both sentimental and implicitly magical: they are attempts to contact or lay claim to another reality.
>
> (Sontag, 1977: 16)

An inherent pathos is invited by the knowledge that the moment has passed. That moment is never to be reclaimed, even if that moment was just seconds ago before the camera-phone was turned to show the image on its tiny screen. The tiny image invites, vicariously through the rehearsed psychology of one's encounters with such images, a fantasy that the moment ought to be able to be reclaimed. The reclamation is of course illusory, especially when the viewer was not the photographer and even more so when the viewer may not have been present when the original negative or file was created. Sontag (1977: 15) reinforces this:

> All photographs are memento mori. To take a photograph is to participate in another person's (or thing's) mortality, vulnerability, mutability.

Photography can therefore contain elements or dimensions of which we are not consciously aware but in which we unconsciously invest in the making of images. Becoming very familiar with one's technique enables this to happen, as much to a mobile phone (cellphone) camera user as to a 5×4 zone system monochrome worker:

> In that sense any photograph, by implication, involves a set of questions and ambiguities endemic to its nature as an act of representation.
>
> (Clarke, 1997: 7)

Ehrenzweig (1967) defines three stages of creative process, arguably valid in the practice of smartphone images. The first stage he defines as *Projection*, the second, *Manic oceanic*, then a third stage, the *Compromise phase*, which would include editing of uploads, creation of mini animations and posting to blogs. At this stage the maker is adapting the image to become digestible or accessible to view to some degree, equating with the *depressive position* in object relations theory.

All three are embodied in the structure of the final work of art, including the display context of a social networking site and its imagined aesthetic: the expectation of what the page will look like to other viewers on their laptops as the smartphone user uploads in the field. Such embodiment is made possible by familiarity with the machinery, not taught technique, so as likely with a well-practised mobile phone photographer as a 5×4 gallery icon:

> It is practice and experience, rather than journeyman training, which enables the unthought instinctual investment of unconscious activity and emotion in the print.
>
> (Booth, 1983: 9–21)

The connectivity of the smartphone might modify context, in that the online viewing community, whether real or imagined, impose contextual forces as powerful as those from family, culture of origin, or those actually present. Does the model described by Burnham (1986) still apply without the collective influence of direct face-to-face human contact?

The 1960s experiments of Stanley Milgram (Milgram Experiment, 2011) encouraged experimental subjects to inflict pain on people they believed to be experimental subjects themselves: 50 per cent of subjects did inflict pain on the 'subjects' (who were actually actors) when instructed to do so by the experimenters, believing they were participating in a very different experiment:

> The social psychology of this century reveals a major lesson: often it is not so much the kind of person a man is as the kind of situation in which he finds himself that determines how he will act.
>
> (Milgram, 1974: 205)

No controlled research has investigated whether similar degrees of influence occur from virtual social pressure and such experiments would be deeply unethical; indeed, the original experiments were deeply ethically flawed by modern standards.

Conclusion

The presence of images stored in phones or on networks has profound effects in the therapist's consulting room, whether or not this is overtly acknowledged. The patients may fantasise about their own phone networks and may also fantasise about the therapists' (imagined) phone in the therapist's pocket or handbag.

These encounters are psychologically complex and as significant, and currently as little understood, as countertransference was in the early development of psychoanalysis. All encounters with photographs invite and involve preconditioning from a number of contexts that begin with the domestic, but encompass news media, documentary, art-historical and cultural-historical dimensions. Reducing this to words demands separating the simultaneous strands and threads and laying them bare. Thus, each thread or strand begins to look like a separate narrative. However, it is the simultaneous presence of these different narratives that endows the smartphone image and social network site image with momentum and power, especially in the context of psychotherapy.

Smartphone and digital images, by their immediately reinforced geometric relationship with the perceived external world, may further develop the *reality trap*, which is both a cultural contextual force (Wheeler and Stein, 2004; see Photo 4.2 for an illustration of a photographic context) and also, by its lifelong repetition, a personal implicative force. From daily encounters and practice of digital (smartphone) photography and networking these forces are reinforced. It is from encounters with photographs in the therapy room that the ideas in this chapter have emerged. The images themselves and our experiences of them are the most powerful evidence to support these arguments, as Jonathan Coe made clear in his description of writing *The Rain Before It Falls*.

Individual printed photographs might invite analyses that consider their capacity to mediate unconsciously the emotional state of their making; the position of the smartphone image in a multiverse of contexts demands consideration of those wider contexts.

Just as photographs may invite the fantasy that viewers would see the same had they been standing at the photographer's shoulder, the shared, networked image may invite a fantasy of pseudo-presence in the depicted event. This is reinforced by the repeated activity of making images on smartphones for immediate viewing.

To view any photograph, analogue or digital, is to invite an emotional response unique to that encounter as well as the core investment in form and content. These processes are all extant in making and viewing smartphone images, and they are equally present in consideration of fantasy images imagined in the phone of therapist or client.

Photographic apparatus extends far beyond the film camera and the explicit contents of latent and developed image, and includes digital and smartphone images and those stored in virtual spaces in hard drives and on the World Wide Web. In the context of phototherapy and therapeutic photography this may be explored and amplified. Narratives may be thickened by these images. As well as the cultural contexts of any encounter with photographs, including those in phones and social networking sites, other unconscious and implicative forces also apply.

The practice of psychotherapists who conduct conversations with clients prompted by photographs, whether present or not, is informed by the psychological aesthetics of making and viewing photographs: Photo-Psycho-Praxis. Such conversations, engaging with images within smartphones and the networks they inhabit, further engender fantasies that may override other capacity for thought if not acknowledged. Equally, the catalyst of such an encounter may precipitate reactions of much greater magnitude.

Ansel Adams defined what we might consider as photographic transference over eighty years ago, in contemplation of photography beyond ideas of content and explicit form:

> Forget what it looks like. How does it feel?
>
> (Ansel Adams, 1927, quote in Booth, 1983: 10)

References

Bartels, A. and Zeki, S. (2000). The neural basis of romantic love, *NeuroReport*, 11, 3829–3834.

Bartels, A. and Zeki, S. (2004). The neural correlates of maternal and romantic love, *NeuroImage*, 21, 1155–1166.

Blakemore, J. (2008). Interviewed by Mark Wheeler, 26 April 2008, recording transcript.

Booth, P. (1983). *Master Photographers*. London: Macmillan.

Burnham, J. (1986). *Family Therapy: First steps towards a systemic approach*. London: Routledge.

Clarke, G. (1997). *The Photograph*. Oxford: Oxford University Press.

Coe, J. (2007). *The Rain Before It Falls*. London: Viking.

Coe, J. (2008). Email exchanges with Mark Wheeler, 19 May 2008, author's record.

Cozolino, L. (2002). *The Neuroscience of Psychotherapy: Building and rebuilding the human brain*. London: W.W. Norton.

Ehrenzweig, A. (1967). *The Hidden Order of Art*. London: Phoenix Press.

Fisher, H. (2002). Neuroendocrinology Letters. Reported in *Los Angeles Times*, 16 December 2002.

Kaplan-Solms, K. and Solms, M. (2002). *Clinical Studies in Neuro-psychoanalysis: Introduction to a depth psychology*. London: Karnac.

Kozloff, M. (1978). *Photography and Fascination*. New York: Addison House.

Krauss, D. and Weiser, J. (2009). Picturing phototherapy and therapeutic photography: commentary on articles arising from the 2008 international conference in Finland, *European Journal of Psychotherapy and Counselling*, 11(1), 77–99.

Lodge, D. (2002). *Consciousness and the Novel*. London: Secker & Warburg.

MacLagan, D. (2002). *Psychological Aesthetics: Painting, feeling and making sense*. London: Jessica Kingsley.

Panksepp, J. (1999). Emotions as viewed by psychoanalysis and neuro-science: An exercise in consilience. *Neuro-Psychoanalysis*, 1, 15–38.

Milgram, S. (1974). *Obedience to Authority: An experimental view*. New York: HarperCollins.

Milgram Experiment (2011). The Milgram Obedience Experiment. Available from: http://psychology.about.com/od/historyofpsychology/a/milgram.htm (accessed 6 January 2011).

Schore, A.N. (1994). *Affect Regulation and the Origin of the Self: The neurobiology of emotional development*. Hillsdale, NJ: Lawrence Erlbaum.

Smith, W.E. (2008). W. Eugene Smith. Available from: www.magnumphotos.com/Archive/C.aspx?VP=XSpecific_MAG.PhotographerDetail_VPage&ll=0&pid=2K7O3R139C2T&nm=W%2E%20Eugene%20Smith (accessed 4 January 2008).

Sontag, S. (1977). *On Photography*. New York: Dell.

Spence, J. (1984). In conversation with the author.

Wheeler, M. (1992). Phototherapy: The use of photographs in art therapy. Unpublished Dip. Art Therapy dissertation, University of Sheffield, University of Sheffield Medical Library.

Wheeler, M. (2004). Photography, fantasy and fine print encounters: An exploration of making and viewing. Dissertation held by Royal Photographic Society, Bath.

Wheeler, M. (2008). Photo-Psycho-Praxis. Text of plenary address to European Symposium on Phototherapy. Available from: http://phototherapy.org.uk/pdf/photo-psycho-praxis-2009.pdf (accessed 1 January 2011).

Wheeler, M. (2009). Photo-Psycho-Praxis, *European Journal of Psychotherapy, Counselling & Health*, 11(1), 63–76.

Wheeler, M. and Stein, N. (2004). Photo Context Levels, image for review of Judy Weiser's Derby Workshop, available from author.

Wilkinson, M. (2006). *Coming into Mind, the Mind–Brain Relationship: A Jungian clinical perspective*. London: Routledge.

Wilkinson, M. (2010). *Changing Minds in Therapy: Emotion, attachment, trauma and neurobiology*. New York and London: W.W. Norton.

Chapter 5

A creative photographic approach

Interpretation and healing through creative practice

Mike Simmons

Introduction

> The power of images to interpret events and emotions is a basic premise of art.
>
> (Bradley *et al.*, 2001: 7)

In 1969, along with the rest of the world, I watched in wonderment, as Neil Armstrong became the first man to set foot on the moon. That 'one small step' represented the pinnacle of human endeavour and the height of technological development. The photographs captured by those lunar pioneers stand as some of the most memorable images in the history of photography, and somewhat reassuringly, the images were shot using conventional (if adapted) cameras and film.

The first live images beamed back from the moon onto our television screens of Armstrong's decent to the lunar surface were like ghostly apparitions. Shadowy and unclear, they were nevertheless captivating and reminiscent, in hindsight, of another image equally commanding when it first appeared over 140 years earlier (Niépce, *ca.* 1827).

With the discovery in the nineteenth century of chemical processes to record and permanently fix the previously elusive image formed by the camera obscura, we were given for the first time, a copy of the real world. The photograph became the index by which we began to measure the things around us, and it set in motion the mechanisms for a revolutionary new form of representation.

1969 was also the year I first began to take photographs, oblivious to the historical legacy I was inheriting as a curious eleven year old, and unaware of the sweeping changes I would witness in the intervening years. However, change has been a process endemic throughout the history of photography; both in terms of the technological development that it continues to experience, but perhaps more importantly in the ways in which photographs can function.

Although the nature of the photograph as documentary evidence remains an important aspect of the medium, advances in digital technology have taken place that challenge photography's core values, shifting the terms by which we experience and read photographic images.

At the Digital World Conference, held in Beverly Hills, California in 1991, Mexican photographer Pedro Meyer premiered a groundbreaking computer-based multimedia photographic documentary, *I Photograph to Remember* (Meyer, 1991). Featuring a slide show of black and white still photographs with an audio track of voice and music, it told an intimate story of his family history and gave a moving account of the death of his parents, offering the viewer a personal window into the 'rituals of love and grief' (Berman, 2001: 52). At the time, the work demonstrated that technology, normally associated with dispassionate mechanical precision, could provide a platform for an emotive human experience (Stein, 2006).

Twenty years later, the impact of the computer has become something of a phenomenon, both in the workplace and more recently within the private and social realms of the individual. Within photography and lens-based media, there are now a wide range of accessible resources that traditionally would have required specialised equipment, knowledge and skills. These developments have effectively widened participation and provided greater opportunities for creativity and self-expression.

Over the last ten years, through my photographic practice and research, I have explored ways in which digital technology can be used to extend knowledge and understanding of personal experiences, in the context of bereavement and grief, to promote health and well-being. Drawing on my own experiences, and those who have shared with me their personal stories, I have examined the impact that the death of someone close has on the continuing lives of the living.

Personal stories provide a context through which we can identify with our experiences, create meaning and communicate with others (Ellis and Bochner, 1992; Skultan, 1998; Walter, 1999). As Meyer has written:

> These days I am blessed with a new little boy, who at the time of writing is six years old. My parents obviously never met him as they died before he was born. I thought many times that this work might some day function for him like a family album.
>
> (Meyer, 2001: 3)

French artist Christian Boltanski equates his role as artist with that of a storyteller. Not in recounting the great stories of history, but the personal accumulated knowledge that makes up the individual, what he considers as 'small memory' (Boltanski in Moure, 1996: 108).

Presented in visual terms, our stories, although specific to individuals, have value beyond the personal. The subjective processes developed through their creation can be extended into inter-subjective experiences, as 'a focus for discussion' (Case and Dalley, 1992: 1), in a broader social and critical context, as the work engages with others.

The nature of a creative photographic approach provides a means to translate and evaluate personal experiences through the creation of original photographic artwork. It is a process that can help place the maker in a new relationship to their experiences, through the development of emotional distance, a term used here to describe the means whereby an experience can be understood, and its implications appreciated, from a more balanced and informed perspective. Placed in a health-related context, it has been employed as a valuable method for the development of personal well-being by assisting the process of 'therapeutic change' (Dalley, 1984: xii). What follows are some insights into how this creative process works.

Photography, memory and meaning

My interest in photography to connect with and explore personal experiences, grew out of a need to understand how the impact of my father's death when I was a child had continued to shape my life. As an adult, I needed to somehow give a material presence to my memories in order to 'see' what was inside my head and give solidity to my 'fleeting and formless memories' (Meyer, 2001: 3).

14 January 1975.

I was sent home from school for not wearing the right kind of trousers.

> *The deputy head glared at me during morning assembly and by 10:00 am I was at home. To be honest, it felt good to be a bit of a rebel. It was a new school and we had been told that uniform rules would not apply to sixth formers; but that soon changed and I felt resentful.*

I hadn't been home long, when a policeman came to the door.

> *My father had been taken into hospital in October of the previous year, with a back problem. Slip disks were a common complaint amongst coal miners, and it wasn't the first time he had spent weeks in traction. They sent him home for Christmas in a pot jacket and shortly after the holidays, he went back into hospital.*

My mother and I waited for a bus.

> *We were ushered into the ward sister's office and left there to wait. I remember thinking how strange and distorted their white coats seemed, through the small wired and frosted glass panel in the door.*

They asked if we wanted to see the body; but I didn't go.

> *My diary entry for the day reads: Dad died today about 10:00 am. Apparently it wasn't his back at all, but lung cancer, which had spread into his spine. It was peaceful, so the nurse said.*

The heart in medieval times was seen to symbolise memory (Carruthers, 1990), and it has been argued that memory is shaped through our relationship with the physical world (Radley, 1990). The 'things' that are left behind when people die 'come to the foreground of consciousness', as 'death reconstructs our experience of personal and household objects' (Gibson, 2008: 1).

Here is a framed photograph of a town clock. It is wintertime and there is snow on the ground. And here an old pocket watch sits on a bed of cotton wool. It has been placed in a round tin, just slightly bigger than the watch itself. The watch face has yellowed and the glass cover has become loose. Here is an old black and white family photograph of two women walking side by side. They are in step and their military gate implies an intimate sense of connectedness. It is sunny and the shadows they cast

Photo 5.1 Photography, memory and meaning (Mike Simmons).

lead the eye to the caption 'Bridlington 1965', printed in a white boarder at the bottom of the image. And here a photograph shows a detail of red leather-bound book; fine grained and gold blocked with the image of a thistle and the date, 1768.

These mnemonic traces form part of a larger artwork (Simmons, 2000), a matrix of specifically created images, photographs of personal belongings, appropriated and selectively cropped family photographs, and real objects. Sealing them in frames became a way to make public the private (see Photo 5.1).

I know the location of the town clock and the significance of its geographical setting. I know to whom the pocket watch belonged and why it was kept in that particular fashion. I also know the identity of the two women and the relevance of the leather-bound book. But there are no clues to any of this information explicit in the work; nor does there need to be.

Removed from their original context, photography has enabled these disparate elements to be harnessed and brought together regardless of scale, location or ownership. They have been juxtaposed to form new alliances; becoming metaphors that link internal emotional states and give them form in the material world. These signs and symbols are not rigidly fixed to a single personal interpretation, but are active and open to multiple readings, allowing others to participate in the creative process. Not by looking *at* the photographs can others identify, connect with and be touched, but by looking *into* them. A photograph becomes something that is experienced emotionally, as a 'participant', not rationally, as a 'viewer' (Viola, 2003: 2). A response from the comments book from an exhibition of the work (Simmons and Hind, 2001) demonstrates:

> You have showed us the significance of what we pass by, and shocked us out of our complacency. You have made us consider our mortality and our creativity.
>
> (Hart, 2001: 9)

No one home: death, relationships and social context

> Understanding is not embedded in the experience as much as it is achieved through an ongoing and continuous experience of the experience.
>
> (Ellis and Bochner, 1992: 98)

The creation of original photographic artwork is a proactive process involving self-reflection, self-evaluation and discussing the outcomes of that process with others in order to inform the creative process. The negative emotional experiences produced through bereavement that include, among others, sadness and anger can be realigned as history, memory and biography, which overlap and resonate, and past experiences become re-appropriated, reinterpreted and articulated in the present.

Engaging in such activity can play a significant role in the creation of positive emotions, such as optimism and contentment, in terms of understanding or defining the relationship between the survivor/s and the death experience. As Fredrickson has observed:

> Phenomenological, positive emotions may help people place events in their lives in broader context, lessening the resonance of any particular negative event.
>
> (Fredrickson, 2004: 1371)

The changes brought about by the death of a significant person in our lives relate not only to the permanent absence of that individual, but also to the social roles associated with them (Silverman, 2000). As Berman has written:

> In her death we were dying as well. Mother and daughters: what had been us was changing, because she was leaving it, she was leaving us behind, she was leaving what we were together.
>
> (Berman, 2001: 52)

No One Home (Simmons, 2005) considers the social context of death. It explores the slippery boundaries of memory and the important role that objects play in reconciling the disrupted emotional and physical states that bereavement and grief can create. Set against the landscape of a home following the death of my mother, the work considers two related but alternative perspectives associated with the broader idea of 'home'. One is external and finds expression in our relationships with people, objects and spaces, and our familiarity and intimacy with the practices we engage in with them. The other perspective is an emotional one, informed by those external influences, but articulated internally, through feelings of reassurance, comfort and belonging.

Home, so the saying goes 'is where the heart is', an adage that stands as a metaphor for a significant personal relationship. Often an amalgamation of many facets, both real and imagined, whatever our individual notion of 'home' may be it remains a symbol of stability, which can be undermined following the death of a close family member, creating a new and challenging context for those who remain.

In the early hours of the morning, at home in her own bed, my mother died quietly in her sleep, silently crossing the threshold into memory. At precisely the same moment, the house too passed mutely into reminiscence, closing the door on over half a century of home life. Along with my mother's body, the house in turn had to be attended to and the process of clearing out and selling had to be addressed.

In an attempt to hold onto what I felt I could not keep, I began to photograph the house. For two months after the funeral, I would visit the house every week to record its details, maintaining a physical relationship with this place, to preserve the constancy it denoted and retain the history created within its precinct. The photographic process became a symbolic embalming of the house against change and decay. Although these photographs depicted a sense of normality, emotionally the reality of being in the house was very different, and the paradox between what the eye sees and what the heart feels became central to the work.

Comprised of four digitally generated photographic montages *No One Home* is a metaphor for change. Presenting the physical landscape of home as a calm, ordered setting, the work seeks to re-create a common bereavement experience, that of expectation and anticipation of finding some reference to the deceased in the reflection of a mirror, through a crack in a door or the shadow on a wall, 'for a long time you expect them to still walk in' (Skevington, 2003: 3).

This intense scrutiny is intended to slowly give way to the realisation that there is *No One Home*, leaving the viewer gazing upon a private space that becomes radically unfamiliar, inducing feelings of intrusion. The anxiety arising from the process of dismantling the contents of the domestic space, revealing intimate aspects of the lives of the dead through the things that they leave behind, is another common and unnerving experience among the bereaved (Hallam and Hockey, 2001).

Portraits taken from the family album, that traditional and universal symbol of memory, which offers tangible reminders of all that is good in our lives, have been digitally altered and their new semi-transparent forms float above the images of the house interior. These familial faces gaze out with unfamiliar intensity to increase the tension and unease. Detailed photographs of objects provide a further layer of biographical information, linking past to present.

Regaining an emotional balance following the distressing experience of bereavement is central to both psychological and physiological health and well-being. Achieving some kind of normality requires the bereaved to move forward 'find[ing] an appropriate place for the dead in their emotional lives' (Worden, 1991: 16).

As a catalyst for change, a creative photographic approach can help achieve this, assisting the bereaved to create meaning from their loss. Research has shown that positive evaluation of bereavement experiences can help to produce 'resilient rather than vulnerable survivors' (Riches, 2002: 8).

Between hope and despair

> [T]he photograph as the frozen trace of life would seem to be the fitting artefact of mourning both the life that was lived and its passing in death.
>
> (Liss, 1998: 6)

Since its inception, photography has had an uneasy relationship with death (Hobson, 1995). Posthumous photography became an accepted ritual in nineteenth-century Europe and America (Burns, 1990; Ruby, 1995) providing a focus for grief, as Linkman has observed:

> A portrait of the dead at peace could help alleviate the anguish caused to the bereaved by a painful or tragic end. While portraits of those who had died a 'good' death could serve as an example and role model for the living.
>
> (Linkman, 2005: 49)

Images of the dead are perhaps at their most valued in cases of infant mortality, where there is often little or no history on which to build memories. Hospital maternity units in the UK have, for a number of years, offered instant Polaroid photographs of stillborn infants, or those who die within a month of birth (Bourne and Lewis, 1991); some hospitals offer a more comprehensive service (Meredith, 2000; Hochberg, 2011). Photographs of such events illustrate 'the importance of photographic images in assisting with [the] grieving process' (Meredith, 2000: 161).

Around a quarter of every confirmed pregnancy in the UK ends in miscarriage (Miscarriage Association, 2006), a term used to describe a pregnancy that ends before twenty-four weeks gestation. This is defined by the UK Stillbirth Definition Act 1992, as the developmental age of a foetus that can survive independently of its mother outside the womb. Deaths before twenty-four weeks are 'often not viewed as proper bereavements' (Lovell, 1997: 29), which may have a direct effect on the way the pregnancy is managed professionally, considered legally (there is no requirement for a death certificate) and perceived within a wider social context.

For most women and their partners, life begins at the moment of conception, with all thoughts, hopes and activities centred on that perspective. Loss at any time during pregnancy is equivalent to the loss of anyone 'who left a mark on the world and occupied a place in the memories of the people who knew him or her' (Lovell, 1997: 35).

Between Hope and Despair (Simmons, 2006) explores pre-term infant death from the perspective of my own family's experiences and seeks to highlight the uniqueness of individual experience in this context. Research has shown that men, women and children grieve differently. Women may become more absorbed in grief than men, becoming more introspective as opposed to their male counterparts, who tend to return to active social involvement at an earlier stage (Strobe and Schut, 1995; Thompson, 1997). Children vary in their response to grief depending on the age of the child, and the relationship the child had to the deceased (Job and Frances, 2004).

The photographs I had taken in the maternity suite at the hospital on the day form the foundational platform around which the story is built. These images bear witness to the event and capitalise on one of photography's key attributes, to record. As Meyer has observed:

I knew full well that my emotions at the time would not allow me to recall further on, the specifics of any given moment. The photographs have indeed allowed me to return many times to those captured slices of my experiences.

(Meyer, 2001: 3)

Between Hope and Despair considers the interconnected roles of the family, wife and mother, husband and father, sons and brothers, and sets these intimate relationships against the broader social context of our lives. It is also a reflection on the professional communities who manage and legislate pre-term infant death, which are often at odds with lived human expectations and ultimate experience. The work conceptualises these complex relationships as borderlines; each playing a part in the unfolding narrative, yet unable to fully understand the other's position.

Comprised of six diptychs the work brings together the personal hospital photographs, which include a post-mortem image, with specifically created photographs and original poetry. The poetry, written to augment the predominant visual construction, provides a tempo within the work based on the symbolic rhythm of the human heartbeat. Together these elements highlight the conflict and contradiction between the physical and the emotional, between the personal and the public experience of losing a child in this way.

The poem reads:

Between hope and despair,
Between damage and repair,
Between bias and fair,

Between beauty and beast,
Between sinner and priest,
Between famine and feast,

Between support and neglect,
Between accept and reject,
Between hurt and protect,

Between love and lust,
Between flesh and dust,
Between doubt and trust,

Between truthful and lying,
Between peaceful and trying,
Between living and dying,

Between father and mother,
Between sister and brother,
Between self and other.

Produced six years after the event, a creative photographic approach has allowed us as a family the time to reconsider our experiences of bereavement and grief, which are never fully resolved, as Freud has observed: 'Quite deep down I can trace the feeling of a deep narcissistic hurt that is not to be healed' (Freud quoted in Jones, 1957: 20). It has provided the family unit with an opportunity to integrate our dead child in the broader context of our lives, to reassess how we feel and create our alternative family album, which has brought cathartic value.

Pictures from life

> For a deceased person in the West today who is mourned by more than one rememberer,
> there is comparatively little provision for the mutual interplay of their memories of him.
>
> (Vitebsky 1993: 259)

Children and young people can often feel isolated in their experiences of loss and grief, which can lead to social exclusion in its widest sense. Children's grief is frequently misunderstood or ignored, which can significantly affect a child's relationships and self-esteem (Job and Frances, 2004). Families may often find it difficult to communicate with each other about their feelings surrounding death.

Pictures from Life is a photographic workshop programme that has been specifically designed to support children and young people (primarily between the ages of eight and sixteen) who have experienced a family death, and whose families have sought support. The programme provides cross-agency collaboration, bringing together a team of qualified, skilled and experienced professionals from the creative and clinical communities, and developed in conjunction with the Children's Bereavement Project, as part of the service provision by the Children's Fund in Lincolnshire.

A pilot project took place with a small group of Year Five children (ten students) at a school in rural Lincolnshire, with financial assistance from Arts Council England, which focused on the terms of bereavement and grief in the broadest sense.

It was in effect a feasibility study to evaluate the following:

*   cross-disciplinary collaboration in terms of project team cohesion and effectiveness;
*   logistical management and cost implications;
*   participant response in terms of skills development, knowledge transfer and increased awareness of project themes;
*   participant group dynamic in terms of the solidarity, integration, and social communication across a diversity of backgrounds, gender and individual experiences;
*   quality in terms of delivery, creative output and experience;
*   repeatability.

The pilot proved to be a conclusive success across all its evaluative criteria, demonstrating that interdisciplinary collaboration was an effective and valuable model in this context.

Much of the work already achieved elsewhere in the UK has been through support programmes based on a counselling model of working, with less emphasis placed on the recognition of creative photographic-based practice or interdisciplinary collaboration. Pictures from Life was the first of its kind in Lincolnshire and has highlighted many benefits for participants including:

*   an alternative to the counselling and support groups currently available;
*   an innovative opportunity for children to create a considered, highly valued piece of photographic artwork to be taken with them throughout their life journey, allowing the family to have a continuing bond with the deceased person through the work produced;

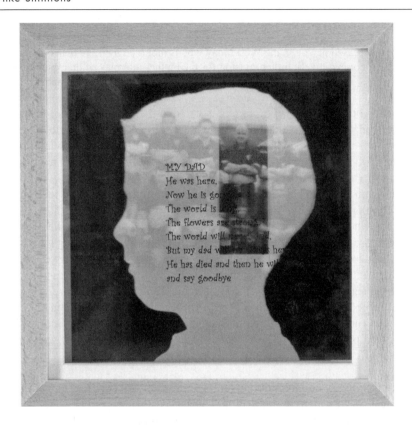

Photo 5.2 Artwork from 'pictures from life' workshop (Mike Simmons).

- safe therapeutic methods to explore relationships within the family, strengthening communication and enhancing and developing opportunities for expression of individual emotional needs and understanding.

The first Pictures from Life workshop ran as a week-long programme following referral to the scheme via the Children's Bereavement Project Coordinator. Participants had experienced difficulties with communication and/or behavioural changes. Four families took part with six children between the ages of eight and twelve.

By encouraging self-expression in a positive and creative way, the workshop provided an opportunity for the children and young people to experience a healthy grieving process, giving them the time to acknowledge and normalise their bereavement journey. Through the creation of original photographic artwork, Pictures from Life (see Photo 5.2) opens up a new and stimulating path to the expression of grief, helping to strengthen family communication and understanding. One of the repeated responses from parents and carers has been the realisation that their children's grief was different to their own experiences. Taking part and sharing with others their individual stories has helped them to construct a new and continuous relationship with the deceased by celebrating their ideas, valuing their memories and acknowledging 'the significance of the life which has been completed' (Riches and Dawson, 1998: 133). It is a process that bridges the gap often encountered between emotion and expression, helping to raise feelings of self worth, which may endure as the child or young person grows through their lives (Aspinwall, 2001; Fredrickson and Joiner, 2002, Fredrickson, 2004). Subsequent workshops have been run, and Pictures from Life has been acknowledged as 'a beacon project' (Willis, 2005). Although it represents only a relatively small study sample, it is interesting to note that, of all the participants who have taken part, none have required additional support or follow-up work. Feedback from the children and their families underlines the important contribution that a creative photographic approach can make in a bereavement context.

Conclusion

Death transforms the lives of those who remain, forcing the bereaved to consider new beginnings through which the acknowledgment and acceptance of emotional significance, shaped by personal events, can be negotiated. Regaining an emotional balance and redefining our personal and social roles are essential to the 'purpose and process of grief' (Walter, 1996: 8).

This chapter has presented the ideas behind the practical application of a creative photographic approach as a core strategy to explore and interpret human experiences. It has considered how photography can connect memories and emotions with aspects of the material world to construct original photographic artwork that has personal meaning for the maker. Examples of how creative photographic approaches have been employed in a personal context and in a health-related setting have been discussed, and the creative process explored to demonstrate how the act of creating could become a catalyst to foster positive emotional change and assist in the enhancement of personal well-being.

Creativity is something inherent in all of us, something that we can choose to do; a way we can choose to be. A creative photographic approach can be used to harness the things that are important to us, enabling us to interpret and express our thoughts and feelings creatively, and place us in a new relationship to our experiences.

References

Aspinwall, L.G. (2001). Dealing with adversity: Self-regulation, coping, adaptation and health. In: Tessar, A. and Schwartz, N. (eds), *The Blackwell Handbook of Social Psychology*, vol. 1 (Intra-individual processes) (pp. 591–614). Malden, MA: Blackwell.

Berman, K. (2001). Elements of the month of our dying. In: *n. paradoxa* vol. 7. London: K.T. Press.

Bourne, S. and Lewis, E. (1991). Perinatal bereavement: A milestone and some new dangers. *British Medical Journal*, 302, 1167–1168.

Bradley, F., Brown, K. and Nairne, A. (2001). *Trauma*. An exhibition organised by the Hayward Gallery, London for the Arts Council England in collaboration with Dundee Contemporary Arts [exhibition catalogue]. Hayward Gallery, London, Arts Council England, Dundee Contemporary Arts.

Burns, S.B. (1990). *Sleeping Beauty: Memorial photography in America*. Los Angeles, CA: Twelvetrees Press.

Carruthers, M.J. (1990). *The Book of Memory: A study in memory in medieval culture*. Cambridge: Cambridge University Press.

Case, C. and Dalley, T. (1992). *The Handbook of Art Therapy*. East Sussex and Philadelphia, PA: Brunner-Routledge.

Dalley, T. (ed.) (1984). *Art as Therapy*. London: Routledge.

Ellis, C. and Bochner, A.P. (1992). Telling and performing personal stories. In: Ellis, C. and Flaherty, G.M. (eds), *Investigating Subjectivity: Research on lived experience* (pp. 79–101). London: Sage.

Fredrickson, B.L. (2004). The broaden-and-build-theory of positive emotions. In: *Philosophical Transactions of the Royal Society of London. Series B, Biological Sciences* (pp. 1367–1378). London: The Royal Society.

Fredrickson, B.L. and Joiner, S. (2002). Positive emotions trigger upward spirals towards well-being. *Psychological Science*, 13, 172–175.

Gibson, M. (2008). *Objects of the Dead: Mourning and memory in everyday life*. Carlton, Victoria: Melbourne University Press

Hallam, E. and Hockey, J. (2001). *Death, Memory & Material Culture*. Oxford: Berg.

Hart, D.A. (2001). *Our Fathers' Childhood Loss and Memory* [exhibition comments book] (personal communication, 23 May 2001).

Hobson, G. (1995). A horrible exhibition. In: *The Dead* [exhibition catalogue] Bradford National Museum of Photography, Film and Television.

Hochberg, T. (2011). Moments held – photographing perinatal loss. In: *The Lancet.com* 377(9774), 1310–1311. Available from: www.thelancet.com/journals/lancet/issue/vol377no9774/PIIS 01406736%2811%29X6016-6 (accessed 16 April 2011).

Job, N. and Francis, G. (2004). *Childhood Bereavement: Developing the curriculum and pastoral support*. London: National Children's Bureau.

Jones, E. (1957). *The Life and Works of Sigmund Freud*. Vol. 3. New York: Basic Books.

Linkman, A. (2005). Taken from life: Post-mortem portraiture in Britain 1860–1910. *Mortality*, 10, Supplement, 49.

Liss, A. (1998). *Trespassing Through Shadows: Memory, photography, and the Holocaust*. Minneapolis, MN: University of Minnesota Press.

Lovell, A. (1997). Death at the beginning of life. In: Field, D., Hockey, J. and Small, N. (eds), *Death, Gender and Ethnicity*. London: Routledge.

Meredith, R. (2000). The photography of neonatal bereavement at Wythenshawe Hospital. *The Journal of Audiovisual Media in Medicine*, 23(4), 161–164.

Meyer, P. (1991). *I Photograph to Remember*. CD-ROM, Los Angeles, Voyager Co. Available at: www.zonezero.com/exposiciones/fotografos/fotografio/ (accessed 28 February 2011).

Meyer, P. (2001). *. . . . some background thoughts*. Available at http://zonezero.com/exposiciones/fotografos/fotografio/work.html (accessed 28 February 2011).

Moure, G. (1996). *Christian Boltanski: Advent and other times*. Barcelona: Edicoines Poligrafa S.A.

Niépce, J.N. (*c*.1827). *View from his Window at Le Gras*. [Heliograph] Gernsheim Collection, Harry Ransom Center, University of Texas, Austin.

Radley, A. (1990). Artifacts, memory and a sense of the past. In: Middleton, D. and Edwards, D. (eds), *Collective Remembering*. London: Sage.

Riches, G. (2002). *Our Fathers: Childhood loss and memory* [exhibition catalogue]. Lincoln: Simmons & Hind.

Riches, G. and Dawson, P. (1998). Lost children, living memories: The role of photographs in processes of grief and adjustment among bereaved parents. *Death Studies*, 22, 121–140.

Ruby, J. (1995). *Secure the Shadow: Death and photography in America*. Cambridge, MA: The MIT Press.

Silverman, P.R. (2000). Research, clinical practice, and the human experience: Putting the pieces together. *Death Studies*, 24, 468–469.

Simmons, M. (2000). *Photography, Memory and Meaning* [photographic composite installation] (Collection of the artist).

Simmons, M. (2005). *No One Home* [digital photomontage] (Collection of the artist). Available from: www.dmu.ac.uk/research/aad/research-projects/photography-bereavement-grief/noh1.jsp (accessed 28 February 2011).

Simmons, M. (2006). *Between Hope and Despair* [digital photomontage] (Collection of the artist.

Simmons, M. and Hind, B. (2001). *Photography, Memory and Meaning, 2000* [photographic composite installation]. Our Fathers' Childhood loss and Memory exhibition. Derby, The Atrium Derby University hosted by Multi-Faith Centre, May.

Skevington, T. (2003). *Conversations*. Video interview by Mike Simmons [mini dvd tape]. Interviewed at participant's home 21 October 2003. Transcript with author.

Skultan, V. (1998). *The Testimony of Lives: Narrative and memory in post-Soviet Latvia*. London: Routledge.

Stein, B. (2006). *I Photograph to Remember moves to the iPod*. Available from: www.future ofthebook.org/blog/archives/2006/09/i_photograph_to_remember_moves.html (accessed 28 February 2011).

Strobe, M. and Schut, H. (1995). The dual process model of coping with loss. Paper presented at the International Work Group on Death, Dying and Bereavement, St Catherine's College, Oxford, 26–29 June.

The Miscarriage Association: Acknowledging pregnancy loss (2006). *Men and Miscarriage* [brochure], MM/02/06, The Miscarriage Association, Wakefield, West Yorkshire.

Thompson, N. (1997). Masculinity and loss. In: Field, D., Hockey, J. and Small, N. (eds), *Death, Gender and Ethnicity*. London: Routledge.

Viola, B. (2003). De profundis. *Art Review*, 1(11), 2.

Vitebsky, P. (1993). *Dialogues with the Dead: The discussion of mortality among the Sora of Eastern India*. Cambridge: Cambridge University Press.

Walter, T. (1996). A new model of grief: Bereavement and biography. *Mortality*, 1(1), 7–25.

Walter, T. (1999). *On Bereavement: The culture of grief*. Buckingham: Open University Press.

Willis, S. (2005). *Picture from Life Seminar* [Chair's statement]. Lincoln Cathedral Centre, Lincoln, 7 March.

Worden, J.W. (1991). *Grief Counselling and Grief Therapy*. London: Routledge.

Part II

The use of photographs in various practices

Chapter 6

Inhabiting the image

Photography, therapy and re-enactment phototherapy

Rosy Martin

Introduction

We live in a culture, in Western Europe, ever more mediated by the visual. Photographic images surround us on all sides: newspapers, magazines, advertising hoardings, the Internet and if one includes the moving image: television, film, video, and computer games. The evolution of digital media now results in the majority of people in Europe always carrying a camera with them, as an integral part of their mobile phone. Within the computer, traditional boundaries between media breakdown and merge with the facility to digitise information and easily combine images and sound, both original and sampled. Individuals can then post their work on websites and publish to the worldwide Internet audience. Social networking sites such as Facebook, video-sharing sites such as YouTube and photo-sharing sites such as Flickr, as well as individual's personal websites and blogs offer the opportunity to share images with family, friends and audiences previously unimaginable. Digital technologies have provided the means to communicate easily through images, text and voice. Is this the longed-for democratisation of the image?

As a cultural phenomenon, does this then speak to a more fundamental desire? Is this a manifestation of the need to be seen, to be heard, to have an audience, and to be noticed? Or is it the reflection of a narcissistic society? While at one level the culture of the spectacle (Debord, 1967) encourages a voyeurism that can be parasitic (Big Brother on Channel 4 could be said to have set the stage for the crowd who gathered and called to a suicidal young man to 'jump' (BBC News, 3 Oct. 2008). However, there are therapeutic approaches that use these visual languages to powerful effect.

Photography and therapy

There are a number of different ways in which photographs can be used within the therapeutic relationship. In the 1970s in the United States and Canada therapists (notably David Krauss, Judy Weiser and Joel Walker) began using photographs as tools in counselling (Krauss and Fryrear, 1983). Photographs offer up a slippery surface of meanings to reflect upon and project onto, and contain a myriad of latent narratives. How someone responds to a particular image at a particular time might provide clues to their unconscious. Using photographs as both a conduit and a catalyst for communication, a therapist, using a nonjudgemental approach with skilful listening and open-ended questions, can enable the client to articulate, make conscious and then reflect upon his/her ways of viewing the world and value systems.

Found images

Found images can be a useful resource to introduce the use of photographs in therapy. They have the advantage of being anonymous and decontextualised. This allows for a much freer reading, since there are then no potential conflicts regarding personal loyalties, nor self-silencing evoked. In my workshops, I use a selection of found old family album photographs, alongside some documentary images, which share the anecdotal captured moment aesthetic of domestic photography. I lay these out, and invite the client to choose one that they are drawn to, quickly, without intellectualising their choice. Clients are invited to tell a story using their chosen photograph as a starting point, by entering the space of the image, identifying with one of the individuals in the photograph, speaking from the first person, thereby inhabiting the imaginary space offered up. I have observed that clients draw unconsciously from their own, or their family histories in this storytelling.

Found images can be used to demonstrate the narrative potential of photographs, and how all photographs are fictions. As chosen moments, edited out from the continuum of everyday life, or highly constructed presentations to the camera, framed extracts from the visual field, all photographs are constructions.

Alternative visual diaries

Photographs taken by the client may offer insights into thoughts and feelings that are of deep personal concern. The practice of loaning out cameras to participants with the brief to document their ordinary everyday lives has been used by community photographers for many years (Dewdney and Lister, 1988). This is particularly beneficial in work with young people on their sense of identities and community (see www.photo Voice.org) and in working with marginalised groups (Mandel and Lemus, 2008). Automatic point-and-shoot digital cameras have simplified image taking. It is important to give a precise brief, and to ask participants to edit to a manageable amount, since people tend to overshoot. I developed a digital identities course in an artist's residency at a girl's secondary school in Batley for Photo98 (Shepherd, 1998). By using image manipulation software (e.g. Photoshop) it is possible to combine creating an alternative visual diary to explore aspects of the self with family album images, self-directed portraits and found images. In the making, choice and layering of these images, complex interwoven 'digital identities' can be created. This then can be a focus for therapeutic processing, as one might use images produced in traditional art therapy.

Family albums

Family albums provide a rich resource for autobiographical storytelling. They may be used to explore familial relationships, and how these early experiences continue to affect the individual.

A family album contains a mini-history of photography as a medium and a variety of genres, as interpreted by a succession of photographers, both amateur and professional (Spence, 1986). Each of us only has the images we inherited; precious, since they offer each of us images of the self, as we grew up, and a fragile framework for memories. Precious too, once family members have died, and their photographic image becomes a means of recall. But the traditional family album is an ideological construct (Spence and Holland, 1991). Editorial control is held by the archivist, usually the mother, whose preferences are shaped by an unconscious desire to provide evidence of her own good mothering. The conflicts and power struggles inherent within family life are repressed. The traditional family album functions like a public relations document, which mediates between the members of the family, providing a semblance of a united front to the world, in an affirmation of successes, celebrations, high days and holidays, domestic harmony and togetherness. It uses established codes of commemorative convention, so ubiquitous that they are taken for granted, even meticulously reconstructed and sold back to us in advertising campaigns. Imaging companies using digital manipulation now propose to 'enhance' the family album mythology by offering 'seamless, permanent, and reassuring solutions to torn and separated memories', 'your whole family together at last', 'cosmetic perfection', and even the opportunity to 'remove any trace of your ex-husband, ex-wife or ex-lover. An excellent idea' (Fleet Imaging, 1996).

Although now people are using digital cameras to document a wider range of activities and take many more photographs, the delete button provides instant editing that facilitates an even more persuasive pursuit of the 'ideal'. One of my concerns is that this editing, followed by tidying up using image manipulation will erase some of the mistakes, aberrations and quirkiness, as if repressing the unconscious of the photograph that can be found in old albums.

Re-enactment phototherapy

Re-enactment phototherapy is a methodology that I have been evolving since 1983, in collaboration with the late Jo Spence (Martin and Spence, 1985; Spence, 1986), and continue to develop. Our innovation was the creation of new photographic representations through performative re-enactments, within the therapeutic relationship.

Jo Spence and I met when we were attending a series of co-counselling training courses. During an exchange counselling session on the third course, we came up with the idea of dressing up and playing with aspects of our identities that had been either hidden or denied, and photographing the results. Within the safety and trust of the therapeutic relationship that we had built during the previous year, we photographed one another, as we inhabited these roles. In some of our earliest work we used an old family album image as a starting point. However, this was not simply an act of replication. Crucially, we used what had been unearthed in the counselling beforehand to structure a session and explore a range of feelings in the process. We worked together in an experimental and creative way and maintained the therapeutic framework to work through the emotions that making and viewing these images released. We soon realised that we had discovered a very powerful technique.

Initially the work was prompted by a lack. In our family albums, either no images existed (film was unobtainable in the Second World War) or the few that survived only showed the child posed for the parent. The work grew from an autobiographical engagement with the complexity of the multifaceted aspects of an individual's identity. We started by deconstructing the existing visual representations of our lives and became acutely aware of the structured absences, and both the paucity and stereotypical limitations of representations within the dominant media that were offered to us as middle-aged, working-class women.

You are the only one who can never see yourself except as an image . . . even and especially for your own body, you are condemned to the repertoire of its images.

(Barthes, 1977: 36)

We used therapeutic techniques to look behind the 'screen memories', the simplifications and myths of others, too long accepted as our histories, as a way of extending this repertoire, by exploring the self as a series of fictions. We began to tell and explore ways of making visible the complexity and contradictions of our own stories, from our points of view, by re-enacting memories, key scenarios with emotional resonance and imagining possible futures. We worked collaboratively, alternating the roles of photographer/therapist and protagonist/client. We were always committed to examine the personal as political within the practice. We aimed to uncover and make visible the elisions that had silenced or marginalised our experiences; for example, as working-class women and, in Jo's case, as someone living with cancer. We showed the effects of institutional gazes and social constructs upon the individual as exemplars, rather than seeing these as only a privatised distress. We highlighted the psychological and social construction of identities within the drama of the everyday.

Then, after Jo's death, I went on to develop this modality further. I no longer worked in the exchange of roles, co-counselling model, but, having trained as a therapist, concentrated on the therapist role. I formalised the methodology by carefully analysing the process of my work with clients, as well as drawing upon my knowledge of what it feels like to occupy the positions of both therapist and client. I use formal contracts and clear boundaries so that the client feels adequately held and contained. I have regular therapeutic supervision and I am much more aware of how I work with the transference and counter-transference that is always present and often actively played out in the photography session. I developed and ran a range of experiential workshops to share and teach these methods (www.rosymartin.info).

Re-enactment phototherapy is about making visible process, change and transformation, by going to the source of an issue or an old trauma, re-enacting it and making a new ending, a new possibility, a new way of being visible. This very powerful intensity, which touches deep, dark and difficult material, is held and contained by counselling at both the beginning and end.

Identity formation and the gaze

As discussed in Martin (1997; 2012), the notion of the gaze has been examined by such differing theoreticians as Winnicott, Lacan and Foucault, in their explorations of how identities are formed through mirroring. Sometimes these gazes are loving or benevolent, but often they are more intrusive and surveillant. Out of the myriad fragments thus mirrored to us, first unconsciously as babies, then as we are growing into language and culture and are subject to the various discourses of society, aspects of our identities are constructed.

The 'good enough mother' offers her face to the baby's gaze, and mirrors back the baby's reflection. 'When I look I am seen, so I exist. I can now afford to look and see. I now look creatively and what I apperceive I also perceive' (Winnicott, 1971: 134).

But if the mother is caught up in her own projective identification, reflecting back her own feelings of despair, hopelessness and rage about the inadequate mothering that she herself had received, the baby finds not itself, but the mother reflected back. The baby then has to learn to predict and respond to the mother's moods and feelings, instead of focusing on his/her own (Winnicott, 1971; Ernst, 1987).

Lacan (1977) theorised the 'mirror phase', which begins a process in which the child will acquire a gendered subjectivity and a place in the symbolic order. The child gazing into a mirror misrecognises itself as the 'gestalt', the totalised, complete external image of the subject. The discordance of the visual gestalt with the subject's perceived reality means that the image remains both a literal image of itself and an idealised representation, since it prefigures a unity and mastery that the child still lacks. The mirror stage initiates the child into identification with and dependence on representations of its own form.

The therapeutic gaze

Unlike the traditional power relationship in portrait photography, the photographer/therapist's gaze does not attempt to control, nor objectify the other. The client, as sitter/director, determines how s/he wants to be represented. It is the photographer/therapist's task to enable this to happen. For clients whose experience of being photographed in the past has felt invasive, or even abusive, it is particularly important to create a different quality of experience. For these clients, I have spent a whole photo-session working on beginning to feel at ease being in front of the camera and articulating what kind of image they want. Within the photo-session, the client is offered a therapeutic gaze, which is akin to that of the 'good enough mother', mirroring back the reflection of what is there to be seen to the client. This gaze is offered within a context of safety, trust and acceptance. The therapist acts as witness, advocate and nurturer. There is also a sense of encouragement and permission giving, if the client starts to become self-censoring. This then provides a containing environment, within which clients can explore the full range of their emotions.

This work was developed before the advent of digital photography. I still choose to work within the limitations of deferral. The trust, even surrender, when asking the other to make images of you that is required on behalf of the client, is most important. Frequently checking back and reviewing during the re-enactment process, as one can with a digital camera, interrupts the flow, the happening in the moment. This may make the client feel self-conscious, and create a critical distancing. It is, however, very useful to show the client how the image looks at the beginning of the session, as a check to ensure it is how the image was envisaged.

Performativity

Since photographs are mimetic, finding the right clothes and props is an important part of the process for the client, and will itself evoke feelings. Setting the staging of the session, in the contained space delineated by the background paper, creates the physical environment in which the action happens. There are clear links to psychodrama. But it is a dyadic relationship, not a group activity, and all the focus is on the client. In the photo session the client 'acts into' role, while the therapist enables this to flow by taking the other role in a dynamic relationship. The details of this role, and the appropriate things to say to enable the client to get more closely in touch with their feelings, are learned within the preceding counselling sessions. The client moves between role-playing different power positions within the dynamic; for example, parent/child, teacher/student, powerless/powerful. The therapist may take the other role, to enable the client to get more closely in touch with their feelings where appropriate. This may include enacting, for example, a surveillant parental gaze, or a judgemental institutional gaze, and photographing from that position. This role-playing dynamic, in which roles are enacted and shifted is contained by the security and challenge offered by the therapeutic gaze.

Re-enactment phototherapy makes visible the performative body. The photography sessions, are about enabling the process to happen, to 'take place', rather than 'capturing' the image. It is about a staging of the selves and knowingly using visual languages, referring to and challenging other pre-existing visual representations. Thus this work makes visible the constructions of identities rather than revealing any 'essential' identity.

Embodiment and transformation

This is a very physical way of working, in which the body expresses the emotions. The chosen role is entered into and the scenario is replayed in the here and now. The body speaks its knowledge through gesture and movement as the emotional stories unfold. Its eloquence is recorded. Clients embody the issues and personal narratives they wish to work on. In re-experiencing a range of frozen and previously repressed emotions in the here and now, and then moving into a transformation, there is a shift and a cathartic release. The transformative aspect is required to create images of the potential for change; for example, finding an inner nurturing part of the self to challenge a punishing super ego. This is crucial to the process, not merely to represent old pains, which could re-enforce distress, but rather to offer and envisage possibilities for other ways of being.

Play

The photo session could be described as a sophisticated and contained form of adult play. It is neither inner psychic reality, nor the external world, but a kind of interim, experimental, spontaneous, creative space that is held by the therapist. There are clear parallels to the ways in which children use fantasy play to re-enact troubling scenarios or to try out roles, gathering dressing up clothes and a variety of objects as props to give form to their desires and fears.

> Playing implies trust, and belongs to the potential space between [what was at first] baby and mother figure . . . Play is essentially satisfying, even when it leads to a high degree of anxiety . . . and is inherently exciting and precarious [because of] the interplay between that which is subjective and that which is objectively perceived. . . . In playing the child, or adult, is free to be creative . . . and it is only in being creative that the individual discovers the self.
>
> (Winnicott, 1971: 60–1, 63)

Case history as example – work with S

This is an edited extract from my case notes, which were made immediately after each session. Exploring current issues within the counselling relationship about authority and the misuse of power by his line-manager at work led S back to a vivid childhood memory. A sadistic teacher, who used his sarcastic tongue as a lash, his rod to beat, to embed his authority in the minds and bodies of his charges, and himself as a young pupil, held in detention, terrified, vulnerable, as he failed again and again to recite 'The Daffodils' (the poem 'I Wandered Lonely as a Cloud' by William Wordsworth). S said, 'He stole my love of English literature.' When S came to a counselling session with the book of poems, I thought – yes, we have the scenario. We then worked on how he wanted to make it visible. S suggested that he needed to take up the role of the teacher, which was great, since I knew that was what would make the session come alive, but it is much better if the idea comes from the client. S said, 'the daffodils are the symbol of my spirit. I never used to like them, I bought some for the first time last week.' He learned the poem for the phototherapy session, and brought boxes of daffodils and child-like clothes, and so took the responsibility of providing what he needed for the work. I provided a tailor's dummy and an academic gown, to represent the teacher. He changed into the schoolboy outfit, scrunched up his tie, ruffled his hair, put on the glasses. He had begun the process of becoming the role.

During the re-enactment, I take many photographs as it happens, nothing is posed. He sits, head down, then rises and begins his hesitant recitation. As he falters, I take Mr H's role and taunt him with the words S had told me in sessions when describing his abuse. He retreats to his chair, defeated, then tries again, falters again. I continue the barrage, he is clearly distressed. Then spontaneously, S puts down the book, puts on the academic gown and picks up the stick (see here Photo 6.1). In role, as Mr H, he is very abusive: 'Stupid boy, fat, lazy boy.' I then play the schoolboy role, a faltering 'Yes Sir'. Spontaneously, he puts the gown back on the dummy, and returns to the schoolboy role. He grabs a bunch of daffodils, recites the poem with an angry passion, confronts Mr H and beats him with the daffodils: 'I am not stupid, I am not lazy, I am not fat.' He is powerful and formidable as the retaliating schoolboy.

He then takes handfuls of daffodils, sits on the floor and recites again, with sadness, tears; he removes his glasses, then, with such joy and release, embracing the daffodils, at the last line he throws the daffodils up, letting them fall with glee. His joy is visible on his face, in his body, relaxed and at ease (see Photo 6.2). I ask him to do it again and again, this throwing of the daffodils. I want the image that will encompass the feeling that is in the room; I want the balance to all the pent-up rage against the abuse S received from Mr H. He lies down, and I cover him in daffodils, he takes the book of poems on his chest, and recites again, playfully, joyously and covers himself more with the flowers.

When equilibrium has returned, he sits up, and slowly we rebundle the flowers that have survived. 'Marvellously resilient flowers – they bend with the wind,' S says. This is a gentle task, and slowly he de-roles. He changes back to his business suit.

We viewed the photos in the next session. He re-visited the emotions within the session; interestingly, he had forgotten that he had cried.

He was struck by one of the Mr H images. 'That's me. I am arrogant. I know that I am superior, I am very articulate and I use that and my intelligence, I put people down.' 'Sarcastic?' 'Very. I am told that I do not suffer fools gladly – which means I am intolerant.' He speaks slowly and considered, I ask him 'what's the thought?' 'I am cruel, verbally.' I pick up the image that he has identified, and pull it to the front; I hold it as he describes himself. I aim to be very there for S, as he slowly acknowledges this part of himself. I am aware this is hard to do.

Photo 6.1 'The authoritarian' (photographer/therapist Rosy Martin, protagonist/client S).
Original in colour.

I take one of the joy images, a playful child, and put it beside Mr H: 'What does he say to him?' 'Control yourself.'

I am more struck by the sad image; I get that and put it beside Mr H.

'I am aware that he (Mr H) is very sad. Is that what he cloaks?' 'And angry too.' 'Which one?' He chooses the one expressing tense anger.

'So, the arrogant side cloaks your anger and sadness?' 'Oh yes. He is in control. I have to be in control. He covers up my anger and my sadness. When I am angry or sad, I am vulnerable.' 'So, you use him? Tell me about your anger.' . . .

So the session continued. There was so much made visible here to work on, as part of the on-going therapeutic relationship. As S said, 'the camera makes me look at parts of me I have suppressed for most of my life. I have begun the journey.'

All the clients I have worked with have an interest in images, and use symbolic and metaphorical ways of thinking. This is a particularly useful method for those who over-intellectualise their psychic distress, since it foregrounds the body as the expressive mode and offers the potential for a connection with the unconscious. This modality would

Photo 6.2 'Then my heart with pleasure fills and dances with the daffodils' (photographer/therapist Rosy Martin, protagonist/client S). Original in colour.

not be appropriate for any client whose grasp on reality was small, or who was lacking any solid sense of identity. The danger is the risk of stirring up too much material from the unconscious when the personality is incapable of integrating it.

Why and how the photographs produced in re-enactment phototherapy are useful in the therapeutic relationship

A productive paradox is created between the projected reality and notions of evidence invested in the photograph, even its very physical existence and the acts of choice and framing required to make it. So it may be seen as either reflecting or constructing a reality. The objectifying eye of the camera offers a blank screen and the necessary distance to see from a different point of view.

The sheer quantity of photographs offers the client a sense of having been really fully seen. The photographs produced provide the possibility of an unfiltered connection with the unconscious; since what takes place within the photo session is rooted in unconscious processes, the session itself grows out of the therapeutic relationship, flowing in the here and now. The photographs provide a mapping of the session, and the possibility of reconstructing and recalling it. This is useful since aspects of what happened within the session can so easily slip back into the unconscious and be repressed again. A dialogue between individual photographs, which represent different parts of the self, or significant others, can be facilitated by the therapist as an externalised gestalt. The photographs produced can be re-ordered at will, giving the possibility of telling many new stories, thereby suggesting new versions of old realities.

Taking up the role of significant others within the client's life, especially that of parental figures, can be very personally challenging. Introjections may be faced up to, projections and projective identifications are suddenly seen for what they are, in a flash of recognition. The split-off disowned parts of the self may be acknowledged as such and accepted back within the self. Maintaining lifelong patterns of shame, secrecy and denial is contested by these photographs that mirror back and give form, size, weight and colour to psychic pain and to its history, its source. Out there and made visible, these aspects can be worked with and reflected upon within the counselling relationship. The photographs may then be seen as transitional objects between inner and outer reality. The therapist bears witness to these previously hidden aspects of the selves. By offering a non-judgemental positive regard, and challenging fixity, the therapist enables the client to work towards integration of all these parts.

As Assagioli (1975) has said of psychosynthesis, symbols are seen as 'accumulators', in the electrical sense, as containers and preservers of a dynamic psychological charge. This 'charge' can be transformed by the use of the symbol, channelled by it, or integrated by it. The use of symbolic re-presentations are especially powerful for connecting with and transforming unconscious belief systems.

Looking at the range of photographs produced and witnessing the mutability of the images enables the client to see how identity is fragmented across many 'truths'. This understanding frees up the client from the search for the 'ideal' self and allows acceptance of the self as process and becoming.

Confidentiality

All the work is confidential. Because photographs are mimetic, this is of special importance. When I run workshops or teach, I always set the limit that the work produced cannot be shown beyond the group itself, unless the participants themselves choose to make it public.

Process to product

The therapeutic process needs to have been finished before any work based on it can be shared or put on display; otherwise the protagonist would be placed in too vulnerable a position and it could be potentially exploitative. Phototherapy work always needs to be based on trust. The photographs are only shown with the expressed permission of the sitter/director, in practice it is nearly always at their instigation. Consequently almost all of the photographs remain private.

Jo Spence and I chose to exhibit some key images from our practice, in an art context (Martin and Spence, 1987), because we wanted to share these ideas. To make this transition, a distancing, an intellectual and objective examination is required to ensure the work has the power to communicate. The chosen images speak to the social and cultural formations of subjectivities and can activate a personal or collective memory for the spectator.

Digital imaging and photography – some considerations

The meanings of photographs are shaped by the ideas and beliefs that are invested in and brought to them, which are culturally, historically and personally determined, rather than by the technology used to produce them. However, the shift from analogue to digital is changing our relationships to the photographic image.

Grazing around Facebook will show that the images uploaded by younger people (say up to the age of thirty) concentrate on posing, performing the self and partying; an extension of the leisure pursuits that have always been the focus of vernacular photography. Holidays, (new-born) babies and pets feature too, just as in the traditional family album. Some users make photo-diaries, photo-stories, carefully constructed sequences, or short movies from stills with music added. Such generous sharing of thoughtful creativity is a delight, and is an enhanced form of communication. But the public/private division can be tenuous on Facebook; legendary stories abound of people losing their jobs when their bosses see images from their private lives, initially shared between 'friends'. Cyber bullying is also rife.

Digital imaging was proclaimed by Mitchell (1992) as a rupture in the discourses of photography. Yet there are parallels to the changes brought about by the introduction of the Kodak camera in 1888, with the slogan 'you press the button, we do the rest'. Then, taking an image was separated from making the photograph. The processing and printing became industrialised. The proud owner of a Brownie Box camera at age eight, I documented our family holiday, as a child with a digital camera might today. However, I was limited to two films, and so each photograph had to be carefully chosen, planned and composed, time of day and light had to considered – in scarcity each was precious. When using an SLR, studying photography on my Foundation Art course in 1968, all settings were manual, so I learned what one could achieve and how, the slow and thorough way. The magic of the darkroom still retains its potency, although the computer is more convenient and precise.

When using a digital camera, there is a tendency to take a huge number of photos, often without thinking carefully first. Excess becomes the norm: snap, snap, download, and maybe never look at them again. The hard drive becomes the depository of visual memories. Editing is an even more challenging task, while also potentially emphasising the desire for the impossible ideal (Martin, 1991; Watney, 1991). The LCD monitor offers instant feedback, which is very useful as long as it does not detract from carefully observing the subject and being present in the moment. What one loses is the deferral, the anticipation and separation of taking from looking at the resultant image. On the mobile phone, images are deleted with the same nonchalance as texts. Ephemeral or taken as a kind of proof that one was there, but rarely looked at again, is the photographic image losing its previous intrinsic value, as a potential container of memories?

What all the different approaches to phototherapy offer is reflectivity, taking the time to really look at and examine an image, and pull out its multilayered meanings. This gives back value to the photograph, its layers of resonance and the opportunity for contemplation. I prefer to work with the physical object for this reason, so I encourage and work with the client to carefully select images from the session to find the key ones to print out and work on in depth.

Conclusion

Re-enactment phototherapy offers a methodology that can make visible and open up aspects of the self to scrutiny. It uses the languages of the body; gesture, facial expression and movement, in an embodied eloquence, which is photographically recorded. It can embrace aspects of play and humour, even joy. The images produced become material for articulation and integration within the therapeutic relationship. There is a profound connection to the unconscious enabled through the photographic and therapeutic exchange, and therefore it needs to be used carefully and responsibly. It is a very powerful modality.

Note

This essay draws upon and develops arguments addressed in:

Martin, R. (1996). You (never) can tell: Phototherapy, memory and subjectivity. *Blackflash*, 14(3), 4–8.

Martin, R. (1997). Looking and reflecting: Returning the gaze, re-enacting memories and imagining the future through phototherapy. In: Hogan, S. (ed.), *Feminist approaches to art therapy*. London and New York: Routledge, 150–176.

Martin, R. (2001). The performative body: Phototherapy and re-enactment. *Afterimage*, 29(3), 17–20.

References

Assagioli, R. (1975). *Psychosynthesis*. London: Turnstone Books.

Barthes, R. (1977). *Roland Barthes*. London: Macmillan.

Debord, G. (1967). *The Society of the Spectacle*. Detroit, MI: Black and Red Books.

Dewdney, A. and Lister, M. (1988). *Youth, Culture and Photography*. London: Macmillan.

Ernst, S. (1987). Can a daughter be a woman? Women's identity and psychological separation. In: Ernst, S. and Maguire, M. (eds), *Living with the Sphinx: Papers from the Women's Therapy Centre* (pp. 68–116). London: The Women's Press.

Fleet Imaging (1996). *The Power to Change Your Photos* (Advertising leaflet). London: Fleet Imaging.

Krauss, D.A. and Fryrear, J.L. (eds) (1983). *Phototherapy in Mental Health*. Springfield, IL: Charles C. Thomas.

Lacan, J. (1977). The mirror stage as formative of the functions of the I. In: Sheridan, A. (trans.), *Ecrits* (pp. 1–8). London: Tavistock Publications.

Mandel, G. and Lemus, A.B. (2008). I pray. But not for myself: *Historias positivos*. Available from: www.guardian.co.uk/world/gallery/2008/aug/04/mexico.aids?picture1/433620992 (accessed 19 October 2008).

Martin, R. (1991). Unwind the ties that bind. In: P. Holland and J. Spence (eds), *Family Snaps: The meanings of domestic photography*. London: Virago.

Martin, R. (1997). Looking and reflecting: Returning the gaze, re-enacting memories and imagining the future through phototherapy. In: Hogan, S. (ed.), *Feminist Approaches to Art Therapy* (pp. 150–176). London and New York: Routledge.

Martin, R. (2012). Looking and reflecting: Returning the gaze, re-enacting memories and imagining the future through re-enactment phototherapy. In Hogan, S. (ed.), *Revisiting Feminist Approaches to Art Therapy* (pp. 112–139). New York: Berghahn Books.

Martin, R. and Spence, J. (1985). New portraits for old: The use of the camera in therapy. *Feminist Review*, 19, March, 66–92.

Martin, R. and Spence, J (1987). *Double Exposure: The minefield of memory*. London: Photographers Gallery (exhibition and catalogue).

Mitchell, W.J. (1992). *The Re-Configured Eye: Visual truth in the post-photographic era*. Cambridge, MA: MIT Press.

Photovoice, *PhotoVoice*. Available from: www.photovoice.org/ (accessed 20 October 2008).

Shepherd, J. (1998). Controlling images for a change. *In the picture*, 33, Summer, 5–6.

Spence, J. (1986). *Putting Myself in the Picture: A political, personal and photographic autobiography*. London: Camden Press. See particularly pp. 172–185 (Spence, J. and Martin, R.).

Spence, J. and Holland, P. (eds) (1991). *Family Snaps: The meanings of domestic photography*. London: Virago.

Watney, S. (1991). Ordinary boys. In: J. Spence and P. Holland (eds), *Family Snaps: The meanings of domestic photography* (pp. 26–34). London: Virago.

Winnicott, D.W. (1971). *Playing and Reality*. London: Tavistock Publications.

Chapter 7

Talking pictures therapy
The therapeutic use of photographs in counselling and psychotherapy

Del Loewenthal

Introduction

Photographs can be used therapeutically in counselling and psychotherapy, both in the short term and long term, open ended and fixed term. This chapter focuses on a description of the use of photographs in brief therapy.

The purpose of this collective case study was to explore and in turn, as described more in Chapter 14, evaluate *talking pictures therapy*, which is the use of photographs within psychotherapy and counselling. The therapeutic work that forms the data of this study was carried out with four children in a UK school on the south coast of England in an area of relative deprivation. The children, who ranged from age twelve to fourteen (Key Stage 3 to Key Stage 4), were informed that *talking pictures therapy* normally involved up to six sessions of one-to-one therapy with the purpose of enabling them to express and explore, during the therapy and potentially through photographs, aspects of their lives about which they would like to talk.

As reported in Chapter 14, alongside use of a suitable quantitative assessment set: PHQ-9, GAD-7 and the Improving Access to Psychological Therapies (IAPT) Phobia Scale (IAPT minimum data set) and CORE-10, the author also wished to consider the 'progress' of the therapy through client's choice of photographs and the individual meanings projected onto them. *Talking pictures therapy* is, in particular, being explored here as a possible alternative to cognitive behavioural therapy which, as in many countries, is currently the most prominent 'therapy' in the UK as a result of the national roll-out IAPT programme, following the Layard report (Layard *et al.*, 2006).

Theory

Phototherapy and therapeutic photography are not completely separate entities but may be classed as existing on the continuum of photo-based healing practices. In turn, the two practices involve making use of the 'emotional-communication qualities of photographs and people's interactions with them' (Weiser, 2004: 1) to enable clients to begin to speak of difficulties they experience that are otherwise difficult to speak of (Weiser, 1999, 2001).

Following an international conference on phototherapy in Turku, Finland in June 2008 (see Loewenthal, 2009), the research project 'PhototherapyEurope: Learning and healing through phototherapy' was established, funded by the EU Leonardo da Vinci Lifelong Learning Fund, with the aim of developing and disseminating phototherapy to practitioners, to promote well-being and social adhesion.

Broadly, phototherapy is the use of photographs within psychotherapy where therapists will use techniques to enable clients to express their concerns during counselling sessions (Krauss and Fryrear, 1983; Weiser, 2002). However, therapeutic photography often involves self-initiated, photo-based activities conducted by a person and sometimes without a therapist guiding the experience for self-exploration and personal growth (Spence, 1986; Martin and Spence, 1987, 1988). This process often involves the taking of photographs, for working through what might be considered an emotional constriction. In practice, the distinctions between phototherapy and therapeutic photography are not always clear, and some practitioners use the methods interchangeably within their practice.

Within therapy, photographs can be seen as a route to an unconscious, with the meanings clients attach to the photograph assumed to be the result of the client's projections, being what may have been previously repressed. Repression is taken to be an unconscious exclusion of memories, impulses, desires and thoughts that are too difficult or unacceptable to deal with in consciousness: 'the essence of repression lies simply in turning something away and keeping it at a distance from the conscious' (Freud 1915: 147). In turn, for Freud (1914:16), 'the theory of repression is the cornerstone on which the whole structure of psychoanalysis rests'. Hence, photographs may be seen as a device through which the clients repressed projections can be realised within the therapy.

Talking pictures therapy may be spoken of as the use of photographs within the various counselling and psychotherapy modalities, such as person-centred and psychodynamic approaches; it is a process that may be incorporated into any psychological therapy that aims to enable the client to speak of what is of concern to them. In turn, *talking pictures therapy* is the use of photographs within psychotherapy and counselling to facilitate this *talk*.

Therapeutic method

Talking pictures therapy involves the use of photographs in counselling and psychotherapy. Each child was asked to select a photograph in the initial and final session, as well as at other times in the therapy if this was deemed useful. The selection of photographs used for this study were 'Spectro Cards'; an associative set of sixty photographic cards created for practitioners to use within therapeutic activities to facilitate the client to speak of their concerns, through captivating imagination, exposing feelings and promoting storytelling (Halkola and Koffert, 2011).

Each of the clients was seen at their school for fifty minutes, usually on a weekly basis for up to six sessions. Regarding the therapeutic method used in the individual sessions with the children, this is termed 'post-existential' (Loewenthal, 2009; Loewenthal, 2011), focusing on individual meanings while influenced by person-centred, existential/continental philosophy and analytic approaches.

Data collection and analysis

With regard to evaluating the effectiveness of *talking pictures therapy* alongside the descriptions from the clients of their chosen photographs, the IAPT minimum data set (GAD-7 and PHQ-9 and the IAPT Phobia Scale) was used, together with CORE-10 at the beginning and end of each client's course of therapy. These were assumed to be the most common methods currently used to evaluate therapeutic effectiveness in the UK.

Results

Each of the four individual cases will be described, outlining the use of photographs as process and outcome alongside the pre and post therapy assessment set; PHQ-9, GAD-7 and CORE-10 data. However, this chapter focuses on qualitative description, whereas Chapter 14 both describes the underlying qualitative phenomenological-hermeneutic case study method and discusses further quantitative results. The names of the children and other content have been changed for reasons of confidentiality.

Charlotte

Charlotte was twelve years old when she came for up to six sessions of *talking pictures therapy* at her school. She had a somewhat soulful air about her and was engaging. Charlotte's chosen Spectro Cards can be seen in Chapter 2 (see Photos 2.1 and 2.2).

Photographs as process and outcome

In the initial session, she chose a photo with what she called 'a twist' in it (see Photo 2.1). She said she found it difficult to talk about her situation, for her father had been run over and killed three years ago, and her mother had never wanted to know her. She lives with her gran and her aunt (her father's mother and sister). Her aunt had been in psychiatric hospitals from the age of sixteen after being in care and was 'in crime'. Charlotte did not have a computer at home, but there was talk that she might get one 'one day'.

We talked about films and she said her favourite one was a story about how three people got killed in a Range Rover in Africa. But there was a 'twist' to it, in that no one is sure as to whether the person taken prisoner did it, or not, particularly as he had a record. We came to speak of how her father had also been involved in some criminal activity, but that didn't necessarily mean to say that there wasn't any good in him. Charlotte seemed relieved when I said there could be bad and good in everybody.

Charlotte had a fifteen-year-old brother whom she was only just getting to know, but who was currently in prison. She also had a sister in care whom she had hardly ever seen, but whom she was hoping to meet through her brother. It later turned out that this sister lived in the road near to the school, but she didn't know which number, and she also worried about what reception she would receive.

She talked about how her brother was in prison because he got some other boy to hold somebody down while he threatened him with a knife. Charlotte said, in a disbelieving voice, 'The boy who had been threatened claimed that his face was black and blue, but it could not have been so.' I was able to wonder with her how, in saying that, she took on the values of her family (which on both sides were notorious for crime in that area, something Charlotte had said she did not want to get into). Charlotte told me her favourite subject was Drama, and how the other children were impressed at how realistically she was able to make up the part of a drug dealer. 'More crime,' I said and she looked crestfallen.

In the fifth session, I again asked her to choose a photograph that called to her. She chose one of some trees with green leaves (Photo 2.2). She said it reminded her of a peaceful place she goes to on her own where there is nobody else. She said it was a lane and there were cars in the first part, and someone had been murdered a bit further on, but here was ok, 'but I suppose one has to be careful'.

In the last session she brought in to show me a photograph of the trees in the lane that she had taken on her mobile.

Overview

I did feel that the *talking pictures therapy* had enabled her to be less depressed and start to talk more of her anxieties. She was able to find places outside her therapy to do more with her friends, and on her own. While she did not want to be in crime, for which her mother's extended family is even more notorious than her father's, she needed to talk about this. But talking about crime was also a currency with which she was able to engage others at her school, and hopefully, more therapeutically, myself, while we also spent a lot of time talking about fashion, films and mobile phones.

Winston

I had been told that Winston was almost mute and at my first meeting with this thirteen-year-old black boy, he appeared obedient but not wanting to talk. When Winston did talk, it was in such a whisper that I had to put my ear in front of his mouth to hear him.

Photographs as process and outcome

The first photograph he chose was of a Catherine Wheel at a fairground (see Photo 7.1) which he said reminded him of when he went there with his parents and two sisters last summer. It appeared that he felt he sometimes played at home with his sisters but not his parents.

At our next meeting the following week, he again found it difficult to talk and I asked him to choose another photograph that called to him. This time he chose one with noughts and crosses (see Photo 7.2) which he said, again whispering, that he enjoyed playing with his sisters. We played noughts and crosses together for about twenty minutes. Then I asked him if he'd like to play another game I had, called 'Connect 4'.

Winston was very interested in this and soon became very proficient. After some time, while playing this, I said to him that I had been struck, when asking him the pre-therapy evaluation questions, that he had chosen the response 'sometimes' for the question 'over the past week, I have made plans to end my life', and I wondered what had made him say that. Winston whispered to me that another student, Linda (whom I was also seeing for *talking pictures therapy*) said that she didn't like Winston because

Photo 7.1
Winston's first choice of photograph (Halkola).

Photo 7.2
Winston's second choice of photograph (Halkola).

of the colour of his skin and that she had also called him a prick and slapped him, saying 'your mother and father . . .' and then 'gave me a sign with her fingers'. I asked Winston if he would like me to tell the SENCO that this had happened. And he nodded vigorously.

At the start of the next session, he wanted to play Connect 4 again. After a while I asked him if the other student had stopped bullying him. Winston nodded with a happy smile on his face, whispering 'yes'. After two more games, I again put my head round the counter stand of Connect 4 and asked him if he'd always spoken quietly? He whispered into my ear 'no'. When I asked at what age he started, he said 'I was five' and went back to playing the game.

At the subsequent session, he seemed more relaxed and cheerful, and wanted to play scrabble, which I had previously introduced to him. While we were playing, I said to Winston that I had found myself thinking about how he had said that he had spoken before he was five and I wondered what had happened to stop him talking. Winston seemed unable to even whisper, so I said, if he wanted to, he could write it down and he wrote: 'My mother tell me to stop talking to [sic] much and I stopped talking.' I asked him if he would like to talk more, and when he nodded I wondered to him how he and I together could help him.

In our penultimate session I asked Winston if he would like to choose another photograph that called to him and he chose one of playing cards (see Photo 7.5).

I asked him how he came to choose that one. Winston replied, 'My mother used to play cards in Africa before we came here a year ago.' He also told me he had spoken French then and now he no longer played with his mother, who also does not speak very much. I asked Winston whether all women of his mother's age didn't speak very much in that part of Africa. Winston shook his head with a big smile on his face as if I was stupid and then indicated that he was keen to carry on our game of scrabble.

At the start of our sixth and last session I asked Winston if he wanted to play games or to talk. Winston unusually replied, 'talk'. Then, hesitantly, and quietly, he said that he had been thinking about how, while his mother does not talk, this was not the same for his mother's sister. Also, in this session Winston told me that his mother did play tennis with him, after he had told her he wanted to be a tennis player. Winston also said, with a happy smile on his face, that he now has a friend at school.

Overview

Over the six sessions, Winston was able to move from being what teachers had described as 'an elective mute' to someone who another teacher commented was now able to look at her. It could be that the increase in scores with regard to CORE came about because he was now able to voice what was of concern to him.

Linda

Linda wasn't there the first week so I could only offer five and not six weekly sessions of *talking pictures therapy*. Linda was thirteen and walked very stiffly; she appeared tall and slightly unkempt. Sometimes, cut off, she would give herself a little smile.

Photographs as process and outcome

Linda had difficulty choosing a photograph that called to her but liked the ones of flowers because they were 'pretty' and the tropical fish (see Photo 7.3) because it was 'colourful'. She had a tropical fish tank at home where she lived with her mother, two brothers and a Rottweiler. Linda also commented on a photograph of a sailing boat. She said it reminded her of when she was four and last went to the seaside. She added, 'It was a happy time.' She also commented, more quietly, on another photograph that 'it looks like someone was hurt', but she wouldn't say any more, including which photograph it was.

The photograph she finally chose as her favourite was because she liked 'the swirl of colours' (see Photo 7.4). Linda seemed to find it difficult, and was reluctant to speak of her feelings associated with the photographs.

At the start of the second session, Linda told me she liked playing computer games and took up the offer to do this in our session. Linda first chose a computer game that required her to take the place of the person (it was actually a black person) and correctly serve an increasing number of customers. I asked her if she could teach me to play and for a short time she did, but ended up wanting to play on her own. Linda was unable to play many of the games she searched for as the school had restricted internet access. Eventually though, she found one where the object was to see how far you could grab

Photo 7.3
Linda's first choice of photograph (Halkola).

Photo 7.4
Linda's second choice of photograph (Halkola).

and pull cartoon pictures of girls' breasts. After she started playing, I said, 'Linda, I don't think that's . . .' 'appropriate', she finished my sentence and changed to another game.

At the third session, she again wanted to play computer games and started with one looking after pets, which subsequently became very popular in our sessions. Again, I said I also would like to play and we did briefly play a computer running game she introduced but Linda soon returned to the pets game, which she played on her own.

Just before our next session, Linda could not be found. Later that morning, I was told that the police had brought Linda into school. Apparently she had come to school, taken her younger brother and gone with him shoplifting. Linda did knock on my door towards the end of the hour. I said that I couldn't see her then but could see her at lunchtime, but she didn't take this offer up. At lunchtime I was told by the SENCO that Linda had said she was sorry about what had happened that morning and that Linda had never apologised before.

At the start of our final session, Linda seemed far keener to engage and started by asking if I would get her a tissue (from out of the room). I said it was perfectly alright with me if she went and got one herself. When she returned to the room I asked her if she could choose again a photograph that called to her. Linda suggested that we could play another game where she would hide two of the cards and I would have to find them, but I would first have to go out of the room and close the door. I said that

I couldn't do that because we were in the room where the teachers left their coats and bags.

Linda replied, 'Let's play with the computer' and she again started with the game where she had to look after pets. She then chose, still playing on her own, another game called 'Destroy the Human'. When this came on the screen I said, 'Is that what you'd like to do?' 'Yes,' she said, but didn't say anymore. During the final session, I did say to Linda, 'You seem to start with games looking after animals but don't stay with them and move on to playing more violent games.' Linda nodded and carried on playing.

In this last session, when asked, Linda chose the photograph with the 'swirling colours'. She again seemed to find it difficult to say why she had chosen it, eventually saying it was something to do with the colour and shape. She then chose photographs of flowers, as she had done previously. When I asked how she came to choose these, she said they were colourful. She then said, 'My mum likes flowers.' Linda said her mum had planted roses. When I asked her if she had any other flowers at home, Linda replied, 'dandelions', and then added that she had also picked flowers for her young brother but she didn't know their name – 'they were small and yellow'. 'Buttercups,' I offered. 'Yes!' she said, and continued, 'I have also bought daffodils for my mother.'

Overview

I did wonder to myself whether I reminded Linda of someone such as her older brother and also whether it might have been better for her with a female therapist. Also, as with the other children I saw for this brief therapy, I did say that it was possible for me to see them on another occasion in the future if there was something really important they wanted to see me about. But, in Linda's case, I found it more difficult to say this as I had felt she was mainly interested in me when she wanted to manipulate me – and it occurred to me that this might have been her experience with other people as well.

Amanda

It was unclear whether Amanda would turn up for her first session of *talking pictures therapy*. I was told that she had not been to her classes earlier that day, although she did arrive outside the door, but kept moving away and coming back. The SENCO who was passing asked her to take the gum out of her mouth and she threw it on the floor and rapidly disappeared, followed by the SENCO. When Amanda returned, she rushed into the room and slumped onto a chair. I asked her if she would come and sit on the chair next to the desk where I was sitting, which she did, but sat in a way that must have been very awkward for her.

Photographs as process and outcome

When I asked her which photograph called to her, she chose the one of the playing cards (see Photo 7.5) which featured a joker. The process of going through the cards also seemed

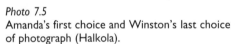

Photo 7.5
Amanda's first choice and Winston's last choice
of photograph (Halkola).

Photo 7.6
Amanda's second choice of photograph
(Halkola).

to calm her down a little. Amanda said, 'I like to make people laugh, but it gets me into trouble.' She also told me how, four years ago, her father died and that was after her parents had split up. Furthermore, Amanda wasn't told that her father had died and was not able to go to the funeral. Amanda said that apparently her father's doctor had told him not to drink because of his lungs and her father had had a heart attack.

At our next meeting, Amanda was standing, waiting, outside at the start but it took her about thirty minutes of going away and coming back to come into the room. Eventually, when she did, she rushed in, diving across the room and ending up horizontally across three chairs. Amanda eventually came and sat on the chair next to the desk, but again sat awkwardly, keeping her backpack on, playing with anything she could find on the desk in a fidgety but deliberate way.

I asked Amanda, as in the previous session, to choose a photograph that called to her. When I asked her what she thought the photograph she had chosen was about, she replied, 'It's a clearing' (see Photo 7.6). Amanda then said, 'I want to sleep,' to which I replied, 'Go ahead.' She moved the cards aside to put her head on the desk and I said, 'You're making a clearing for yourself.'

We then talked about football. Amanda said that she didn't play for the school (though it turned out she did for a Sunday league). When she spoke about not playing for the school team, she did it in a way that seemed to devalue it but she also sounded as if she really did want to play for the school. I asked her how come she doesn't play for the school and she replied that she wasn't allowed to because she had previously forgotten to bring her kit for PE. I said 'I'm not making any promises, but would you like me to speak to the school and tell them you would like to play football for them?' Amanda said, 'Yes.'

At the start of the next session, I was told that Amanda had been suspended the previous Friday for throwing the contents of a soft drink can over the Deputy Head, and as a further consequence, she was now in a meeting at the school with her mother but wanted to see me afterwards. When she did arrive, Amanda said 'I'm tired' and she took a piece of paper from the desk in an aggressive way and made a concertina.

She then screwed up the piece of paper and threw it on the floor. I asked her if she would put it in the bin. Amanda replied, 'When I've finished reading' as she took one of the magazines from a side table, but followed this a few seconds later with, 'I need to go to the toilet.' I said, 'Ok, but first pick up the piece of paper.' As Amanda went out, she picked up the paper she'd thrown on the floor. When she came back, she wandered round the room in an agitated way and started picking at a plastic notice on the wall, saying, 'These could easily break off.' I said, 'Don't do that – you'll get me into trouble.' Amanda stopped and sat down again in the chair next to the desk. We talked about her chances of staying on at school. Amanda said she knew she'd need to show some improvement to stay on. At the end of the session, she said abruptly, 'You will be here next Thursday, won't you.'

At the next session, Amanda still had her bag on her back but was getting easier to talk to. I said it seemed difficult for her to go after the things she wanted and wondered whether that's why she played the part of the joker. Amanda didn't say anything but what I said seemed to reverberate within her. Again, at the end of the session, she wanted reassurance from me that I would be there the following week for what she knew would be our last session.

In the final session, she sat down in the chair next to the desk without first wandering around, though she still seemed to find it difficult to speak other than in monosyllables. When I asked her once more to choose a photograph that called to her, she straightaway said 'the one of the clearing'. Amanda also told me she had been asked to join the school football team but had said no. At first, the reasons for this did not appear clear, but what eventually came through was that Amanda wanted to train in the week for her Sunday football when the school team met, and that lots of other girls no longer wanted to play with the school team.

I still wondered with her that this might well be the case, but whether it might also be because she found it difficult to go after what she really wanted.

Overview

I think it was important for Amanda to be able to see a man who was supportive but able to hold the boundaries with her. I think she would have particularly benefited from longer-term therapy.

Discussion and conclusions

The *talking pictures therapy* approach overall seemed to provide a useful way of opening up a therapeutic encounter. By being able to get quickly to the client's concerns, it also provided a way that the actual looking at photographs enabled the client to manage their own therapy. In turn, the findings may suggest that *talking pictures therapy* enables clients to quickly bring to mind and explore that which is troubling them and is in contrast to the current dominance of CBT, which focuses more on taking the clients' minds off the problem.

With regard to the evaluative data measures (see Figure 14.2 in Chapter 14), three clients (Charlotte, Amanda and Linda) saw a decrease in the PHQ-9 score between pre and post evaluation, alongside a decrease in CORE-10 score. Further, both Amanda and Linda scored higher on GAD-7 at pre than post evaluation. With regard to Winston, both PHQ-9 and CORE-10 scores increased between pre and post therapy evaluation.

To return to the photographs chosen, both Charlotte and Amanda, who initially chose photos that could be seen to have indicated their turbulent states of mind, at the end of therapy chose photographs that may be found to indicate they had found safer places sometimes to be, and to speak from. They both started with photographs that showed what was of concern to them – for Charlotte, the metal with the twist in it, and for Amanda, the joker in the pack of cards – and they were both subsequently able to find another place, a lane with some trees where Charlotte could be on her own. Similarly, Amanda chose a photograph that she described as a 'clearing', which enabled her to rest and eventually become more present, at least in our sessions, in a more ordinary way.

Winston has now found his voice and through this, works with material that is important to him. At first, he had started by holding on to the precious memory of playing with his sisters and parents; but he was eventually able to voice, through the picture of the playing cards, how his mother does not speak and his experience of how his mother told him not to speak. Contrary to the evaluative measures, Linda, by staying with the same photographs, perhaps showed she has not moved very much, though there may be the possibility of her becoming clearer in acknowledging how she cannot stay with ordinary pressures such as looking after pets but moves instead to games that are violent and sometimes sexualised. There is also the possibility that she may come to see how she attempts to manipulate the world in a way that she feels she has herself been manipulated.

The evaluation tools PHQ-9, CORE-10, GAD-7 and the IAPT Phobia Scale were used as they are the main culturally accepted approaches to evaluation in the UK. It was found that they can, however, work against more phenomenological approaches to therapy. For example, the asking of questions can produce an expectation that the therapist is then going to solve the problem, as in, for example, a medical model, which therefore only suits a particular type of therapy. There again it was found that having such a framework that starts with asking questions can be a way, for both clients and therapists, of temporarily reducing the anxiety of 'two frightened people in a room' (Bion, 1990: 5).

In turn, there was also the feeling of further violence being done to the client in both asking clients to respond to such questions as 'whether they have made plans to end their life' and then moving on to the next question. This appeared to mitigate against a therapy evolving through a human relationship.

In comparison, it was found that the photographs, in the context of the therapeutic dialogue of the client's projections, may be a more useful descriptive device, not only for the therapy itself but also as an evaluation of it. For example, Charlotte and Amanda both started with photographs indicating their turbulent states of mind and over the course of the brief therapy chose photographs indicating calmer places to be speaking from; while Linda's choosing similar photographs at the start and end of therapy may indicate that she had moved very little at all. Furthermore, this evaluation does not have to be potentially distorted by the pre-imposition of medicalised notions of anxiety, depression, phobias and clinical ranges, thus enabling a more phenomenological/post-phenomenological approach to evaluation. Importantly, the photographs were used within a psychotherapeutic process (in this case a post-existential one, particularly influenced by psychoanalysis) and not as an ongoing theory of phototherapeutic technique. While there are opportunities generally for clients individually and collectively to take photographs, the clients seen here were not in a place where it would have been considered helpful, or probably even possible, as they were too distressed.

However, with regard to the use of photographs in the psychological therapies, there are, nevertheless, some potential disadvantages to a *talking pictures* approach. The first is that clients might say too much too soon for them to be able to manage its representation in the photograph as this may prevent healthy repression. The second concerns whether photographs or projective techniques (in a digital era where photographs are so commonplace) could be used consciously or unconsciously by, for example, a teacher, in order to make one person carry out the agenda, or any other person or even the State. It is therefore recommended that *talking pictures therapy* is carried out by a therapist who has at least some basic therapeutic interpersonal training that also involves the therapist gaining personal insight (for this reason CBT, Systemic and some Group trainings may not be sufficient on their own).

In particular, teachers and SENCOs should not be assumed to have these abilities (even though many will have gained much through their work experience). In schools and other settings, it is important that the phototherapist is independent though, with the young person's permission, able to share some aspects that emerge. This can be very delicate, involving, for example, both teachers' inappropriate curiosity and own anxieties, as well as their desire to help, and the complexity around, for example, the ethical notions of what it might mean to put the other first (Loewenthal, 2011). However, with these provisos, phototherapy as part of our digital culture is considered a helpful and cost-effective way of reducing constrictions in people's lives.

This chapter has attempted to explore both how photographs can enable clients to speak in brief therapy (and should be equally applicable to longer-term therapy) about that which they find difficult to voice, and the use of the photograph chosen and the resulting projection evaluating the therapy itself. More generally, *talking pictures* could be offered to most people who wish to explore what is of issue to them, and CBT offered to those who want to find strategies for not allowing thoughts to come to mind.

References

Bion, W.R. (1990). *Brazilian Lectures*. London: Karnac.

Freud, S. (1914). *On the History of the Psycho-Analytic Movement*. S.E., 14, 7–66.

Freud, S. (1915). *Repression*. S.E., 14, 141–158.

Halkola, U. and Koffert, T. (2011). The many stories of being: In: *PHOTOTHERAPYEUROPE: Learning and healing with phototherapy – A Handbook*. Turku: University of Turku, Publications of the Brahea Centre for Training and Development. Also available from: http://phototherapyeurope.utu.fi/photoeurope_handbook.pdf.

Krauss, D.A. and Fryrear, J.L. (1993). *Phototherapy in Mental Health*. Springfield, IL: Charles C. Thomas.

Layard, R., Clark, D., Bell, S., Knapp, M., Meacher, B., Priebe, S., Turnberg, L., Thornicroft, G. and Wright, B. (2006). *The Depression Report: A new deal for depression and anxiety disorders*. London: The Centre for Economic Performance's Mental Health Policy Group, LSE.

Loewenthal, D. (2009). (Editorial) Can photographs help one find one's voice? The use of photographs in the psychological therapies. *European Journal of Psychotherapy and Counselling*, 11(1), 1–6.

Loewenthal, D. (2011). *Post-Existentialism and the Psychological Therapies: Towards a therapy without foundations*. London: Karnac.

Martin, R. and Spence, J. (1987). New portraits for old: The use of the camera in therapy. In: R. Betterton (ed.), *Looking On: Images of femininity in the visual arts and media* (pp. 267–279). London: Pandora.

Martin, R. and Spence, J. (1988). Phototherapy: Psychic realism as a healing art? *Ten*, 8(30), 2–10.

Spence, J. (1986). *Putting Myself in the Picture: A political, personal and photographic autobiography*. London: Camden Press.

Weiser, J. (1999). *PhotoTherapy Techniques: Exploring the secrets of personal snapshots and family albums* (2nd edn; 1st edn 1993). Vancouver: PhotoTherapy Centre Press.

Weiser, J. (2001). PhotoTherapy techniques: Using clients' personal snapshots and family photos as counseling and therapy tools. *Afterimage: The Journal of Media Arts and Cultural Criticism*, 29(3), 10–15.

Weiser, J. (2002). PhotoTherapy techniques: Exploring the secrets of personal snapshots and family albums. *Child and Family*, Spring/Summer, 16–25.

Weiser, J. (2004). PhotoTherapy techniques in counseling and therapy: Using ordinary snapshots and photo-interactions to help clients heal their lives. *The Canadian Art Therapy Association Journal*, 17(2), 23–53.

Chapter 8

The self-portrait as self-therapy

Cristina Nuñez

Background: about being seen

I have been taking self-portraits for more than twenty years. At the beginning I did not realise I was doing self-therapy. I felt really good when I photographed myself, but I thought I was just being vain, or later, that it was part of my artistic project. Only in the last few years have I understood that this practice was an intuitive response to my childhood and teenage suffering.

I was born in 1962 in Figueres, Spain, the fifth of six sisters. During my first three years of life I was the centre of the family's attention and was thrilled by my sisters' and parents' loving gaze and cuddles. However, when my little sister was born, all the attention and caring shifted, naturally, to her and towards my older sister, who then suffered from rheumatism. I loved being photographed, but family snaps show my little sister getting in the way between the camera and me. Very soon I started to feel an invisible child, and probably this was the beginning of my low self-esteem.

In my teenage years these feelings of inadequacy generated huge rage. When my father left my mother, she fell into a deep depression. I was only twelve and began to feel even less *seen*. My sisters were beautiful, creative, famous and revolutionary, and I wanted to be like them; but I did not feel good enough. I remember very well thinking 'You'll see, I'll do something important too' – it was then that I started taking heroin.

I was an addict from the age of fifteen until the age of twenty. I have been a thief, a drug dealer and a prostitute in order to get money for heroin. On the one hand I wanted to attract my family's attention, on the other, to explore my limits and start a process of inner awareness. When I was nineteen and I hit rock bottom, my father asked my sister to tell me he did not want to *see* me anymore if I didn't quit. After a year and a half of rehab in France and Belgium I completely stopped using heroin, but back then I had not realised that it was precisely my dad's statement that had urged me to quit. I realised the truth of this sixteen years later when talking to my sister Isabel at my father's funeral.

I returned to Barcelona, resumed my studies and started psychotherapy. In those days I started acting, which satisfied my need to be *seen* as I loved being onstage. A short time later I met an Italian photographer, we fell in love and I moved to Milan. Seeing him work, I felt the camera could be used to understand myself better and so I turned the camera lens to myself and took my first self-portrait. It was 1988. Through self-portraiture I had found a way to re-create the loving gaze of my mother – and I was now able to be independent; to become adult.

In 1994, after a long series of self-portraits, Freudian psychoanalysis and group therapy, I started to photograph other people. I received the Marangoni Foundation Award with my project 'Body and Soul', a series of portraits, nudes and self-portraits that showed my aim to see others as I had seen myself. Now I know that those six years of self-portraits and therapy had allowed my 're-birth' into the world (the project can be seen at www.cristinanunez.com).

During my years of success as a photographer, I continued to take self-portraits, but in times of crisis I photographed myself more often. After my separation from my husband and my father's death, both of which happened during the autumn of 1998, I started a new period of introspection and self-search, for which the self-portrait became the daily instrument. Six years later, following a new crisis, the failure of my young photographers' agency, this helped me realise that I had intuitively discovered my own method. Moreover, a year of self-portraits allowed me to overcome the crisis, find a new love and a renewed passion for my work.

Building the method

My daughter Yassine is half Senegalese. One day, after I had taken a self-portrait with her and her sister Diana, Yassine said 'Mom, I want to take one on my own.' She was three at the time, and she had just come back from Senegal, where she had spent three months without me. I placed my Rolleiflex on the tripod, Yassine chose a leopard cushion – as if expressing her African roots – and she took her clothes off. I was amazed at the wonderful series she took that day. Her gaze was incredibly intense, full of willpower and pride. I understood that not being white like her sister and me, or black like her father and her African family, she needed to affirm her differences. Moreover, her decision to represent herself could have arisen from her need to feel that she was an individual, separate from her mother; something absolutely normal for kids of that age. The contrast between her brown skin and the dark blue wall seemed to express the great difference between Africa's warmth and Europe's coldness.

Yassine's self-portraits inspired me to study and to understand the dynamics of the self-portrait. Stefano Ferrari (2002: 79) in his *Lo Specchio dell'Io* quotes his theory on the 'third phase of the mirror':

> The child recognizes the image in the mirror as his own and identifies with it, he becomes that image. This identification of the child with the image in the mirror is a primary identification, and the matrix of every other subsequent identification.

Therefore, I thought that facing the camera and pressing the shutter can take us immediately to that first process of definition of the self, and in children this is even more intense in their being relatively new to the world.

Convinced that my method could be as useful for others as it had been for myself, I started to ask others to take self-portraits with my camera. At the same time, I built the method: a series of self-portrait exercises for individuals, couples and groups, based on my personal experience. The exercises were accompanied by a series of criteria for the perception and choice of the work to stimulate a dialogue with the images. In 2006 I used the method systematically to improve it, and now I teach self-portrait in therapeutic contexts, in companies, schools and prisons, and in individual counselling workshops in Italy, Finland, Spain and the USA.

Transforming pain into art

Self-portrait, with the method I propose, allows anybody to take an active part in the creative process and produce a work of art. I believe that difficult emotions are the raw material for art, and if we seek deep contact with them while taking self-portraits, this will stimulate the unconscious to 'speak' with the language of art. Standing alone in front of the camera is the easiest way to stimulate our deepest emotions and transform them into artworks. The work is produced in the moment and therefore the subject is least conscious of the act of taking the picture, because he is immersed in his interior.

A work of art, as I understand it, is an image that contains multiple meanings, often contrasting: it deals intimately with the human condition, it contains a rich diversity of stimuli to thought and feeling, and it possesses a special relationship with time, all within a harmonious configuration of aesthetic and formal elements.

Facing the camera lens can bring about an opportunity for a unique experience and a deep non-verbal dialogue. My human eye scrutinises the mechanical eye, gazing into the bottomless pit, in search of an image that captures my vision of myself, or one that shows the 'other' in me (see Photo 8.1). Shot after shot I live through all my different personas, looking for something that I still do not know about myself. I might judge myself, or control my behaviour so that the image will be more acceptable to others. Whatever I do, I always succeed: my sheer humanity will always be expressed in the picture.

Facing the void, experiencing the feeling of being lost, is a precious state. I might suffer, it might be painful, but precisely because of this, it will help activate the creative process later on. By touching the emptiness where I seem totally unable to create, I reset my 'guts', wipe them clean like a blank canvas. The secret is to look inside, suffer from it, face it and photograph it. It is a sort of meditation. Introspection is essential to find inspiration to fill my mind and heart once more with new ideas and projects.

The decision to represent oneself can provide what I call a 'state of grace': the feeling of centredness that happens in moments of creative work where the emotions are naturally retained because our creative self is in command. There is a positive and pro-active tension and an emotional detachment in which actions and thoughts are flowing freely. In *The Power of Now*, Eckhart Tolle (1999: 42) writes: 'All true artists . . . create from a place of no-mind, from inner stillness'; and 'a state of absolute presence in the Now . . . that intensely alive state that is free of time, free of problems, free of thinking, free of the burden of personality.' The self-portrait, by forcing us into the Now, can help us perceive and express our essential Being in a photograph.

Where does art come from?

Let's talk about 'guts'. . . . I imagine our guts to be the place where creativity comes from: meanders of intestines, warm fluids and microscopic life, an atmosphere similar to the primordial broth from which life originally sprang on Earth, as described in Hermann Hesse's poem *Narcissus and Goldmund* (2008), from where all earthly creatures as well as angels and demons originated, since the 'guts' are also the reproductive area for men and women, where children are conceived and are born. According to Kanō Jigorō (1922), the founder of Judo, the centre of our body, the *hara*, is the source of all vital energy. In the meanders of our guts we keep our most profound emotions

Photo 8.1
Self-portrait in Mauthausen (Nuñez, *Someone to Love*, 1995).

Photo 8.2
Blonde Cris (Nuñez, *Someone to Love*, 1998).

and memories, even those forgotten or dormant. Kristeva (1995: 204) redefines Plato's 'chora, a matrixlike space that is nourishing, unnameable, prior to One and to God, and thus defies metaphysics'.

As Noreen O'Connor (1991: 46) states:

> The notion of chora also helps us to consider the genesis of psychic pain, suffering, sadness. Kristeva specifies the chora as the place where the subject is both generated and negated, where the unity of the subject is fragmented by the changes and stases that produce him.

The self-portrait, as proposed with this method, can take us to our own chora; can stimulate a healthy 'movement' in our guts, which helps us liberate emotions or needs that need to be expressed cyclically during our lifetime.

Another metaphorical image I love to use is that of the 'cavern'. I imagine our identity as a huge cave. To enter it we must go down a narrow tunnel of cold earth. After several metres we get to a huge aperture, a dark cavern with many small caves, water dripping and forming little lakes, other tunnels. We cannot see the end of it: the more we explore it, the more we discover that it is enormous and complex. My metaphor corresponds to the fourth stage in Plato's (2010) myth, in which man detaches from 'reality' to perceive the idea of 'good', truth and intelligence.

I have seen the cavern 'appear' in many collaborative self-portraits. I remember a ten-year-old girl who took five pictures, all of them with her eyes closed, smiling and moving her hand forward as if feeling her way in the dark. In most of the collaborative self-portraits taken in my studio, pictures show the 'cavernous' expression, in which we often do not recognise ourselves because we seldom see ourselves when we are immerged in our inner life. A twelve-year-old girl recognised herself in a picture only after I suggested that she remember the moment just before falling asleep. Maybe then we recognise this expression, even if we have never seen it?

There is another element that influences the creative process, and, I would say, the therapeutic process: the studio and its creator and guardian. The artist is able to create the place in which he will immerse himself in his inner life with the right state of mind – the 'state of grace'. The art-therapist or the artist who, like me, becomes a facilitator for people's creativity, activates, as McNiff (2004: 30) states, 'the energy of the community, setting in motion a dynamic interplay among the people, the space, the images, and the spirits of expression. This creates the atmosphere of authenticity and healing only available in a safe and sacred space.'

As an 'activator' of the creative process, the self-portrait project can become a sort of 'mother project' – an artistic body of work that makes visible the raw material that will generate new projects or creative ideas. Every time our identity is challenged by great changes in life, we must return to our 'guts', to our 'cavern', to reactivate the dialogue with our thinking mind, to start the 'gut' movement to find new emotions and needs that must be expressed. During our work on the 'mother project', or after it is completed, new 'child' projects will emerge until the 'mother' will exhaust its fertility, that is, when our identity will be 'updated' after a new crisis or life change. Then we will have to return into introspection and find a new 'mother project'.

Portrait of our higher self

Anthony Bond (Bond and Woodall, 2005) states that, through his gaze, symbol of his creative power, the self-portraitist acquires a triple role: he is, at the same time, author, subject and spectator of himself. As I see it, each of the three roles makes a statement: the subject says 'Yes, I am – and I'm ok as I am'; the author says 'I am creating, I am the creator,' and the spectator says 'I am looking at myself, I can see myself.' All these statements imply acceptance to some degree. The dynamic of relationships and gazes between the three roles also establishes a dialogue with the viewer. This is what gives the self-portrait its communicative power: the author involves the viewer as if whispering in his ear 'Hey, this concerns you too!' He invites him to identify himself as the author, subject and spectator at the same time, and through this deep exchange, he ensures his own immortality for posterity.

I imagine the powerful dynamics of gazes between the three roles acquired in the self-portrait push the unconscious to speak, to communicate a multiple message so strongly that a work of art is created, almost unknowingly, and it is perfect: all of the elements in the image acquire significance, as if guided by a superior energy. But this can happen only when the subject abandons himself completely to the expression of his interiority. Tournier (1986) states that the self-portrait is the only possible image of the creator and his gaze, in the very moment of the creation of the image. Bond (Bond and Woodall, 2005: 12) says the self-portrait is a sort of 'alter ego of the creative subject'. Gell (1988: 45) writes that the self-portrait 'acts like a person, a surrogate of the artist'. It means 'this is me, the creator of this image', and therefore it allows our affirmation as artists, as creators.

According to Woodall (Bond and Woodall, 2005), the self-portraitist possesses an intrinsic power and freedom of action that is akin to that of the gods. Many artists have represented themselves as Christ or other divine figures. In his *Specchio dell'Io* mentioned above, Ferrari (2002: 11) talks about Albrecht Dürer's 1500 self-portrait and quotes Lotman's (1988) statement: 'Christ's face is placed exactly in front of the spectator's face, so that their eyes are on the same axis: Christ's face represents the viewer's mirror reflection.' Therefore, far from a blasphemous narcissism, the artist's message could possibly be, 'The Christ in you, in all of you'.

These concepts support my idea that the self-portrait, with the method I propose, is the portrait of our creative self, that is, our 'higher self': a sort of divine self, able to create, present in every human being. Spanish poet Jiménez conveys this concept in his poem *I am not I* (2005).

The Chinese oracle *I-Ching* (*The Complete I-Ching*, 2004) often mentions our 'inner wise man' as that part of us who can guide us because he is in contact with the cosmos. Spinoza (2001) felt that God is the deterministic system in every living creature, plant or stone, and that everything done by humans and other animals is excellent and divine. Feuerbach (2008: 48) claimed that God is the outward projection of man's inward nature: 'If man is to find contentment in God, he is to find himself in God.' For Nietzsche (2006) God is dead, and the *Übermenschen* possess godlike qualities. Theosophist H.P. Blavatsky (2000) talked about the 'higher self' as the immortal human soul, what reincarnates from life to life and accumulates the experience, the lessons, the virtues. Freud's (2001) 'super-ego' is a similar concept: a father figure who takes care of our more childish selves, but Freud does not consider any spiritual dimension. Steiner (2009: 176) does not use the words 'higher self', but talks about the 'ego' as the spiritual body of the human being (other bodies are 'ethereal', 'astral', 'physical'), which reincarnates in different bodies or lives on earth to complete its spiritual evolution. Steiner's vision found inspiration in the Indian Veda's concept of *atma* (soul). In *Antropologia Scientifico-Spirituale Vol. I* he explains his interpretation of the first commandment: 'I am the eternal Divine you feel in you.'

Tolle (1999: 3) narrates his own story:

> This false suffering self immediately collapsed, just as if a plug had been pulled out of an inflatable toy. What was left was my true nature as the ever present I AM: consciousness in its pure state, prior to identification with form.

In many self-portraits people have taken in my studio, I have seen images that seem to express this concept: while engaged in the expression of extreme emotions, another 'being' seems to appear, different from the subject, making solemn statements that, as I see it, very often relate not only to the subject but also to the community at large.

The epic of suffering

The objectification of the 'higher self' in the self-portrait through the expression of difficult emotions immediately makes the author–subject–spectator a 'speaker' for the community. We are all speakers of something, we express what others do not, so that they can learn more about the human being's multiplicity and potential. Our actions have an effect on others and the community, and can mirror something in our actions. The self-portrait work of art certainly strengthens and makes visible this important social role.

In these times of privacy obsession and image-usage hysteria, making your life public with an autobiographical self-portrait project is a heroic action, both extremely liberating and empowering. On the one hand, you become a speaker for many: you have a mission in life! On the other hand, converting your own suffering, your difficult past into a useful and communicative object stimulates your inner life: you can detach from it and pass on to something else, letting life flow and transform like a mountain river, while at the same time influencing others. Moreover, the feedback and critique you get from people makes your action powerful and significant. You become a hero.

'Epic' is defined in the *Concise Oxford Dictionary* (1982: 324) as 'a story narrating the achievements of one or more heroes, ordinarily concerning a serious subject, significant to a culture or nation'; and in *Wikipedia* (entry for 'epic poetry': http://en. wikipedia.org/wiki/Epic_poetry) as 'majestic depictions that capture impressive struggles, such as stories of war, adventures, and other efforts of great scope and size over long periods of time'. If we manage to understand that these epic stories are, to a great extent, symbols of our own inner life, since they help us perceive the greatness of the human being – even in extreme circumstances, and that, for example, the inner conflict of a husband forgiving his adulterer wife is an 'impressive struggle and requires an effort of great scope and size, (often) over a long period of time' (Wikipedia entry for 'epic poetry': http://en.wikipedia.org/wiki/Epic_poetry), then we can start perceiving ourselves as heroes.

We all need the 'epic', especially adolescents. Drugs are epic; I recently realised that heroin, the drug I took in my teenage years, has a very epic name. Music, pop stars and movies convey a lot of the modern epic to young people, but when the concert or movie is over, the epicness is gone and we are thrust back into our grey normality. This is because we are convinced that either we cannot be heroes unless we take what we consider to be heroic actions, or that our society does not allow us to be so.

Now, more than ever, after almost a hundred years of psychoanalysis, we need to feel our greatness. We Western men and women – although it is extending to the entire planet – are, like the hero, lonelier than ever, because the protective community is an endangered species, and each individual is fully responsible for what they will do with their lives. Therefore, we cannot delegate the part of the hero to anybody else than ourselves.

In Spain, the bullfight *toros* live for five years in uncontaminated pastures, surrounded by several cows and seldom seeing a human being; until they arrive in the arena, where they will face the human torero, fight, and probably die in a very solemn, epic way. But the corrida, which should not be considered a show, is obsolete: not so much because of the openly visible violence (keep in mind the 'un-epic' and horrible life and death of the millions of animals we eat, which seldom see a green pasture or a blue sky, is unanimously accepted, but not acknowledged and remains unseen), but because we must go through the same process inwardly, not symbolically, but in our own reality. Being heroic today is confronting our own inner beast, through pain and suffering.

The method I propose is like a modern corrida. Some 'violence' is still there, but it is interior and self-inflicted: we do what we are able to deal with so it's safe. We grab the inner bull by its horns, since we go directly to where the problem is, without distraction, deep into the very bottom (as much as we can in that moment) and we convert it into art. Just like the corrida, as Hemingway (2005) saw it.

Then, by looking at the artwork we have produced, we discover the competency of the beast and the suffering and find the beauty: our greatness. By converting the pain into art we enter into a process of deep knowledge, not only regarding ourselves, but the whole of humanity. This is heroic in itself, since we are confronting our inner beast through pain and suffering, but it becomes an epic story when we communicate and share with others our heroic action.

Performance and catharsis

The expression of difficult emotions in the self-portrait is particularly therapeutic. Rage and despair often cannot be externalised, so we become accustomed to repressing them. But if we concentrate hard enough, tune in to listen and try to push them out, these extreme emotions can help us move our 'guts' and express ourselves fully. By objectifying our 'dark side' in a photograph, we separate ourselves from what is painful and open ourselves up for catharsis or renewal. The barriers to our essential Being fall away (see Photo 8.2). Sometimes, before an important meeting or job, I take enraged or desperate self-portraits to release the tension and I come out calm and satisfied, ready for any challenge ... It is similar to a punching bag, but the picture itself gives me back an image I can see and introject again to accept myself fully.

As Weiser (1999: 130) asserts in her *Photo-Therapy Techniques: Exploring the secrets of personal snapshots and family albums*: 'Self-Portrait Photo-Therapy work can help clients clarify their self-images and raise their self-esteem and self-confidence through making, viewing, and accepting images of themselves and owning their positive perceptions.'

Besides looking inside, every self-portrait is always a sort of performance. What we do in front of the camera is certainly mediated by what we want others to see of us. Performance in art is based on the concept of the relationship between the artist's mind and body, with the collaboration of the spectator. The artist performs to communicate, to share his/her message with the public and involve them in a universal issue. Nevertheless, there is a space, a relationship between me and my self which is, I believe, independent from the other's gaze, and which implies an intense inner dialogue of judgement, perception, thought and acceptance. A wonderful process that needs no words, because the work of art contains everything and does not need to be translated to hit the target.

The work of art, or the sequence of two or more images, can bring interesting inner activity to light: natural self-healing processes that every human being is capable of undertaking, often unconsciously, even though this might not be visible to others. In a sequence of self-portraits, there is often a great difference between the first and the last in terms of the subject's well-being and awareness. McNiff (2004: 114) also describes these processes: 'I also observed, in my studios, that someone who is suffering might begin by expressing the hurt in a picture, but then in subsequent pictures treat and transform the condition.' According to McNiff (2004: 115), 'The pictures themselves could function as angels who minister to the wound.' I believe that man certainly possesses the capacity to heal himself, even if it is not visible to others, but the production of art of any kind can activate, accelerate and bring these processes to light. Performance also means stepping outside of oneself, imagining oneself as someone else. I once asked a young Swedish drug addict to take a collaborative self-portrait representing a character he liked. He chose Aragorn, from Tolkien's *Lord of the Rings*, who felt inadequate in his role at the beginning, but became the King of Gondor in the end. In his self-portrait my Swedish friend transformed himself completely and expressed a huge charisma, a *super partes* quality and love for 'his people'. This beautiful picture proved that he actually possessed these qualities. He hung the picture on his bedroom wall, and one year later he quit taking drugs.

Art critic and curator Daniele de Luigi (2009) states about these collaborative self-portraits:

> The extraordinary fact is that these iconographies are not created in an intentional artistic and intellectual action which voluntarily refers to codified formulas, but they spring from a creative process in which, in the precise moment of creation of the image, there is no control on its shape or composition.

The iconic image – the subject's 'higher self' – seems to make solemn statements that very often relate not only to the subject but also to the community at large. A very powerful example of this is C.R.'s collaborative self-portrait – taken under my guidance – in Milan's prison San Vittore (www.self-portrait.eu).

At first sight, these images are often disturbing for the author, who does not recognise himself. Sometimes the eyes are half-closed because of the flashlights. That is the moment of least control, of profound abandonment into one's 'cavern'. The strange gaze suggests complete attention towards one's own inner life. That expression, which I recognise immediately and which moves me very deeply is the face of he who is in deep contact with himself.

Inner image, outer image

In the self-portrait, the body of the artist can convey the pure expression of human needs and thereby serve the community. Calle (2002) puts her own life into an artistic performance by anonymously asking a detective to follow her or working as a cleaning woman in a Venetian hotel. Spence (1986) turned her calvary with breast cancer into a work of art with a social and political intent, publishing a manifesto about the freedom of showing one's own ugly body in a work of art. Jenny Saville (Schama, 2005) transforms herself into a grotesque and monstrous being as a political statement against the idealisation of the perfect body by the media. Korean artist Kimsooja (2004) films herself as a panhandler in the middle of the street in her photo and video work *The Needle Woman*.

Many of us fear the camera lens. In most cases I believe this stems from the gap between how we see ourselves (which remains more or less unchanged from adolescence or infancy) and the image that we see in the mirror. For Barthes (1993), photography neither represents nor reflects reality, rather it gives it meaning. We are not our self-portrait, we are much more: the self-portrait does not define us, it is simply what needs to come to light; it is the voice of our unconscious that tells us what we need to know today.

Since its invention, photography has changed completely. In those days, to have your picture taken was for most people a rare event: it meant being immortalised, so pretending to appear at one's best, according to the period's style and values, was understandable. Today, digital technology allows us to record our lives continuously. Therefore, I ask myself, does it make sense to show ourselves always at our best? Why are we still afraid of being photographed in difficult moments? Why do we always want to communicate happiness, harmony, well-being? Can we still imagine ourselves in life's album as always impeccable and smiling? Photography has become an indispensable instrument to express *all* of our emotions, even, and especially, the most difficult ones, to let them out and fully accept them. This requires using photographs creatively, regardless of whether we intend to communicate our emotional photo-diary to the world.

Disturbing images often carry important messages. According to McNiff (2004: 97), 'If an image . . . agitates the person who generated it, it is likely conveying a message that needs attention.' If the self-portrait contributes to creating a correspondence between our inner and outer images, if it is a journey into our unconscious, the work of art can be surprising or scary but need not be dangerous or harmful, because the acceptance it carries will bring out an essentially positive outcome. Working on the perception and choice of the self-portrait works according to precise artistic criteria, and creative storytelling from the chosen image helps participants detach from their usual self-image and acquire an imaginative vision. This vision often triggers new discoveries regarding one's own identity and its unknown potential, which result in the subject's immediate empowerment. The whole process is often cathartic and continues to resonate in time: participants will keep on seeing different issues and statements in the photographs throughout their lives, depending on the moment they are living.

This is the era of the self-portrait

Like Rembrandt and Van Gogh, there are millions of people today who experience a compulsion towards self-representation. As Stefano Ferrari suggests, it might respond to a need in certain moments of crisis, when our ego is being questioned, or to our contemporary identity, always in a state of becoming. Ferrari also affirms that the desire to represent oneself surely springs from a deep need to leave an image of ourselves, of our body, but above all, of our face. Flickr, YouTube, MySpace and Facebook are full of self-portraits and are a sort of collective self-portrait themselves, especially for teenagers and young people.

An example of this is Matthias Preti (Nuñez, 2010: 113) who started taking self-portraits with his mobile phone at fourteen, when his parents divorced and his father moved to China. He and his mother were living in a friend's house and he wasn't doing well at school. His self-portraits always show the rap gesture 'respect' – an open hand with two fingers together, surely meaning 'respect for myself'. During the workshop he managed to express his deepest emotions and explore his relationships with his family and friends. He produced a powerful series of images, including urban landscape, calling his project 'Metropolitan Rap'. He later improved his performance at school, and his passion for photography is becoming a profession. He has grown into a very smart and emotionally stable young man.

Art and therapy, two sides of the same coin

Art and therapy are intimately connected. Most artists need to produce a work of art in order to feel better – writers are a good example of this: Tennessee Williams (Rader, 1985) once said, 'You have no refuge but writing.' Emotions are their raw material: ideas spring from emotions or needs, or even from inner pain. The decision to create art might come from the need to express emotions, to define identity or to fulfil a sort of social mission (we have something to say to the world, and this must be said). Troubles and inner pain can increase the need to create and communicate not only in artists, but in all human beings. McNiff (2004: 47) points out 'how emotional states profoundly influence expression, how art may be an expressive lifeline in periods of crisis, and how difficult times and emotional upheaval offer a gate of access to the archetypal flow of artistic expression and its medicines'. When producing art, besides channelling and transforming pain and thereby raising their self-esteem, mentally disturbed patients, prisoners, drug addicts, extremely poor people and other outcasts can perform a valuable social role: by expressing essential human needs, they inspire us to remain connected to our inner selves, in a society largely and unhappily focused on materialism and economic growth.

In 'the self-portrait experience' we are the subject of our art: we are in front of the camera, at our most vulnerable, and the inner dialogue that occurs is similar to the inner process of therapy at length: self-perception, self-questioning, judgement, thought and acceptance. The multiple meanings of the self-portrait work contribute to the union of the different aspects of the self. In the method's first and most important exercise, the attempt to express extreme emotions requires full attention on our interiority, and full attention when looking at ourselves in the photographs! And, according to Eckhart Tolle (1999: 99), 'Attention is the key to transformation – and full attention implies acceptance.'

To complete the process, however, it is necessary to communicate the discovery of the self to others. By his constant introspection, the artist – like many people today – separates himself from the outside world. This is often the root of his existential suffering. Tolle (1999: 150) states:

> The ego perceives itself as a separate fragment in a hostile universe, with no real inner connection to any other being, surrounded by other egos which it either sees as a potential threat or which it will attempt to use for its own ends.

By intimately sharing our work with the public we have the opportunity to free ourselves from the confines of the ego and, as in Zen, become one with the cosmos.

Acknowledgement

This is an extended and modified version of a paper published by the *European Journal of Psychotherapy and Counselling*, Routledge, London (March 2009), of another article, published in the book *Autofocus* by Prof. Stefano Ferrari of the University of Bologna and of a chapter of my book *Someone to Love* (2010), Private Space Books, Barcelona.

References

Barthes, R. (1993). *Camera Lucida: Reflections on photography*. London: Vintage Classics.
Blavatsky, H.P. (2000). *The Key to Theosophy*. Boston, MA: Adamant Media Corporation. Available from: http://en.wikipedia.org/wiki/Higher_self – cite_ref-0.
Bond, A. and Woodall, J. (2005). *Self Portrait: Renaissance to contemporary*. London: National Portrait Gallery Publications.
Calle, S. (2002). *Double Jeux*. Arles: Actes Sud.

Concise Oxford Dictionary: 11th edition revised (2008). Oxford.

De Luigi, D. (2009). Higher self: A journey towards the origin of emotions and of images. Available from: www.self-portrait.eu.

Ferrari, S. (2002). *Lo Specchio dell'Io, autoritratto e psicologia*. Bari-Roma: Laterza.

Feuerbach, L. (2008). *The Essence of Christianity*. New York: Dover Publications.

Freud, S. (2001). *Complete Psychological Works of Sigmund Freud*. London: Vintage Classics.

Gell, A. (1988). *Art and Agency: An anthropological theory*. Oxford: Clarendon Press.

Hemingway, E. (2005). *Fiesta: The sun also rises*. London: Vintage Classics.

Hesse, H. (2008). *Narcissus and Goldmund*. London: Peter Owen Modern Classics.

Kanō, Jigorō. (1922). Jiudo: The Japanese art of self defence. *Living Age*, 314, 724–731.

Kimsooja. (2004). *Conditions of Humanity*. Milan: 5 Continents Editions, PAC.

Kristeva, J. (1995). *New Maladies of the Soul*. New York: Columbia University Press.

Lacan, J. (2007). *Ecrits: The First Complete Edition in English*. London: W.W. Norton.

Lotman, J.M. (1998). Il ritratto. In: *Il Girotondo delle muse. Saggi di semiotica delle arti e della rappresentazione*. Bergamo: Moretti & Vitali.

McNiff, S. (2004). *Art Heals: How creativity heals the soul*. Boston, MA: Shambhala.

Nietzsche, F. (2006). *We Philologists: Complete works of Friedrich Nietzsche*, Vol. 8. New York: Public Domain Books.

Nuñez, C. (2010). *Someone to Love*. Barcelona: Private Space Books.

O'Connor, N. (1991). The an-arche of psychotherapy. In: Fletcher, J. and Benjamin, A. (eds), *Abjection, Melancholia and Love: The work of Julia Kristeva* (pp. 42–51). London: Routledge.

Plato (2010). *The Allegory of the Cave*. London: Createspace.

Rader, D. (1985). *Tennessee, Cry of the Heart: An intimate memoir of Tennessee Williams*. New York: New American Library.

Schama, S. (2005). *Jenny Saville*. Milan: Rizzoli International Publications.

Spence, J. (1986). *Putting Myself in the Picture: A political, personal and photographic autobiography*. London: Camden Press.

Spinoza, B. (2001). *Ethics*. London: Wordsworth Editions.

Steiner, R. (2009). *Antropologia Scientifico-Spirituale, Vol. I*. Milano: Editrice Antroposofica.

The Complete I-Ching: The definitive translation by the Taoist master Alfred Huang (2004). New York: Inner Traditions Bear & Company.

Tolle, E. (1999). *The Power of Now*. London: Hodder & Stoughton.

Tournier, M. (1986). *Petites Proses*. Paris: Gallimard.

Weiser, J. (1999). *Photo-Therapy Techniques: Exploring the secrets of personal snapshots and family albums*. Vancouver: Photo-Therapy Centre.

Chapter 9

Community phototherapy

Carmine Parrella and Del Loewenthal

Introduction

'Hello Del, I am going to die, and I am scared.' This was said to me by Roberto from a hospital bed in Lucca, Italy, looking at me with eyes sometimes rolling and at other times as if pleading with me to say that it was not true as his teeth chattered with anxiety.

I had met Roberto one year earlier (pictured in Photo 9.1), before he had liver failure, when visiting the community phototherapy programme run by the psychologist Carmine Parrella at the Mental Health Centre in Lucca. This was when Roberto was a mental health patient and a particularly keen and able photographer. During that year he had come to my house in Brighton, where he met his cousin, to see the photographs my son had put up for him as part of our PHOTOTHERAPYEUROPE exhibition (see Photo 9.2).

Going to see Roberto dying in hospital was difficult – in facing his death (and through this, my death). However, he had visitors, many the result of friendships built through our phototherapy community. What was too difficult, was that I could not, and I don't think any of the other visitors could, face the old man in the next bed, dying alone.

This chapter describes community phototherapy as practised by Carmine Parrella at the Mental Health Centre in Lucca, Italy. The chapter arises from Del Loewenthal interviewing Carmine, mainly in Lucca, particularly when on his visits to learn about Community Phototherapy as part of the EU funded Leonardo Project, PHOTO-THERAPYEUROPE.

This chapter has started by describing the last occasion Del went to Lucca, when Carmine and Del visited Roberto who was dying in hospital and to whom this book is dedicated. The chapter ends with the transcript material from the photo diary that Del made on community phototherapy with Carmine's help. However, the central part of this chapter is Carmine describing to Del his work developing Community Phototherapy. (Del's questions have been omitted so as not to break the continuity.)

There is a certain integrated chaos in Carmine's work and sometimes this interweaving makes it difficult to describe. However, among the themes considered here are: what Carmine understands by community phototherapy; the influences that have led to his approach; his use of still photography, video and digital storytelling in a community context; and his development of various therapeutic groups. At the time of visiting, these therapeutic groups were as follows: a large multi-family social group (Monday evening), the group of the multi-media journal (Monday morning and Wednesday

Photo 9.1 Roberto Brunini (Loewenthal).

Photo 9.2 Roberto's wall (Loewenthal).

lunchtime), the Photo biographic group (alternate Mondays), the After Effects group for learning about advanced digital techniques in editing video (Thursday evenings), the Clubbing group for evening and weekend activities (twice a week), the Play Back Theatre group and the Zephiro group, which is a company that employs patients, trained as photographers, to work particularly in schools.

Why community phototherapy – engineering the social boundary

For Carmine, photography has to do with communication and narrative. He considers this is the way the world functions and is increasingly based on visual communication. Photography can be a powerful key to represent the world, to tell a story to the world (digital illiteracy is now a form of exclusion).

There are levels: individual (looking through the camera plus mirror); social/small group (what we do together with our cameras); larger levels such as schools in Lucca (what we can do with our cameras), City of Lucca (for our communities), Italy (how we can communicate with other communities fighting on the same issue); and international (how we can join others doing the same thing internationally) – 'the client, their families, my daughter and you from London can be part of this'.

Carmine considers that phototherapy is a medium to activate the healing process. The psychological sense of community – this is the theory of McMillan and Chavis (1986) – is that if it works at a social level it will bring about a change at the individual object level. Community phototherapy is part of a wider therapeutic process. Social therapy (Kreeger, 1975) is the engineering of the social boundary. As a consequence, Carmine works to modify, not the people, but the way people meet and connect. Carmine says he is interested in the way that these connections affect the minds of people. However, he doesn't attempt to go through the minds of people, but through their basic need to be part of the community. For Carmine it is of prior importance for we all need to be part of something to exist.

Carmine is also influenced by Mark Spivak (1974; 1987) and his multi-contextual model (1992). 'This is to base the programme on what they have, not what they do not have. The mental health organizations have to adapt to the person, not the other way around. The community can do this, not the institution.'

One of Carmine's strategies, after a few minutes, is to offer people the option of being part of something and at a level that can be acceptable and sustainable, but open to possibilities of development. What is new in this programme is that people can modify the setting. Carmine starts with a project with rules, but he does not know after six months how the therapeutic process will change all these rules. So he thinks he knows where he starts, but he does not know where he will end. It is as if this creates a massive, useful, therapeutic tension while recognising that it can be a strong boomerang if it is not managed properly: 'If you do not manage a team properly, they turn into a nightmare and you are in a mess if they feel manipulated.'

> Phototherapy, the medium I use to activate the photo, could be gardening, sport, theatre, fashion – but I decided to use video. So why such photography? What is specific about photos? First, photos are an act of seeing – this is very important for psychiatric patients because they are seen by others in the community as dirty and

dangerous. We can change the direction of the sight so the patient has the right to see the other and objectify the other, whereas usually, they are on the receiving end of being objectified. We give them back the power to see the other. The camera gives the same world as being on a bus – you can see the world but the world cannot see you. So the patient feels protected by the camera – the camera is like a mobile shield but lets these people be touched by reality, with sunglasses that protect them. At the same time, photography is a creative act and there is something about this, and their relations. Photography can happen just through a relational process. Phototherapy is the intentional use of the therapeutic potential of photography. I choose photography as it is a cultural object and can be used after the shooting session. So, I have a cultural object, for example, a school's yearbook which enables to be activated, or revitalised, in the new situation what was active in the previous situation. So, photography can help create a connection between what is here and now, with what was there and then. This can be educational or therapeutic. Educational is when I want to improve certain skills to reach a competence or expertise for social roles. Whatever helps me be part of the community – for example, doctor, journalist, father – this role must be internalised for the society we want.

I speak of therapy when the sense of the personal entireness is broken. When the identity is broken, then from this process starts the psychopathology. Something is happening to me which is not me, but which affects me. So there is a gap between what I am and how I am feeling and how I would like to be. So the therapeutic process is in the middle of deep, personal, family, social and cultural processes, because I can find photographs in every field, for example, everyone has an identity card which you always keep with you.

The early work in schools

Before coming to Lucca in 1992, Carmine had worked for several years as a psychologist in a substance misuse unit where over time it became clearer to him that the people treated had had no one with them in the critical moments of their lives as adolescents and, while a lot of effort was put into the substance misuse unit, there appeared relatively few results. So in 1995, he began work with a school in Lucca and attempted to create a system that could include everybody in a 'community growing process'. He states:

> Here, I could work with those with serious problems as part of a community rather than them being seen as the black sheep of the school. The schools were also interested in prevention: I said you don't need psychologists, but you need psychology. You need to be competent in psychology – if everybody works together you will not need to see, individually, psychologists.

Carmine described how he attempted to develop 'active listening' for everybody; for example, during seven years in one school, he was only called once by a teacher to an individual situation.

> The community managed situations of emotional crises on their own, with supervision. This was through the belief in the potential of the therapeutic community. Here, a target is declared in the community and then everyone agrees to be committed to that target, no matter who they are.

Carmine suggests that it is easier to start with the school and then take this outside. The students can use the school for the community, as is now happening with the Centre for Mental Health where people who previously have had nothing to do with mental health can come in the evening and learn, for example, how to use the Special Effects programme when making videos. Within the school, Carmine saw his role as promoting a process of participatory democracy (particularly influenced from South America). Here, for example, he trained teachers to use focus groups of students to devise the agendas and targets for assembly meetings. At the time the Italian government had a law for student participation and such community approaches helped achieve this. In 2002, Carmine started to put this community approach into the Mental Health Centre. Also in that year he volunteered to take part in a programme putting psychiatric patients back into the community in Romania and used video as part of the therapeutic approach in combination with the drama therapy approach of Sue Jennings (Jennings *et al.*, 1993) who was leading the project.

For Carmine, the video tool has to be for the community, otherwise he is concerned that psychotherapy creates exclusion for those who cannot afford it. The rehabilitation programme in Lucca has the same goal as individual psychotherapy, but on a community basis.

The camera as a mirror

For Carmine, the use of photography is to provide a mirror. In the process of mirroring, something happens of importance for a person as the image enters into resonance.

> We try and expose clients to emotional similarities but we have to deal with their defences. The photo easily goes round the defences, so if there is a person who is scared of the world and it is difficult for them to manage their relationship, they put a distance between themselves and the world. The camera generates a positive attitude to the world. I am seeing the world, rather than the world is seeing me. I am no longer passive as the camera gives me power. So having a camera is something about having the power to represent the other. And the other is now scared as their image can be manipulated.
>
> There is something in your life that is important. The question is how does one focus on it? As with psychoanalysis, one speaks of what comes to mind. The camera breaks the psychological process so that everything is confused or something is so important it destroys all other things.

Carmine had a patient who, in three sessions, made a photo diary of his dream to have a dog that could find truffles, whereas previously no one could find out how to motivate this patient.

> The focus can be emotional or aesthetic. Visual diaries speak to the person making them. In family therapy it is said that 'I understand what I said when I see the effect that it has on the listener'. In individual therapy, the person talks to the therapist and the therapist acts as the mirror – whereas here, the photo diary acts as the mirror and the person making it is affected by this. Most of the work is to

help the other make a dialogue with their deep self. We search in the world for images of ourselves that are abandoned and forgotten.

Carmine considers that day after day he tries to reveal patients' capacities to see and feel. For him, this is the core: so the patients can feel again the personal vision of themselves and their lives through seeing and feeling.

> The skills are present in the community so the community can cope with their own problems. This is the concept of social capital – the community processes the self-activated resources. The setting can be changed by the group and the culture. When a client says 'I have nothing to do all day long,' I ask, 'Do you have a lot of time? This capital – it's like having money.' The question is how to use the capital and how, through phototherapy, I can change this capital into social capital. The mirror is more the photo and you discover something about yourself as in phototherapy. The mirror here instead is the social dynamic that is activated from making a photo project.

The key experience in sharing

Carmine, influenced by Jung (1995), remarks:

> I am trying to distinguish the image my mind makes under my own wishes from my own destiny. You can have images but these can be of one's ego, not of one's destiny. The key is experience and sharing, so I take the responsibility to read the signals that appear on my path when, for example, I pay attention to what I have dreamed regarding the representation of a message that I will try to understand. Photodiaries, as digital memories, can take many forms.
>
> In Romania there was a psychiatric patient spending a lot of time lost in HIS portrait photograph, and then I realised that the photograph was the only thing that told him he was alive. He, as with all the psychiatric patients, could only go outside the hospital in pyjamas, so that they could be easily recognised. But only a few had family who could afford to visit. They were forgotten. The nurses were few and only provided for basic needs. Two questions arise: the first is, what gives this man the proof and sense that he is existing? The second question is, what gives this man the feeling that he does not just exist to suffer? Some psychotic patients feel they are immersed in suffering and think this is their life. Basaglia (1997) writes of a patient's asking whether we are mad because we are suffering so much, or are we suffering so much because we are mad?
>
> We are trying with phototherapy to give to the person a tool to experiment with the feeling of existing. Sometimes the people who are mental health patients don't think they exist and can't have the luxury of seeing if psychotherapy helps their experience of existing. For too long, nothing happens. Also, even when occasionally there are resources, in psychotherapy, being in front of another person is too much for them. Today I told a client whom I had not met previously, 'you know you have beautiful eyes – like those of Gregory Peck. And I would like to take a movie of you in a way that Fellini would.' I was not trying to seduce him. I know nothing about him and his psychiatric illness. Just that he has beautiful eyes.

Our entireness

Again, for Carmine, the website that comes from the Mental Health Centre at Lucca has the same function as the photograph in the Romanian hospital. A place must be created where the person can put some part of themselves that they cannot keep inside them by themselves. So everyone is encouraged to put in this space an object that represents part of themselves, that cannot live inside them. The client can then go every day or every week to where they have projected something of themselves and can feed from this with the help of others. This is common to all art therapies but, through photographic digital media, whatever the client produces becomes a cultural object and has a cultural effect. There is a story that if someone broke a window that is not repaired then in a short time, all the windows will be broken. If you want people not to destroy the windows, then you have to transform the windows into something the community can identify with and they are then not aggressive towards them. This is not just aesthetic beauty, but relationships as art. So through the attempt to create a good object in an artistic way, a new model of relations between people is created – the group.

The attempt to create the object gives the relation between people a new chance. So the idea is that, through the wish to build this good object, an impetus is given to the individual and the group. It is necessary to build an ideal that is possible. For clients to attempt to build between what they think they are and their ideal is too big. So the ideal of the self disappears. At the other extreme, they have to maintain an ideal of themselves as low as possible – anything else is usually too much, from within themselves or within their environment.

> We have to help people to relate to their thoughts. This is our job as psychologists. If you are in a wheelchair and your spine is broken, I have to work with your feelings about your legs. I have to help people with their internal situation, whatever that is – for example, schizophrenia. If you want to meet yourself and your spine is broken, you have to meet your entireness. This is a project that is common to all human beings, whether clients of the mental health service or not. Both you and I are the same – what keeps one entire in one person's life can be different in another. The volunteers in the Mental Health Centre are here for their own entireness. Community phototherapy has to find a process that is able to work contemporaneously on two levels, because they are two sides of the same coin. One is the therapeutic side and the other is the evolution of the human being. The more one focuses on the therapeutic and the more one focuses on the technique, the more one loses connection with the environment and the community resources. There is a volunteer who was a firefighter, who has a critically ill brother. This might be seen in terms of there being a force in the community that is guilty – he loves his sick brother, but cannot do anything for him. Maybe he can return, in time, to volunteering, to helping with photography and video for our Lucca Mental Health Service. Without this opportunity, there just remains a pain for him – yet this can be transformed into a resource for the community. One becomes like a gardener who doesn't know what seeds will appear. Nobody is refused, even if they may be seen to create problems.

Technology and participatory democracy

Carmine considers that their website and journal are transitional objects between the individual and the community.

> So it is not so important how many people click onto the website for the clients are able to click onto this and for them it is proof enough that they exist.

There is the evolution of technology. In every field we have different kinds of techniques. A large collectivity is able to use all the resources, including technology to valorise their own human potential (Levy, 1999). For Demetrio (1996), the book is as a self-object. This is a place where therapy, education and culture can meet with the narrative of self. Therapies without hope create chronic patients (Spivak, 1992). Paulo Freire (1993) writes of the pedagogy of the oppressed. This is at a time of the same cultural wave of Basaglia (1987) and also, from Brazil, the idea of participatory democracy. There is also the human being as a social performer. Performative photography would be a kind of photography that helps people perform. This is similar to what Basaglia has written about with the difference that we are now facing and working with new forms of repression/stigma and aggressivity, which in the past were dealt with in psychiatric hospitals.

> We must focus on the psychological aspects of this – the way the people organize their relationships: the mind of the person. If I am a psychologist, I have to study forms of marginalization – which stops and destroys human potential. The thinking is of the group. A collective approach means you have to lose your power.

This is from Mariano Loiacono, director of the Centre for Social Medicine for Alcohol and Drug Addiction and *disagio diffuso*, who Carmine finds a most important influence (Loiacono, 2000).

> Healing has to be made with everybody in terms of what needs they really have. When I think of phototherapy, I do not think just of techniques. But this can be strange for a therapist – it always needs to be community based and it cannot be institutional – it's like a flower that comes out and is destroyed continually.

Case studies

Case study 1: Digital storytelling and the effect of mirroring

Carmine initially used photography in psychotherapy in digital storytelling, where one creates a story with sounds, music, voice and text. Here the images are chosen by the client from magazines, then scanned and the client speaks of her associated feelings, adding text and music. The potential richness of this approach might be seen from the following fragment. The client chooses a photograph of a child sleeping:

> This is me as a child and the cover has been put on me by somebody to protect me from what others are saying, and this is a photo of me as an old man. I would have liked if my grandfather had put the cover on me (but he didn't). When I was a child I needed to be caressed.

Carmine: 'What do you need now?' Client: 'Still to be caressed.' For Carmine, these photographs are like symbols in a dream, only the storyteller has the key. The aim of the storytelling is to let the symbols dialogue between each other, as in the young child and the old man. And then, between the symbols and what they mean for the storyteller.

> In this case the object is not on photographic paper, but multimedia which can also be projected onto a screen. The object is what continues the symbol for the client. What does it mean for the client to have the object? It is a space where at least something is clarified, where something can be symbolised. It is like a transitional object – like for a child, if I have the teddy bear, which is like the safety of the mother. It can, for example, contain the destructive part of me, or activate the part of me that can protect it. It can help where people cannot. These clients are so depressed and this digital storytelling is a way we can dream together.

Case study 2: Community phototherapy

One practice here is to give a camera to each client and they take photos during the week and then make photodigital stories. Carmine recounts how in the first group everyone took photographs – first in the corridors and then outside. When they saw the photos, there was great satisfaction. Later, they moved into the town. Compliance became high and more people arrived and kept asking, 'When are we going?' One of the clients was a shepherd when he was young, who experienced lot of violence from his family and he developed obesity, so eventually he could not walk or go to the bathroom. He joined the group and though he could barely walk, with the stimulus of making photographs, he came to photograph the town, despite his difficulties. He did this for two years but the problem was then he went back home and the family did not want to let him go because of the money they received. But eventually he was able to live in a community apartment and he was able to walk and have self-esteem. Before, he was illiterate and had hardly been to school. At the end, there was a photographic exhibition in the town that showed his photographs, and he was part of a community and recognised as a photographer. There is a photo of him looking happy in front of his photos and he was known for being particularly able in photographing people.

Since then, a complex weave of changing therapeutic groups has been established. Thus for example, those who do not possess the social skills to take part immediately in the above described community phototherapy, can first work on a one-to-one basis with, for example, a tutor helping them develop their writing skills. Clients and family members can take part in the regular Monday evening therapeutic group. They can also look at particular issues arising between them in the Play Back theatre group and can eventually, through the cooperative Zefiro, work as photographers in schools. They can further attend social groups where people working at the mental health centre and their families can, for example, all go and have a pizza with their clients and their families and friends. Such groups involve people saying to each other, 'how are you?', 'what are you doing', 'if you can come, or don't come, it makes a difference'. And this is different for, as one client said to the group, 'I believe in you because you believe in me.'

Conclusion

Carmine works more on a community than an individual level; though, as someone coming from a more individual perspective, I (Del) have concerns that sometimes what is right for the system may not be right for the individual. However, Carmine's work shows the importance of looking for optimisation as well as when individuals may need to free themselves from some system – for example, their family – and maybe need to be part of another – for example, work. The response is overall more positive, coming from a more positive psychology approach influenced also by humanism, rather than existential or psychoanalytic. There is more of an expectation that individuals can work things through by being in groups rather than where, initially, they may get one-to-one work in terms of skills training. Also, by being caught up with the group, there is sometimes less space left for dwelling on individual concerns. Confidentiality is expected to be maintained by all, including visitors, with which I found it very hard to feel safe. Elements of the work such as patients and staff often socialising and carrying out the photographic work together reminded me of my early days at the Philadelphia Association (established by R.D. Laing, see for example Laing, 1970), but with the significant difference that the patients in Lucca are under medication and that this experiment is taking place within the medical system.

With regard to transferring community phototherapy to somewhere such as the UK, three factors seem important. First, the ideas themselves: on more than one occasion Carmine said to me when we talked about a particular therapeutic situation, 'this could heal the community'. This is radically different to just working on a one-to-one basis. The second important factor is the motivation of the people using community phototherapy. Much of what happens at Lucca in terms of community intervention would appear to rest on Carmine's ability to have relationships with mental health patients, which the patients want to sustain.

I was struck by both how families can drive someone mad (Laing and Esterton, 1970) and how the community has the potential to alleviate this. On the detrimental side, there were situations I encountered that might have been further helped by a more analytic understanding. Furthermore, the medical model ran alongside this community phototherapy in an unquestioning way. There was also the question that mental health patients look more normal if they are photographers, in that it is expected that photographers will move out of step with those they are photographing. Nevertheless, does this sometimes lead to inappropriately reinforcing unsocial ways of being?

I found myself caught up in this last aspect when I was taking photographs. I tended to look for when these patients' humanity might be glimpsed through their pharmaceutical haze, rather than take what might be more representative of their experience. But, there again, there was little medical interference with the activities taking place as community phototherapy. So, for example, the community made videos where they chopped off each other's heads or where the seaside photographer kept asking his customers to take a few steps back until they fell over the edge of the cliff! It is difficult to imagine such activities being funded by the National Health Service in the UK. Also, I went to an after-school meeting where teachers considered the proposals for psychiatric patients who had trained as photographers to work through a cooperative as paid school photographers, often unsupervised with the young children, helping them produce photographic year books, etc. Not only did all the teachers after a discussion vote unanimously for this to happen, but a regional politician wanted to be seen to be there to support the idea. It is difficult again to see this happening in a UK context, where it is increasingly difficult for a child to be alone in a classroom with a teacher, let alone with a psychiatric patient.

There seems a greater acceptance in Italy that everything is part of politics, as evidenced for example by Carmine taking his patients to live in an imprisoned mafia boss' house in Sicily. Carmine is also not reticent in acknowledging such more obviously 'political' influences as McMillan and Chavis' (1986) sense of community and social capital and Paolo Freire in the *Pedagogy of the Oppressed* (1993) with his concepts of entireness, and thinks that we should 'make something together and learn what is happening between us and within us from experience and not from a course'.

This is not to say that such work is easy and always successful in Lucca, but there does seem to be a more general sense of a community. To give just one example, a particular pleasure for me was to go along to the mental health centre on a Tuesday night where the director who has a particular interest in opera can be found singing with the patients.

On that first day in Lucca the year previously, I went with patients of the centre who were learning to be photographers. In photographing them I ended up identifying with them and realised that we all have barriers to being with one another that these photographic projects, whether for the teacher or learner, therapist or client, help to dispel through a sense of community. On the Friday evening, Carmine phoned round to invite people out for a pizza. There were about twelve of us made up of clients, parents, staff, Carmine, his daughter, me, a brother and the boyfriend of a patient – this had some similarity with my experience of the Philadelphia Association in London, many years previously (Cotton and Loewenthal, 2011). At the end of that first week I used digital storytelling, facilitated by Carmine, to describe that first day. It consisted of photographs I had taken that day, with the following text:

> . . . *Soon more people arrive . . .*
>
> *Including Roberto, one of the Centre's official photographers*
>
> . . . *and we are ready to set off!*
>
> *To go outside . . .*
>
> . . . *onto the City wall*
>
> . . . *with the opportunity to meet others!*
>
> . . . *which sometimes looks like it might happen . . .*
>
> *The next photo might symbolise potential loneliness and the barriers to the vitality that is also there . . .*
>
> *Will a meeting be possible?*
>
> *Yes? Sometimes?*
>
> . . . *and other times we can at least be together walking towards our project . . .*
>
> *Even though some may only be able to see it through a pharmaceutical haze . . .*

Our project is to photograph an exhibition at the Cathedral and to put it out in the newsletter which is also on the web for everyone to access

We are all in the world but there is a watchful eye from those who have 'less of the haze' though perhaps we are all there for our 'entireness'

One of us points out another member of the city's attempt to communicate!

Nearly there . . .

Another volunteer, Alessandro, joins us

Now the photographers begin to work . . .

We are on our own . . .

But sometimes there is a meeting

Other times the haze lifts less . . .

But there can be glimmers . . .

Yet enclosures . . .

But at least there are chances to meet

And experience the beauty (and pain) of each other, nature and art . . .

But to what extent do we need to explore what we dread?

And that which we are unsure of is help or hindrance

How can we keep open for those who experience wretchedness the possibility of a better way of being?

Digital photography provides one way we can share being creative together

. . . even though we may not find it easy to meet . . .

Perhaps some are starting to see more clearly . . .

. . . ways through

Most of us experience barriers . . .

Here there is a potential meeting

. . . and perhaps here even more so?

To be able to experience something of Spring . . .

. . . and to walk (sometimes beautifully) together . . .

Back to the Mental Health Centre . . .

First for lunch . . .

And then to start putting the stories on the web page where all our views can act as a digital mirror (for safety and discovery) and be shared in the group and with the larger community.

In learning more about digital photography (photobooks, photo-diaries, video-diaries, web pages) in Lucca it is hoped that all may find further ways of healing and meeting.

Here's to future meetings!

References

Basaglia, F. (1997). *Che cos'è la psichiatria*. Milano: Baldini Castoldi Dalai.

Cotton, T. and Loewenthal, D. (2011). Laing and the treatment is the way we treat people. In: Loewenthal, D. (ed.), *Post-Existentialism and the Psychological Therapies* (pp. 87–114). London: Routledge.

Demetrio, D. (1996). *Raccontarsi: l'autobiografia come cura di sé*. Milano: Raffaello Cortina.

Freire, P. (1993). *Pedagogy of the Oppressed: New revisited 20th anniversary edition*. New York: Continuum.

Jennings, S., Catternach, A., Mitchell, A., Chesner, A. and Meldrum, B. (1993). *The Handbook of Dramatherapy*. London: Routledge.

Jung, C.G. (1995). *Memories, Dreams, Reflections* (recorded and edited by Aniela Jaffe). London: Fontana Press.

Kreeger, L. (1975). *The Large Group: Dynamics and therapy*. London: Karnac.

Laing, R.D. (1970). *The Divided Self*. London: Penguin Books.

Laing, R.D. and Esterton, A. (1970). *Sanity, Madness, and the Family: Families of schizophrenics*. London: Penguin Books.

Levy, P. (1999). *Collective Intelligence: Mankind's emerging world in cyberspace* (translated by Robert Bonomo). New York: Perseus.

Loiacono, M. (2000). *Verso una nuova specie. Disagio diffuso, metodo alla salute, comunità globale*. Foggia: Edistampa Nuova Specie. See also www.nuovaspecie.com/IT/files/associazione foggia.php.

McMillan, D.W. and Chavis, D.M. (1986). Sense of community: A definition and theory. *American Journal of Community Psychology*, 14(1), 6–23.

Spivak, M. (1974). A conceptual framework for the structuring of the living of psychiatric patients in the community. *Community Mental Health Journal*, 10, 345–350.

Spivak, M. (1987). Introduzione alla riabilitazione sociale, teoria, tecnologia e metodi di intervento. *Freniatria*, 111(3), 522–574.

Spivak, M. (1992). Un modello interpersonale per capire e neutralizzare I processi cronici nei pazienti psichiatrici. *Freniatria*, 116(2), 179–195.

Chapter 10

The photographic genogram and family therapy

Rodolfo de Bernart

Introduction

Throughout this chapter, the discussion around why photographs have held such a significant place in the family therapy field will be considered. In turn, the important consequences concerning the development of audio-visual based therapeutic techniques will be outlined, with particular reference to the photographic genogram.

Photographs and family therapy

We have been influenced by early practitioner–researchers in the field of systemic therapy, such as Bateson (1972) who made use of video in exploring schizophrenic patients and their families. The use of the camera also extended to the actual therapy. As early as the 1950s, video was used in exploring the interactions between patients and their families. However, then, owing to the initial cost of filming, only those sequences considered significant were recorded. This method also had too great an influence on the family, who were alerted by the red light on the camera that something important was occurring. This kind of recording was soon abandoned and substituted by a continuous recording of the whole session, which was then re-examined by the therapeutic group in selecting significant sequences. However, here the importance of non-verbal behaviour emerged as well as the need to train trainee family therapists in its analysis:

> If you want a therapist to be able to use correctly the analysis of non-verbal language, you need to make him/her accustomed to confronting with it from the commencement of his/her training.
>
> (Bodin, 1978)

It is acknowledged that the analysis of non-verbal behaviour may help uncover the 'unofficial' story of the family as opposed to the 'official' cover story portrayed in the session. The family, when they come, gives us an image of themselves; however, the therapist must become accustomed to searching for what is not shown. It is just as important for the therapist to become familiar with their own official/unofficial family photographs: to search within one's own family as opposed to continually searching for and finding them in the treated family (de Bernart, 1987). This led, in the training of family therapists, to supplying the student with many images of the 'normal' family so that he/she could then accept with appropriate flexibility all he/she should encounter in the future. As happens too frequently, the concept of the normal family is confined inside the student's own family image or more frequently in the opposite image.

The first tool used with students and then by the student is the use of pictures, slides, 8mm films and video-recordings of events within the student's family. The aim here is not therapeutic but to enable the student to begin to acknowledge difference and description as opposed to judgement. The multiplicity and variability of the norm is obtained just through the comparison among the different families. This method is connected to the work of Kaslow (Kaslow and Friedman, 1977), to the 'Photo-video-scopie genealogique' suggested by Bleandonu (1986) and to the 'family picture' of Ruben (1976). However, it is also different in that it is specially applied to non-clinical use. The significant aspect of this method consists, in my opinion, in the 'journey' inside and outside of one's own family, similar to the one that Bowen (1972) proposed to his students. As a matter of fact, the student returns to his/her family to obtain the photographs (with all the problems connected with this), chooses among them and puts them in order following his/her own criteria. Next the group is shown the photos, which will give a new interpretation of them based on a multiplicity of normality criteria. In this phase, an effective work of consciousness may be completed with a 'geographical–historical' interview with the student's family, which will clarify the methods of tri-generational transmission of the family's culture and the student's functional positions. The use of films (Gladfelter, 1972) or of video-recorded plays is the second instrument used in order to enlarge the concept of normality even further and to enter into 'other realities' through images (de Bernart, 1990). The films are never shown in their entirety, but specific sections or scenes are viewed. The students then build up the characters' stories from these little sequences. Thus, from the very beginning they become accustomed with the activity of imagining familial stories. But it is important to note that to watch does not yet mean 'to be able to watch' as it is still necessary to develop one's own method of observation and to choose what you want to observe, because not all of what is perceptible is equally significant. The student develops the ability to use him/herself in the interaction to detect significant aspects in other relationships in the family. Further, each individual has a unique perception and organising structure by which they view and perceive these interactions and, as a result, they need to become aware of their own prejudices and presuppositions.

In the third clinical phase there is more attention paid to the stimulation of the student's ability to continually pass from general to individual aspects of the treated family. In fact, learning how these elements are connected one to another in behavioural sequences and what their structure is in a relationship allows us to individuate the connections of communication.

The main theoretical reason on which the use of images is based is that it is considered the most useful tool for gaining knowledge of the internal family of the patients and of the students, in that images allow us to understand how these internal relations within the family interact with the external world. According to Stern (2005), 'implicit relational knowing' is nonverbal, non-symbolised, un-narrated and non-conscious (unconscious but not repressed or removed, as Freud describes). The vast majority of all we know about how to be with others (including the transference) is implicit. So this part of the communication heavily influences our relations with other people.

So how do we build 'implicit relational knowing'? Stern says that it is done directly and without knowing. For example, a pupil in the school gets conscious material through meeting with teachers and other pupils, building his/her unconscious through different procedures (repression, removal), described by Freud, when he/she is emotionally disturbed by some negative experience. He/she experiences implicit relational knowing in everyday life understanding (without speaking of it), such as how to connect with people he/she likes or how to avoid people he/she is afraid of. This material is then memorised in the amygdala as implicit or procedural memory. This is our first memory, starting from birth.

According to Stern, you can access implicit relational knowing only through non-verbal behaviour or body language. Another reason for using the non-verbal channel is aesthetic, as Hillman (1997: 56) suggests:

> Life, intended as images, doesn't know what to do with family dynamics and genetic predispositions. Before becoming a story, each life offers itself as a continuum of images: and it asks to be seen, first of all. Even if each image is for sure full of meanings and could be analyzed, when we jump to the meanings without considering the image, we lose a pleasure which cannot be recovered by any interpretation no matter how perfect.

Most importantly, the verbal channel is too saturated, and because of this, one should use the non-verbal channel as it is less controlled by patients and can allow us to enter into the internal image of the family. A way to enter into it is by using a metaphorical language (built through images) that holds the capacity to trigger the affective component of the personality that normally is defended. Memory and historical and cultural identity are preserved through images. Representation is the time–space, through which absent becomes present, not only through a magical evocation, but also through a real substitution of the object. This means, for example, that a photo of a grandfather is not only a photo, but something more: a metaphorical object that presents the grandfather in the session.

Another important element is that human beings have two types of intelligence: holistic and sequential. The first is generic, not defined, global, simultaneous and not sequential. The second one is analytic, structured, referential and sequential. Human beings used the first for centuries before the 'invention' of writing and reading – 2,500 years ago more or less – (first phase). Then we developed the sequential in order to read. For this purpose, we need to see letter by letter, then word by word, then sentence by sentence, analytically. Only through this sequential intelligence can we read using the left-brain (at least in the Western world, as in the Eastern world things are sometimes different because of the use of ideograms and, subsequently, the right-brain). Our Western world has had an increasing prevalence of sequential intelligence, because people learn more through reading (second phase). However, over the past ten to twenty years our children have begun to learn again – as before – more through seeing than through reading, but now in a different way, through TV, computers, films, etc. We can introduce here the distinction proposed by Sartori (1999) between Homo sapiens and Homo videns. Homo sapiens learns by reading and decoding signs, with an autodriven rhythm and mediated emotions. Homo videns learns by seeing, looking at images ,with an ethero-driver rhythm and immediate emotions, using simultaneous intelligence (holistic). This is another important reason to develop tools that use the non-verbal, visual channel in therapy. The principal tools are based on the use of images, both in family therapy and in training family therapists. They include: photographic genograms, sculptures, conjoint family drawings, metaphorical objects, collages, art pictures and films.

I will now outline the use of photographic genograms in training and in therapy. I hope that the examples given will enable an understanding of the photographic genograms as a tool, even if writing on these procedures can be seen as contradicting the need for the visual.

The photographic genogram in training

I have used images in therapy since 1982–83. Maurizo Andolfi decided to start a new introductory course for the students of Psychotherapy named Relational Psychology that focused on the functioning of the 'normal family'. I found the theoretical teachings difficult to grasp – hence, why I proposed a new method of teaching through photographs and films. At the same time there was little literature available on the topic, and so this new method was largely inspired by Berman's (1996) work on the therapeutic use of photos. There were three further references, 'Photo-video-scopie genealogique' by Bleandonu (1986), 'Kaslow's family picture' by Ruben (1976) and Friedman's 'Family photos and movies' (Kaslow and Friedman, 1977). The theory suggested that memory, history and cultural identity are preserved through images. Representation is in turn the time–space through which absent becomes present, not only through a magical evocation, but also through a real substitution of the object. And, as Walter Benjamin (1931/2005) wrote, pictures make us aware for the first time of the 'optic unconscious', just as psychoanalysis opens the 'instinctive unconscious'. The 'optic unconscious' is a part of the 'implicit relational knowing', later thus named by Daniel Stern, as mentioned previously. Roland Barthes (1980: 87) too stated:

> Photography is a reverse prophecy: like Cassandra but with eyes turned to the past, which means literally that if we look at our photos of the past, we could be able to understand our present and maybe preview something of our future.

The significant aspect of this method consists, in my opinion, in the 'journey' inside and outside of one's own family, similar to the one that Bowen (1972) proposed to his students.

The Bowenian training for a family therapist was carried out essentially through working in groups to understand how much each student was part of the relational triangles in his family of origin. Once completed, the student then often takes what they have learned back to the client's family, in order to personally deconstruct these relational triangles and to differentiate them from his family.

In order to prepare the photographic genogram, the student 'returns' to the family to obtain the pictures, for example looking for the pictures in different family households and meeting different relatives in order to hear stories about his/her family. Then the student chooses from the photos and stories and orders them according to his/her own criteria (first view), and finally shows them to the group (second view). He/she shall choose a method for showing the photos: for example, simply passing them around in the group of colleagues, or pasting a number of them onto cardboard (family of origin of his/her father, of his/her mother, his/her nuclear family, his/her family after marriage) or via slides, PowerPoint, or recorded via video. Each of these choices has of course a different meaning in relation to whether, for example, one allows those present to touch the pictures. Another question that arises is whether the student gives a spontaneous and unprepared comment to each photo versus prepared and practised comment. The group being presented to will then ask questions about the genogram but these questions must be restricted only to the photos. The trainer should be very precise on this rule, not allowing deviations from this. The presenter will answer the questions, deciding how deep he/she wants to go. The level of intimacy will of course vary very much from the first to the last genogram made in the group. When finished, the members of the group will give comments (often verbal and making use of photographs), which will help the presenter to obtain a new interpretation of their original understanding based on a multiplicity of normality criteria. The presenter cannot comment on this 'restitution' in order to keep the emotional moment open and allow a continuation of the elaboration later at home (fourth view). If the presenter answers or says something, in fact, the process will probably be closed.

The number of photos requested for the genogram is traditionally thirty. They should represent the dynamics of the presenter's family in at least three generations. However, sometimes a presenter will bring more than thirty pictures and here it is the role of the trainer to ask the presenter to choose the pictures he/she wants to take out in order to leave only thirty photos on the table or on the carpet (the place where they are usually put after having been passed around). This choosing of photographs is sometimes quite difficult, but always very useful for the student. For example, once I remember helping a student to select thirty photos out of a genogram of 160 she had brought to the training session. The whole exercise is finished off through the student recollecting in silence over the pictures he/she has brought to the group.

The number of photos (thirty) seems small in comparison to the number of photos usually kept at home by the family (between 3,000 and at least 30,000 over, on average, 100 years). But this particular figure was chosen to allow a reasonable time for questions and discussion. Usually a 'training photographic genogram' takes at least three hours.

Clinical photographic genogram

The same method can be used in a variety of clinical settings with individuals, couples, families and groups. The photographic genogram is often used as a way of bringing the family into the session when they are not present. However, it is useful to work on the families of origin in individual and couples therapy.

Working with couples and families from a systemic relational approach, we should naturally take account of the particular kind of setting. This approach requires more time and different interventions in maintaining the therapeutic relationship compared to individual psychodynamic therapy. The interpretations are replaced by questions and humour will be channelled by verbal and non-verbal use of metaphors (images and body language) – see de Bernart and Buralli (2009) and the film *The Last Tycoon* by Elia Kazan, where in a scene (the nickel) a producer explains to a scriptwriter what cinema is and shows that it is the best way of building a therapeutic relationship.

Photos become very important when we get to the second part of the therapeutic process, after the first three or four sessions where we collect the stories of the individual members and of the couples and try to establish a diagnostic definition of the problem. After that, the couples start a long period of 'noise' in which they tell their therapist a lot about themselves individually and as a couple but, in reality, they do not increase the knowledge of their situation. On the contrary, they confuse the therapist by introducing quarrels, reciprocal accusations and many other unuseful matters, wasting their own time and ours and building a trial context. In this moment it can be very useful to change the channel of communication from the verbal to the non-verbal one. This can be done with different tools. Usually the first we use is the collage, which allows us to get a fresh and rich image of the internal image of the couple or/and of the couple's sexuality (de Bernart and Buralli, 2009).

When we move from what we have learned about symptoms and their reciprocal functions, to an understanding of the 'family wounds' that cause the functions and create the symptoms, we need then to first gain knowledge of the trigenerational story of the two families of origin. This can be done by asking the two partners to bring members of their family (each family member separately) into the session. Framo, Canevaro, Andolfi and I have used this technique over time. However, many years ago I realised that it often became very difficult to obtain the family of origin in sessions where there was a problem of a sexual nature, such as when one of the partners was having an affair. This was particularly difficult as the partners felt unable to confront themselves in front of their parents and siblings. Here I introduced the family photographic genogram as a substitute for the 'real live presence' of the two families of origin in a modified way.

The method for couples is similar to normal clinical use and includes a prescription that is very similar to the one used in training: a journey back home in order to look for photos of their own families (each client will do his/her own research) and to make a choice of a number of photos that represent the relation of themselves to their families in three or four generations, depending on whether they have children. It is important for partners to locate their own family photographs; ten of their family of origin and childhood and ten of their adolescence. The third phase starts from their meeting as a couple, so the approach to the photo selection is different. Here, the couple decide together which ten photographs represent the period of their life as a couple as well as, separately, five photographs each, which are 'the photos you would like to bring but that your partner refuses'.

When couples are older, have been married over a longer period of time and have children, a fourth session is often required. Here ten photographs of the marriage and family life with their children are chosen together and, again, five separate photographs for each, defined as 'the photos you would like to bring but which your partner refuses'. All photographs brought to the session are analysed by the couple and therapists who will raise questions about what they see in the images. However, it is important to note that the interpretations are restricted to the couple with the therapist only questioning what they see. By allowing the couple to do cross-interpretation reciprocally, we also have the opportunity to evaluate the level of knowledge each partner has of the story, of the other, and of the capacity to listen to one another and to accept the information and knowledge each partner can offer to the other. This can facilitate an important understanding of the prognosis, gaining knowledge of the flexibility of the couple, which is connected with the possibility of resolving their problems. It is through this that one begins to create a 'self-therapeutic couple'.

Methods of reading the genogram

In order to understand what happens in therapy, we often use three parameters that are also utilised to read the photographs. The *interactive* parameter, which in therapy is the tool to read interaction among different members of the family, of the couple and of the group. Observing pictures is used mostly to understand interactions among members in the photos in which different persons are present. If there are similar positions in many pictures we can build some interesting hypotheses on family members' roles and functions, and emotional links in the family. The *relational* parameter includes the story and the value of time. If a specific pattern is repeated over time, we can think of a relational function stabilised into the family, which then should be explored through further questions.

Just to give a small clinical example, in a photographic genogram session, a thirty-three-year-old lady brought at least five pictures in which she appeared to be in an identical position with her brother. The photographs showed this position with her at the age of three, seven, fourteen, twenty-one (just married) and thirty (when she already had her own children). In each of the photographs, her brother was putting his arm over her shoulder in a protective manner. Of course this could have been by chance, but questions put to her and to her brother revealed that there was a specific myth within the family relevant to the protection of women.

The *symbolic metaphoric* parameter is more difficult to use. We often see photos that have special meanings as they bring out a myth or a peculiar belief of that family or couple. One example was in a holiday picture of a couple, now seeking marital therapy. The photograph of the couple had been taken many years previously at a Greek temple in Southern Italy, just after an affair of the man had come to light. When I asked why the wife had brought that specific picture she answered that the choice was owing to a thought she had on that holiday, where she was very angry with her partner and felt he was doubtful about their future as a couple because he felt very attracted to other women he met occasionally. She concluded this by saying, 'I should have understood that that relationship was dangerous at that time, before marrying him . . .'

The pictures of the genogram as a whole must be observed longitudinally to see if there are repetitions over time and transversally to see if there similar events over the same time period in different members of the family. We can also observe changes in time and different behaviours in different members over the same period of time. In the photographs of a family group, we can observe the positions of members, the occasional absence of important members (the mother of the husband wasn't present at his marriage, an unexpected illness, etc.) which are particularly important if they show a pattern or repetition over time.

Individual photographs are useful in order to observe similarities and patterns across different members of the family. Sometimes, even if patterns are evident, they are often denied, especially when the resemblance is with a member of the family who is not appreciated and thought of highly within the family. The number of individual photos of a single member in the genogram can also be important. For instance, if we have four pictures of the mother and only one of the father, this is often significant.

The proportion of black and white photographs versus colour can be important, as it may show the number of photographs of the families of origin compared to the nuclear family or the actual family. The proportion of photographs at certain ages or absence of photographs should also be considered. For example, many people present fewer photographs of themselves in adolescence, as, in my opinion, we do not like ourselves during that period and therefore do not like to bring those pictures to the sessions, or alternatively have got rid of them previously. The proportion of the pictures of the family of origin and of the nuclear or actual family are also important, in order to understand which concept of family is more important for the couple.

I have spoken mainly of the use of pictures in couples' therapy; however, the approach described here can also be very useful in individual therapy. In this case, of course, the therapist will be responsible for asking questions relevant to the photographs and locating emotional nodes that are usually very evident in the genograms.

Conclusion

Audio-visual material and family or individual photographs can be important tools in a therapist's training. In such clinical work, the use of words and the art of talking remain important in psychotherapy, but, particularly following the discovery of mirror neurons and other findings from neuroscience, the use of non-verbal tools could well be shown to become more important in the development of the therapeutic relationship.

References

Barthes, R. (1980). *Camera Lucida: Reflection on photography*. New York: Hill and Wang.

Bateson, G. (1972). *Steps to an Ecology of Mind. Collected essays in anthropology, psychiatry, evolution, and epistemology*. Chicago, IL: University of Chicago Press.

Benjamin, W. (2005). *Walter Benjamin: Selected writings, volume 2, 1931–1934*. Eiland, H. and Jennings, M.W. (eds). Cambridge, MA: Harvard University Press.

Berman, L. (1996). *La fototerapia in psicologia clinica*. Trento: Erickson.

Bleandonu, G. (1986). *La video en therapie*. Paris: ESF.

Bodin, A. (1978). Uso del videotape nella formazione di terapeuti della famiglia. In: Watzlawick, P. and Weakland, J.H. (eds), *La prospettiva relazionale* (pp. 132–148). Roma: Astrolabio.

Bowen, M. (1972). Toward the differentiation of self in one's own family. In: Framo, J. (ed.), *Family Interaction: A dialogue between family researchers and family therapists* (pp. 111–173). New York: Springer.

de Bernart, R. (1987). L'immagine della famiglia, *Terapia familiare notizie*, 6, 3–4.

de Bernart, R. (1990). Video et therapie familiale, *Bulletin de psychologie*, XLIII(395), 564–568.

de Bernart, R. and Buralli, B. (2009). Le lit de six personnes. In: *Cahiers critiques de thérapie familiale et de pratiques de réseaux*, 1(42), 175–205.

Gladfelter, J. (1972). *Films in Group and Family Therapy*. New York: Brunner Mazel.

Hillman, J. (1997). *Il codice dell'anima*. Milano: Adelphi.

Kaslow, F.W. and Friedman, J. (1977). Utilization of family photos and movies in family therapy. *Journal of Marriage and Family Counselling*, 3(1), 19–25.

Ruben, A.L. (1976). The family picture. *The Journal of Marriage and Family Counselling*, 4(3), 25–28.

Sartori, G. (1999). *Homo videns*. Bari: Laterza.

Stern, D. (2005). *The Present Moment in Psychotherapy and Everyday Life*. Milano: Momento Presente.

Chapter 11

'The time we were not born'

Experimental archaeology – working within and beyond the photographic archive with photography students

Julia Winckler

Introduction

I have experienced first-hand the transformative power of photography, both with my own archival-inspired project work and while teaching photography and facilitating participatory art projects. In 2004, I developed a new module entitled 'Experimental archaeology: within and beyond the archive' for the second year students on the University of Brighton BA Photography course. What makes this 'Archives' module distinct from their other electives, is that over the six weeks it runs, students are encouraged to engage with a wide range of archival materials (family or found photographs, objects, documents, etc.) as a starting point for new photographic projects. This chapter will describe the module structure, methodologies and production techniques. Focusing on a small selection of student projects, I will describe how the photographic process has led to artistic and therapeutic outcomes for some of the students, which were, at least initially, unintentional and unexpected.

Archives module structure: engagement with emotion and history

The module begins with a three-hour project briefing. The introductory session presents photographic projects by artists who engage with archives and archival materials, resulting in a range of possible themes. We explore what constitutes an archive and/or a collection and how to define this, with particular reference to Jacques Derrida's *Archive Fever* (1996). We discuss his definition of an archive's role to order and categorise information; as a collection of things with an implicit structure, that follows a system of classification and an inbuilt taxonomy. We acknowledge an archive as a collection or storage system for memories and data that was started at a particular point in history; for example, by an explorer, collector, institution or government body (thus using Derrida's insights on the origins of archives, deriving from the Greek *arkhe* meaning both commandment and commencement). From the onset of archival collecting, processes of exclusion, omission, discarding and forgetting are intrinsically linked with practices of acquisition and accumulation. The structure and order are defined by the processes of how an archive is kept. We explore why we collect things and students are asked to remember when they became collectors themselves. Usually, this is around the age of six, shortly after starting school, and stickers, stuffed toys and action figures are most commonly collected. This affords children the control and expert knowledge in one small area of their lives, at a moment in time when they sense control is slipping away as they begin to realise how little they actually do know. We briefly touch on the history and fate of specific archives and collections, exploring the vast potential of the archive to expand our own understanding of historical situations: 'In these memory-obsessed times – haunted by the demands of history, overwhelmed by the dizzying possibilities of new technologies, the archive presents itself as the ultimate horizon of experience' (Comay, 2002: 8).

Some archives, upon becoming defunct, were 'rescued'; but entire collections have also been discarded or lost. The idea that collections are 'safe' when they are part of an archive, museum or gallery collection is challenged. I show examples of material being lost forever through theft or accidental fire, such as in the artist's projects *Fantômes* (2000) and *Disparitions* (2000) where Sophie Calle photographed the remains of historical artworks destroyed by fire and empty museum walls from where artworks had been stolen. We also look at artistic approaches to found collections, and their ability to speak of social and cultural practices: for example in the form of artist Mark Dion's project *Tate Thames Dig* (1999) where pottery, bone, glass, fossilised sea urchins and twentieth-century rubbish were excavated from the river Thames next to the Tate Modern in London over a two week period by archaeologists and volunteers and subsequently displayed inside the gallery (Putnam 2001). We look at examples of accidentally destroyed collections: during the London Blitz, a bomb fell onto Holland House library in Kensington in 1940; more recently, in 2003 the National Library in Iraq was severely damaged – out of the ruins, some items could be saved. Other destroyed collections include the brutal Nazi book burnings of works by artists and writers who had opposed the fascist regime.

Photographic work and large-scale projections by artists Shimon Attie (*Sites Unseen: European projects*, 1998*)* and Christian Boltanski (*La fete de Purim, The Missing House, Sans Souci*, 1989–91, see Gumpert, 1994) are discussed alongside film-based work by Susan Hiller (*J-Street Project* 2002–5); each artist employing a range of archival approaches and reflecting in unique ways on the Shoah and the void left behind. These artists are also cultural archivists, historians and archaeologists who work with artefacts, archival photographs and documents in order to mediate the past through creative and imaginative investment.

Attempting to recall or recover memories is, of course, slippery and unreliable work. In Jean-Luc Godard's 1998 film *Le Controle de l'Univers* the French cineaste experimented with the idea of the photographic darkroom being a space where an image is reanimated, recalling a past. But the image is not able to represent this past it is trying to conjure up, as each image is annulled from one second to the next as new footage flickers across the screen.

We look at a short extract from Stephen Poliakoff's film *Shooting the Past* (1999*)*, which focuses on the stories and secrets of personal photographic collections. This leads on to a discussion of the most common, visual archive that almost every student has: the family album. Family albums are mini-archives, time capsules, with huge emotional value attached to them. For some, they are the only trace that remains of a dead relative, and as Marianne Hirsch notes, often the only 'means by which family memory would be continued and perpetuated' (Hirsch, 1997: 7). Martha Langford further discusses the compelling relationship and potential of both the visuality and orality of family albums:

'[the album's] oral-photographic framework greases the wheels of retrieval, reinstating and expanding the repertoire of remembrance as the images are seen and heard in a rolling present' (Langford, 2001: 20).

Max Dean is an artist who works with found family photographs; he asks whether images that have lost their original owners and contexts have become devoid of meaning, or whether we have a responsibility to 'rescue' them from final destruction and whether they can be infused with new life. Dean's *As Yet Untitled* (1992–95) shows a robot machine that shreds found photographs. But Dean's installation piece invites viewers to step in and stop the machine from shredding. The images then can be claimed and become the responsibility of the new owners. A key question posed is whether they have already lost their meaning and this rescue comes too late, or whether they can fulfil a new function (Ingelevics, 2005).

Project themes, methodologies and techniques: from *punctum* to *studium*

The students then spend a week on the core readings, including Elizabeth Edwards' (1999) work, which emphasises the importance of going beyond the content and surface qualities of photographs – what the photographs are of, what or whom they represent – foregrounding instead the physical presence of photographs and their existence as objects with an archival smell that have been handled, touched, and have varying scales and changing usages over time.

Students read extracts from *Camera Lucida* (1980), where Roland Barthes discusses the emotional power and potential of photographs to make it possible for viewers to strongly identify with them, even though the experiences depicted are not their own. When Barthes introduced the concept of a photograph's *punctum*, he speaks about an immediate, personal and emotional connection that can be felt between the viewer and a photograph, which brings the photograph's pastness to us into an immediate present. This personal experience of a photograph's *postmemory*, to use Marianne Hirsch's term, and the sense of connectedness to the past, make it possible for the students to embark on their own archival projects.

Using archival source material as a starting point, students respond creatively to a range of themes, working with the notion of archaeological excavation of traces from the past. These include exploring traumatic memories, loss, mourning, illness, the dynamics of family relationships, and trying to understand, or piece together another person's life through photography. In the second week of the project we visit an archive; here the students have the opportunity to learn about archiving processes, meet archivists and curators and handle collections. Five weekly critique sessions culminate in a final session, when students present their work to the whole group.

When exploring their own archival sources, the students work primarily with two complementary methodological concepts; the first being that of an archaeological excavation, where they dig into the past. This archaeological process is not altogether dissimilar to a psychoanalytical and Freudian approach. Refracting the archaeological method through the work of Michel Foucault, Adrienne Chambon writes that this involves starting 'from the surface and work[ing] down through sedimented layers of accumulated knowledge and practice. It is fragmentary work' (Chambon, 1999: 54). This slow, delicate but rewarding approach enables the student researchers/photographers to make a range of connections and new constellations. And, like the archaeologist, 'the psychoanalyst had to work slowly, with great care, gradually uncovering buried "objects" and reconstructing the relations between them. . . . Like archaeology, psycho-analysis dealt with uncovering the past, with fragments, and with interpretation or reconstruction' (www.freud.org.uk/education/topic/40037/freud-and-archaeology).

The second key archival methodology uses the techniques of the genealogy approach, which starts 'with the present and works its way in the opposite direction, retroactively through a descent in time. It is a "history of the present" as Foucault called it' (Chambon, 1999: 54).

Only then do the students decide whether to work with a personal archive or an existing public collection and what their approach will be. The first steps are usually similar: collecting materials; establishing genealogies and making connections; discover-ing artefacts that have lost their original function, value and/or meaning. From being functional objects they have become *signs*, or semaphores; a term Krzysztof Pomian uses to refer to objects collected for a vast range of different reasons: their aesthetic qualities, collector's value, emotional attachment rather than their original functional or usage qualities (Pomian, 1994).

Each student then develops a framework and/or order for the selected material. For example, a genealogy: how does the material (e.g. old photograph from a family album collection) connect to the student/researcher; what is its original value; what are its conditions of production, its origins or its relationship to other objects?

It is important for the students to make the material their own for the duration of the project; tapping both into the emotive qualities and personal connections (*punctum*) as well as the information value and context of the material (*studium*) (Barthes, 1980). A period of *studium* involves a range of experimental processes, construction and reconstruction of the material, which is informed by but also in turn informs the choice of photographic techniques. Barthes considers this the provision of a context, the exploration of how the photograph came to exist, how it was made. Repressed experiences, forgotten, unconscious experiences, both personal and external, and a student's emotions are worked on, and through this process can be explored or better contextualised.

Photography, archival work and the digital age

Digital photography has much to offer in terms of image manipulation, duplication, layering, copying and modification of the original image. But since the arrival of digital photography, we are also in great danger of losing images forever when a computer's hard drive gets damaged or discarded or when one storage medium supersedes the next. This has recently been the case with floppy discs, zip discs, and at some point in the future CDs and DVDs will become redundant formats and potentially unread-able as their surfaces deteriorate. It may become more difficult, if not impossible, to run the Archives project the way we have done. There will be fewer images for students to find in family albums or flea markets or charity shops; fewer hard copies, slides and found images as a consequence of digital photography. The way we work in the Archives project is particularly productive when we have material objects in front of us to handle, explore, investigate. Perhaps students will start collecting com-puter hard drives and will go through people's image folders; maybe we will soon see second-hand CDs and floppy discs for sale leading to an excavation of material from the digital era. Digital archivists, researchers and artists may specialise in image retrieval and analysis. But will this seem remote and counterproductive to the way we have worked thus far?

The digitisation of archival materials continues; as leading institutions make specific records available through a single web portal (e.g. Britain's National Archives and Germany's Federal Archives) it could become easier to access significant source material. However, as Katie Hafner cautions in an article on 'Knowledge lost in a digital age' (2007), if archives follow the trend of the British National Archives, the repository for nine billion documents, only a small fraction are likely to be digitised and put online. On the other hand, the constant increase of new affordable devices to record data (starting with basic camera phones) has led to 'a new explosion of archiving human existence' and the drive to record each moment, leading to millions of new digital images being created and uploaded to the World Wide Web daily (Amies, 2011). This new wealth of information in turn makes it necessary to develop new research skills to, literally, dig through all the available data and learn to discern information that matters (Hencke 2011). Rob Blackhurst discusses 'a new breed of digital archivist [who] is tracking the e-mails, computer files and electronic ephemera that might otherwise be lost forever', commenting on digital texts (e.g. emails) being both easy to create and easy to discard. He argues, 'They constitute an increasingly large part of our cultural record – treasures which, if not properly archived, could soon be lost to future generations' (2007: 20).

Archives projects: student examples

The title of the chapter draws on a comment by Kerry Symes, who took the Archives module in 2004. In the final session, she explained that she had never before consciously thought about 'the time we were not born'. Kerry's response to the project briefing was to work with photographs of her mother, who had died when Kerry was very young, trying to get to know her mother better and reflect on her loss by creating a memory box in which she placed a small selection of her mother's photographs. The project helped Kerry realise that her mother had herself been a young woman once, and that the photographs offered some small insights into her mother's life, both prior to Kerry's birth and as a young parent.

Through Kerry's work, and subsequent projects, I was able to observe that some of the projects had significant developmental and therapeutic effects for the students, triggered by the use of archival source materials, and a combination of experimental processes and artistic presentation. They have come to represent significant turning points for the students, affecting their sense of self, their relationships to other family members and their understanding of the past.

This section describes seven projects that exemplify these effects, discussing how each student approached the project briefing with a different emphasis and technique. Recent correspondence with this group (several of whom have since graduated and are now working as professional photographers) indicates that projects with an archival starting point have been experienced as 'freeing', as they have brought situations, experiences and feelings to the surface. Each has kindly consented to my presenting their work here.

Always look back

Holly Oliver

Holly explored her mother's family albums, searching for photographs of her sister Amber, who had died following a short illness at a young age before Holly was born. Holly's mother still lives in the same family home in South London. Holly decided to ask her mother for permission to work with a small selection of photographs of Amber, a process that Holly found difficult. Fortunately, her mother's response was extremely positive and supportive.

While looking through the photographs, Holly discovered that despite a 20-year interval, many features both inside and outside the home had remained virtually unchanged. In one of the photographs, Amber can be seen sitting on the kitchen floor (Photo 11.1). Holly decided to reinsert the photograph within the kitchen interior. Holding the photograph with her left hand, she pointed the camera downwards towards the floor; choosing an angle that gave an adult perspective. The original photograph was thus extended within the contemporary space of the kitchen.

Holly repeated this process with the other photographs, using the locations around the home where they had been taken originally. Each new image showed her own hand inserted on the left side of the frame.

The photographic distance was dictated by the fact that Holly had decided that she would take the new photographs herself; she had to hold her camera in the other hand to focus in and press the shutter. Holly further paid close attention to the light and

Photo 11.1 Daniel and Amber (Oliver).

emulated the muted and natural colours of the original photographs. The camera focuses in close, leaving the background slightly blurred. As the past is anchored firmly in the camera's frame and is foregrounded, the present slips away. Holly's dual role (as family archivist and contemporary image maker) reintroduces her sister Amber into the home. It further makes possible the simultaneous presence of both Holly and Amber within that space. Holly's working methodology literally contains and preserves her sister's photographs – as Holly physically holds the archival photographs within a new context, articulating a relationship with her sister.

Holly shared the new photographs with her mother and older brother, who agreed to be recorded, reminiscing around the kitchen table together. This sound recording became the starting point for a short film, in which Holly's own photographs come in and out of view, and the family can be overheard talking about Amber. Conversation is interrupted by the occasional teaspoon being stirred in a teacup, or someone getting up from their chair. For the viewer/listener, this makes for a very intimate experience. One feels present at the table, or eavesdropping in on a personal conversation about the loss of a young daughter and sister.

Holly's decision to exhibit both the film and the photographs in her final year show was courageous and extremely hard as she explained later:

> Sharing the work at times, was difficult . . . I think for me one of the most important, if not actually the crucial part of the project was using the archival photographs. . . . It was important to have left home . . . And to have returned and to have taken out the albums. The prints I made are on the wall in the staircase now. My mother put them up. She wanted a set of them to display in the house.

My heart is hurting

Amelie Desbiens

Amelie's parents separated when Amelie was only three years old. She has no memories of her parents together, and wanted to use the Archives project to attempt to get an understanding of her parents' life as a couple before Amelie was born.

Her mother gave her access to photographs and letters, beginning with her courtship and leading up to her engagement and wedding day. Amelie began reading the letters and scrutinising the photographs, trying to find clues of her parents' feelings for each other during that time. Amelie became interested in the gestures and interactions, in how her parents looked at each other in the photographs, their facial expressions, which were inquisitive, curious, loving. She realised how young her parents had been, how attracted they were to each other.

Amelie decided to zoom in closely to a small number of photographs and selected only tiny extracts from them. She also photographed the handwriting of the letters. This close attention to detail and Amelie's technique of entering into the photographs with a macro lens, of trying to literally get under their surface, developed into a poignant series of still images. These spoke to many students in the module about young love, disappointment and loss.

Amelie's final piece was a short animation, without sound, for which she resequenced her close-up photographs to create new relationships between them. In one such close-up, the viewer can only see Amelie's parents' hands; her father is putting his wife's wedding ring on her ring finger, her hand in his hands. It is poignant that Amelie has been wearing her mother's wedding ring on a necklace for many years.

Reflecting on this project, she wrote:

> I found that using an existing family archive was very therapeutic and cathartic, it allowed me to search in to an issue that has affected my life but that I was never a part of. While using the images and letters I was able to piece together my own understanding of my parent's life together.

Absent loss and misplaced mourning

Donna Clark

Arlette Farge likens a photograph to a passage where the viewer fluctuates between desire and mourning. Desire that 'what was will be again one day, and mourning that what was will never come back' (2000: 4).

It was this combination of desire and mourning that inspired Donna's project, which developed out of the loss of Donna's grandmother's family albums. When Donna's grandmother passed away in the early 1990s, Donna and her family had been living in Israel for some years. By the time Donna's father returned to the UK, the local council, with the permission of Donna's uncle, had already cleared out the flat and Donna's grandmother's personal belongings, including all family photographs had gone. This meant that Donna had no photographic memories of her grandmother or grandfather, or other relatives on her father's side, aside from the snapshots existing in her parents' family album, which only showed her grandmother in older age. Having been inspired by Christian Boltanski's work, Donna decided to work with found images to recreate memories of her grandmother.

In a box at a local antique shop, Donna found a series of related photographs, depicting the same woman from childhood to older age – ranging from about the 1930s to the 1990s. She bought all the photographs of the woman that she could find but the woman herself remained anonymous; no text or captions on the back of any of the images (other than a date on a baby photo and a much later image, which confirmed this could be the same woman).

As Donna attempted to reassemble the photographs to stand in for the lost photographs of her own grandmother, she realised that she could not create a substitute for her family's loss of the originals. She also grew quite fond of the woman whose images she had reanimated and saved. She started wondering whether her grandmother's photographs might have ended up in a similar box, incurring the same fate, when they were removed from her grandmother's flat. Donna hopes that they have been passed on to a charity shop, rather than thrown away. To address the impossibility of the other woman's photographs replacing those of her grandmother, Donna wrote a letter. In it, she reveals how the process of working with the found images triggered a renewed sense of loss for her grandmother:

> Dear Grandma, it has been a very long time since I last saw you, and unlike the missing photographs I have somehow rediscovered this feeling of loss for you.

To find these anonymous images, also lost and forgotten and give them meaning, when pictures of you could have had the same fate, felt like the only thing I could do to grasp onto the past I can no longer reclaim.

Donna also sourced an anonymous amateur recording of a song performed in Yiddish by a female singer about a girl talking to her grandmother. She then assembled her selection of found images, displayed in chronological order, into a 2-minute film, which had a soundtrack beginning with Donna reading out the letter addressed to her grandmother, followed by an extract of the song. For the final group presentation, Donna projected this film into an empty frame to emphasise her sense of loss.

Reflecting back on this project a year on, Donna wrote:

I had not realised before doing this how much I missed not having a substantial historical photographic record of my Grandparents and distant relatives; doing this project helped me to accept this reality. To find this way of working, in using photography as a means to both work through and process unresolved emotions was refreshing at a time when I was questioning how and why I wanted to make photography work.

Tempting relations

David Clark

The idea for David's project was triggered by a desire for a deeper connection with his father, which had come about following the death of a close family friend, and the friend's family discovering a family mementoes box. In David's own words:

While the friend's family were sorting through his belongings they came across a box where he had saved every father's day card, letter or note that was ever given to him by his family; he had kept this secret from everyone. This made me start to wonder if my father might have a possible collection of similar mementos to which I expect the answer to be no. As this happened I started to wonder if my neighbour's death would make an impact on the relationship between my father and me.

David's starting point was his supposition that his father would not have kept any family mementoes. To see whether it could help create a stronger relationship, David took portraits of his father in the family home, which David had moved out of when he started university. He also photographed some of his father's personal belongings. He thought that this process might potentially influence his father's own views on photography, and help structure and bring greater understanding to their relationship. David was dissatisfied with his images, feeling that they did not communicate anything about his father, whose biggest passion was competitive angling.

When his father agreed to let David accompany him to Stoneham Lakes in Hampshire, one of his favourite lakes close to where he grew up, David took along a video camera. Throughout the course of a Wednesday in early March, and in freezing temperatures, David filmed the surface of the lake; his father's fishing pole, occasionally zooming in on his father's face, which showed deep concentration, and intermittently recording his father explaining how he got into fishing at the age of seven and talking about fishing techniques, sharing his deep knowledge of Stoneham Lakes. The short film that David made is reflective and understated. For the next stage of the project, David shared the film with his father, and asked him if he would respond to it, which he did by email.

David's final project included the film, his father's response and a sealed letter from David to his father, all presented in a mementoes box addressed to his father. Reflecting back, David writes that, for him:

> The content of this archive is an extension from the family album, focused more on sociological problems and relationships. In this instance, the impetus is not in the content of the archive, but the questions that are raised about such an archive existing . . . For me, it has been a way of finding out who my father is, and in turn, showing my father who I am.

Back to a time before I was born

Richard Clayton

In another project that probed familial relationships, Richard, a mature student, focused on his parents' early life. As his parents had passed away some time ago, Richard searched for a way to reconnect with them. Through this archival process, Richard was also hoping to find out more about himself.

To start, Richard brought a large number of photographs, a stack of letters and personal documents to our group session. There was an envelope from Italy, addressed to his father and sealed with his mother's lipstick kiss on the back, and a letter in which his mother longs to be with Richard's father in England. They had met in 1945; Richard's father was a young English soldier with the Engineer Corps in Italy, Richard's mother a nineteen-year-old Italian girl with a young brother and widowed mother. They met and fell in love and within weeks had married. But when the war ended, Richard's father had to return to England without his new wife. Richard was particularly interested in exploring:

> the motivations that drove two people, in a time of chaos and destruction, to start to build a new life together . . . By searching through the chaos of my family archives I will try to piece together a memory of two people I never really knew. Two people who, to me, are so different from the ones I called mum and dad.

At first, the volume and weight of Richard's family archive seemed overwhelming. What to work with, which images to choose. He thought about making a memorial collage, similar to one he had inherited from his grandmother. The following week, Richard moved into the photographic studio with just a few snapshots of his parents, which he had made into digital scans, and projected these onto the studio back-drop, working with another student/assistant and experimenting with exposure times, re-photographing the projections, inserting himself within the projected images (see Photo 11.2):

Photo 11.2 Back to a time (Clayton).

I experimented with projecting my parents' features onto my own, sometimes placing myself into the picture with them. Whereas the images projected were sharp and clear I was the one who was poorly defined. Using this idea I became the ghost in the image and imagined myself as being projected back to their time.

This led to a layering of past and present, collapsing different moments and places into a new constructed space, with Richard stepping into and out of the space, and deciding to have his face overlaid by the projected image of his father. Richard describes the impact this experience had on him:

I attempted to reflect myself back to the time when my parents first met. It was the most serendipitously important event that I will ever know and I will cherish it forever. As I project myself back into their past, I do not recognise the people I see before me. But my mother seemingly looks up, smiles and sees me. Even though I would not be born for another twenty years she recognises me as a ghost from her future life. A life she is just beginning to imagine.

Betrayal

Alison Beetles

Alison's archival photographs had already been scratched and damaged many years previously by another family member, when Alison decided to work with them.

She wanted to document and bring to the fore the marks and interventions. In an act of anger and frustration with the person depicted, Alison's grandmother had taken a biro and knife to the originals, scratching into them and damaging them in the process. Rather than focusing on the content of these photographs, Alison decided to highlight her grandmother's gestures, and used a macro lens to zoom in on the scratch marks themselves.

Alison arranged the images on a table she had set up in her living room, to create a still life studio, and then lit them carefully. Because of her lighting technique, Alison's photographs appear to be almost three-dimensional. The marks look like scars, the photographic paper has the colour and texture of skin. The pain, frustration and anger that had led to the photographs being damaged is foregrounded; yet Alison's reworked images also have a strange beauty to them – they seem to be floating in space. Her photographs reveal as much as they conceal what had originally been done to them.

Betrayal illustrates the power and potential of photographs' indexical and symbolic qualities: the capacity of photographs to stand in for the person depicted, to infer presence. Alison's own mediated photographs reveal what has been done to the originals, and highlight the presence of the keeper of the photographs. As none of the original image content is visible any longer, only the marks remain.

In a group tutorial, we discussed the different types of damage that can be done to photographs. We noted that almost all of us had at different times in our lives thrown some photographs away, cut off a person from a picture, ripped an image apart, and, since the introduction of digital photography, have simply deleted image files from our hard drives, Flickr, MySpace and other social networking accounts. Photographer and archivist Joachim Schmid has for years collected people's mutilated and damaged personal snapshots and has hosted international exhibitions showcasing found photography. Curator and photographer Vid Ingelevics explores these acts of destruction, discussing a range of artists who have consciously destroyed either their own negatives, or have inflicted serious damage on them through scratching, chemical spillage or tearing (Ingelevics, 2005).

What made Alison's project even more moving was the fact that the damaged photographs had been kept inside the pages of a family album, rather than thrown out and discarded. Alison reflects on this contradiction:

> The photographs have remained a type of secret, mutilated inside a family album, kept in a drawer. I still have the photographs, even though they are damaged . . . I think that they are something that I will dispose of, as my children won't look upon them as I do. They won't hold that same force or essence as they do for me.

The fundamental makings of a solitary voyager

Hannah Laycock

Hannah's project came about because she wanted to be able to spend more time with her father, who lives on the east coast of Scotland. The dynamics of their relationship had changed following Hannah's move to Brighton, and she wanted to get to know her father better from an adult perspective and also learn more about his earlier experiences in life through his anecdotes and personal archives.

Originally from Skipton in Yorkshire, her father had travelled the world as a young man. He had crossed Australia and Asia alone, often camping out in the wild, working, teaching himself foreign languages and keeping a diary. In Asia he bought himself a black Raleigh bicycle, and cycled part of the journey back to Britain. He later inspired his children to become independent and adventurous, and they went on many cycling trips as a family on a tandem and the well-travelled Raleigh bike.

Amazingly, he kept this same bicycle throughout his life, now safely stored in the family garage and still in working order. The bicycle became the starting point for Hannah's project and she made several trips up to Scotland to photograph and interview her father and ask him questions about his travels. He shared artefacts with her: a creased travel map; old travel money; his own photographs; a small travel book *Manuel du Voyager*, passed on to him by his grandfather. Hannah photographed these objects against a black background, using her father's own descriptions of them as captions. Discussions between father and daughter kept coming back to the bicycle, so Hannah decided to make a photograph of the bicycle as well. This image has now come to represent both Hannah's father's adventurous spirit and his resilience.

Hannah's father had been feeling unwell, but up to that point, his illness had not yet been diagnosed. He underwent a series of medical tests and was diagnosed with Motor Neuron Disease. Sadly, he is now mainly in a wheelchair and cannot use the bicycle anymore.

Hannah has continued to photograph her father and mother:

> Motor Neuron Disease is a progressive neurodegenerative disease that creeps beneath the surface, slowly attacking the upper and lower motor neurons. I began photographing my parents in September 2009 . . . since this time all our fears were confirmed, and so began our journey, as we came to terms with the present situation and thoughts on the future.

Summary: the work of mourning (*Trauerarbeit*) and therapeutic impact

The rawness and immediacy of the students' experiences were palpable in the group tutorials and are manifest in the outcomes presented here. Each Archives project described above has worked with notions of absence and presence; with an emotional response to the strong pulls of the past (a person, experience, absence, loss) combined with a more analytical *studium* and artistic mediation that has led to a transformation of the initial concerns explored. Commenting on these projects, Adrienne Chambon has observed that: 'these are and are not narratives all at once, they are narrative links with fragmented trails that disappear in the sand – narrative departures to replace narrative foreclosures, openings, invitations. Kinds of narrative acts, gestures . . .' (Chambon, 2011).

The methods, interventions and visual narratives called upon a wide range of aesthetic devices, including digital manipulation: the presentation of archival pictures within new staged photographs; the cropping and zooming into photographs to focus purely on details and gestures; the extreme close-up and fragmentation of already damaged photographs; the scanning and digital projection of old photographs into the arena of the photographic studio; and working with found images whose original context was unknown; working with historical objects that held and continue to hold symbolic significance and speak to the restorative powers of photography; being inspired by the absence of an archive prompting the creation of one. In responding imaginatively to source materials, immersing themselves within the archive, taking up the challenge of unpacking, handling, reorganising an old box found in the attic, or a family album tucked away in a cupboard, students have understood that a new photography project can be inspired by existing photographs, exploring their tangible, haptic qualities, rather than having to produce new images each time. An emotional response combined with an intellectual approach (*studium* and archaeological/genealogical method) can lead to powerful and often lasting therapeutic benefits. Most poignantly, perhaps, *the past is now part of one's present and the present now has a palpable past.*

The students' own observations and insights broaden over time. In recent exchanges, several graduates wrote that they have continued working with archival sources. They have an enhanced consciousness of what these projects were/are about: working through one's own or someone else's history, dealing with past traumas, relating history to our own lives. Some projects come full circle: an emotional trigger (*punctum*) leads to an enquiry, which students articulate in material–aesthetic ways; and at the end of the project a return from a structured exploration (*studium*) to the initial emotions (*punctum*) that have been addressed and often feel less immediate. As we have seen, it is usually the conscious engagement with an archival object, with what it represents, that can be beneficial, rather than the object itself.

The dialectical process of mediation, and a deeper awareness of the interlinkedness of past and present, which the Archives module aims to achieve by emphasising both an emotional response and a historical study, result in informed, critical and engaged projects. One problem with this kind of project is that archival material can potentially become overwhelming. Also, projects have at times become too idiosyncratic. It is the students' capacity to mediate and universalise their experiences that make it possible for others to relate to their work.

Archives projects are rarely finished, complete. One year on, even ten years from now the initial questions and their artistic responses might be reinterpreted in new ways – there is the potential of alternative archives; of correcting archives emerging; fresh explorations and new insights that all offer exciting possibilities. The archive can, and perhaps needs to, be 'opened up' over and over again, heeding Derrida's *Archive Fever* text, which discusses the importance of the archive in our shared, collective future:

> The question of the archive is not a question of the past . . . it is a question of the future. The question of the future itself, the question of a response, of a promise and of a responsibility for tomorrow. The archive: if we want to know what that will have meant, we will only know in time to come.
>
> (Derrida, 1998: 36)

References

Amies, T. (2011). How to archive yourself. Radio programme, BBC Radio 4, *Archive on 4*, producer Sarah Jane Hall. First broadcast: Saturday, 9 April 2011.

Attie, S. (1998). *Sites Unseen: European projects*. Burlington, VT: Verve Editions.

Barthes, R. (1980). *Camera Lucida*. London: Fontana.

Blackhurst, R. (2007). Will history end up in the trash? *FT Magazine*, 17/18 March, pp. 20–25.

Calle, S. (2000). *Disparitions*. Arles: Actes Sud.

Calle, S. (2000). *Fantômes*. Arles: Actes Sud.

Chambon, A. (1999). Foucault's approach: Making the familiar visible. In: Chambon, A., Irving, A. and Epstein, L. (eds), *Reading Foucault for Social Work* (pp. 51–81). New York: Columbia University Press.

Chambon, A. (2011). Personal communication with Julia Winckler, author's record.

Comay, R. (2002). *Lost in the Archives*. Toronto: Alphabet City.

Derrida, J. (1996). *Archive Fever: A Freudian expression*. Chicago, IL: University of Chicago Press.

Edwards, E. (1999). Photographs as objects of memory. In: Kwint, M., Breward, C. and Aynsley, J. (eds), *Material Memories* (pp. 221–236). Oxford: Berg.

Farge, A. (2000). *La chambre à deux lits et le cordonnier de Tel Aviv*. Paris: Seuil.

Gumpert, L. (1994). *Christian Boltanski*. Paris: Flammarion.

Hafner, K. (2007). Knowledge lost in a digital age. *The New York Times*, *The Observer Supplement*, 18 March, p. 1.

Hencke, D. (2011). Digging through data. National Union of Journalists, *The Journalist* magazine Feb./March issue, pp. 16–18.

Hiller, S., *The J Street Project 2002–5*. Available from www.susanhiller.org/Info/artworks/artworks-JStreetVideo.html (accessed 6 February 2012).

Hirsch, M. (1997). *Family Frames: Photography, narrative and post-memory* Cambridge, MA: Harvard University Press.

Ingelevics, V. (2005). Damage done: Materializing the photographic image. *Prefix Photo*, 11, 34–49.

Langford, M. (2001). *Suspended Conversations: The afterlife of memory in photographic albums*. Montreal: McGill.

Pomian, K. (1994). The collection: Between the visible and the invisible. In Pearce, S.M. (ed.), *Interpreting Objects and Collections*. London: Routledge.

Putnam, J. (2001). *Art and Artefact: The museum as medium*. London: Thames & Hudson.

Chapter 12

Photography and art therapy

Alexander Kopytin

Introduction

This chapter explores therapeutic possibilities and paradoxes that concern the use of photography within art therapy.

Art therapy was a term first used in such countries as the UK and the USA in the 1940s during the post Second World War rehabilitation movement. From this, we see the development of two separate strands: one as a sensitive form of art teaching applied in clinical settings and the second as an aspect of psychotherapy through art. Nowadays art therapists are considered to be qualified specialists who have a considerable understanding of visual art processes and the ability to communicate with a wide range of clients, both individually and in groups, using both visual and talking forms of therapy (Liebman, 1996). In fact, the art therapists' non-verbal communication with clients is believed to be crucial in developing the therapeutic relationship (Weiner, 1999).

In therapeutic work, art therapists aim to provide a secure environment for their clients, which stimulates them to express their ideas and feelings through art. Art therapists also encourage their clients to respond to art products so that long buried feelings can be brought to the surface, understood and acknowledged. Art therapy is often considered to be a dialogue between a client and a therapist mediated by art materials and products. In that art therapy is rooted in visual arts, it is natural to expect that art therapists would use photography as one of the instruments for their clients' creative expression. This is especially apparent today, given that high-tech instruments (such as computers, digital cameras and video) are used not only by professional artists, but also by many people in their daily lives.

However, through reading art therapy literature and contacting many art therapists in my country and abroad, I noticed that few practitioners use photographic instruments in their clinical practice as a powerful vehicle for their clients' artistic endeavours. Though there exists a selected number of art therapy publications that reflect original forms of expressive use of photography in clinical work, its vast therapeutic potential is still underestimated by art therapists. Therefore, I am intrigued as to why most art therapists don't apply photography in their clinical work and to what degree their use of photography in a therapeutic context is different from how it is used by other mental health professionals, psychoanalysts, family therapists, counsellors, ergotherapists, etc.

I introduced the idea of conducting a study of various forms of artistic and therapeutic use of photography by art therapists to George Platts from the United Kingdom who is a registered art therapist and multimedia artist strongly linked to photography and video-art. He was inspired by the idea and as a result, helped me to circulate a questionnaire in the UK.

First of all, however, I would like to present some ideas that will facilitate an understanding of why photography can be considered a potentially powerful tool for clients in art therapy in the 'digital era'.

The nature and the role of 'technical images' from a cultural anthropological viewpoint

Some time ago the Czech-born philosopher Vilem Flusser (2008) paid attention to the phenomenon of so-called 'technical images'; that is, images created with the application of technical devices such as photographic cameras. Recognising the increasing influence of these images on humanity, he claimed that the general culture experienced a profound change. Further, Flusser, on describing the mechanisms that support and define industrialised modern culture, argued that, whereas ideas were previously interpreted by written accounts, the invention of photography allowed the creation of images (ideas) to be taken at face value as truth, not interpretation, in a way that can be endlessly replicated and spread worldwide. The influence of 'technical images' on people seems increasingly important as images not only establish universal codes of modern culture but they also overcome language barriers. They accompany people in their everyday lives and become general denominators for art, science and even politics (in the sense of general values). 'Technical images' also promote connections and dialogue between people and communities, on the one hand, and highlight the risk of erosion of local cultures, on the other.

My own presumption, based on Flusser's ideas on 'technical images', is that such images also serve as a tool for creating a virtual reality (cyber-reality) as 'dwelling environments' of modern people, as well as becoming powerful tools of the socialisation process, serving as instruments for the construction of psychosocial identities. Finally, 'technical images' may be considered to establish visual cultural texts that provide people with behavioural programmes. Since visual images, unlike speech, tackle not only consciousness but the unconscious as well, they are capable of overcoming psychological defences and their influence can be very profound and long lasting. Early familiarisation of modern children with various means of technical communication and self-expression (computers, mobile phones, digital cameras) is one of the significant factors contributing to mental and physical development. Further, the important role of technical images in the formation of the psychosocial identity of the modern person can be seen from the point of view of the concept 'symbolical interactionism', which considers the operation of symbolical representative systems as the key factor for establishing and changing people's notions about the world and themselves.

The second of my personal presumptions is that the influence of 'technical images' on the existential, spiritual and sexual drives of modern people is becoming increasingly important. The creation and use of these images can give people the sensation of managing time, because 'technical images' can 'conserve' the reality. The 'temptation' of omnipotence and the control over reality, human relations, one's own mental processes, as well as others', not to mention various objects, by their reflection in the 'universe' of 'technical images' (a cyber-reality, the media environment) is typical for many modern people. To commemorate oneself in this universe is one of the most desired existential goals. And it is through reaching this goal that fear of personal physical and spiritual annihilation can be diminished. 'Technical images' that can be infinitely duplicated reflect the reproduction or 'cloning' process. In turn, the creation and accumulation of 'technical images' that reflect both individual physical characteristics and the experience of the person can be considered a peculiar form of realising one's sexual–erotic desire. Creation and use of 'technical images' can be considered similar to that of play as they allow 'playing' with reality and its visible displays, combining different elements of reality with each other through the creation of other fantastic realities.

It is natural to believe that the creative drives of modern people can be satisfied through their use of 'technical images'. Thus, like many other tools and products of civilisation, 'technical images' tackle fundamental problems of modern people's lives, their deep motives and fears. Today, 'technical images' are inseparably linked with the development of persons and communities in their dynamic exchanges with each other. Such images are also closely connected with play and creative activities. Through the concerns of the phenomenon of 'technical images' and the creation and perception of visual images, we see the close connections with other art forms, such as music, role game, body expression and movement, and storytelling.

Therefore, understanding the influence of 'technical images' and information technology, as a whole, on art therapists and their clients appears to be very important. I believe, however, that such understanding demands an interdisciplinary approach and application of different theoretical perspectives: for example, the philosophical, anthropological, cultural, sociological, psychological, psychosemantic.

Why photography can be important for art therapy clients

Fryrear and Corbit's book (1992) is one of the early examples of integrating photographic images into art therapy process. Central to their procedure of work with active imagination is the 'graphic elaboration' technique, when the subject of the photo is cut out from the background and glued to a piece of drawing paper (see Photos 12.1 and 12.2). The client is then encouraged to elaborate on the image in various ways. Wadeson (2002) refers to the art therapy work of Bettina Thorn (1998), who combined writing with photography and art in a phototherapy group she established at a psychosocial rehabilitation facility. The group visited locations around the city in order to take photographs. Through photography, art and writing members of the group learned new skills that improved their self-esteem and confidence. In her pioneering work with photographic images Landgarten (1994) explored photo collage as a quick and economical way to evoke descriptive accounts and ventilate cross-cultural themes. Art therapist Barbee (2002) presents a visual-narrative approach, which he used with a small group of transgender clients in San Francisco. Participants were asked to photograph their 'gender story'. Photographs later became the basis for open-ended interviews leading to a narrative portrayal of participants' experiences. In Barbee's study, photographs proved a valuable stimulus for eliciting individual meanings of transsexual experience. Andreyeva (2007, 2008) used the visual-narrative approach in her clinical practice while she was a student at the post-graduate diploma course in art therapy in St Petersburg. She conducted a brief art therapy with ex-offenders discharged from prisons and who

Photo 12.1 Graphic elaborations of a photographic technique (Kopytin).

were undertaking a rehabilitation programme. Andreyeva accompanied her clients on their way through the city according to the route and goals discussed in advance. Clients took photos and she recorded their verbal narratives for analysis and in-depth discussion in the following sessions. An art therapy graduate, Ashastina (2006) presented an original method of using photography in individual art-psychotherapy. In order to help her client to cope with psychological crisis, she asked her to make photographs of the interior of her house. This practice promoted in-depth discussion and revealed the clients' attitudes to her present and future relationships and eventually helped her to rearrange her living space according to her needs. Sventsitskaya (2006) led interactive art therapy groups in a closed psychiatric unit and used various photographic techniques. Some techniques included written narratives and dramatic enactments based on images chosen by patients from photographs and photo collages. Svistovskaya also introduced a wide range of activities based on the use of photographic images in art therapy groups with children with behavioural disorders (Kopytin and Svistovskaya, 2006), as well as in her individual art therapy with an anorexic fifteen-year-old girl (Svistovskaya, 2008).

Photo 12.2 Graphic elaborations of a photographic technique (Kopytin).

Bogachov (2008) presented his work with drug abusers, implementing photographs of his clients as a significant resource, stimulating self-disclosure and insight into interactive art therapy groups. Additionally, there exist publications by art therapists on therapeutic application of video, which may help us to understand how photography may be beneficial (Henley, 1992; McNiff, 2004). David Henley in particular (1992) used video with the developmentally and learning impaired. He indicates that video can 'encourage therapeutic insight and reflection' through 'attending behaviour, cause and effect and language development' (Henley, 1992: 442).

McNiff (2004) writes on video enactment in the expressive therapies. He makes some useful points as to how video may promote self-understanding and self-organisation in clients. In a similar way, photography may have a similar effect. His idea of self-confrontation through art is especially useful in that 'the immediate reply of a real-life process made possible through video technology allows this confrontation to happen in a way that cuts through verbal defences, perceptual denial, wishful and idealised self-images' (McNiff, 2004: 244). Through photography, as through video-documentary, clients may feel validated. McNiff (2004) also writes about the different ways of implementing video in an expressive arts therapy context. One of the ways is when video is just used in the service of other arts, or for feedback. Another way of implementing video into an expressive arts therapy context is when video recording becomes art in itself.

The above writings indicate that art therapists sometimes use photography in the forms that belong to phototherapy or therapeutic photography; for instance, when they ask their clients to take photographs and later discuss their memories and feelings evoked by pictures (Andreyeva 2005, 2008; Ashastina, 2006; Barbee, 2002). However, sometimes they also introduce certain forms of artistic activities in their work with clients that are more typical for art therapy, such as photo-collage of 'graphic elaboration' techniques (Fryrear and Corbit, 1992; Landgarten, 1994).

The convergent agreement of the literature does state that the goal of using photography in art therapy can be very different and may include:

- stimulating and expressing feelings;
- recognising needs and feelings, integrating unconscious material into consciousness;
- improving self-esteem and promoting self-acceptance, strengthening the ego and its boundaries;
- empowering, stimulating activity, self-directedness and ability to be responsible for one's actions;
- developing spontaneity and ability to experiment with new roles and experiences;
- developing interests and motivations, recognising one's attitudes, beliefs and values;
- improving interpersonal competence – ability to accept and understand others and to be involved in constructive interaction with others;
- improving skills in collaborative activity;
- recognising and accepting group norms and values, universality of problems and experiences.

The study

The questionnaire

In order to explore the scope of the use of photography by art therapists, as well as their experience and beliefs with regard to photography as a creative and therapeutic instrument, a special questionnaire was developed and sent to practitioners in the UK and Russia (Kopytin, Platts). One of the rationales for selecting questions was, on the one hand to explore the link between art therapists' personal interest in photography as a cultural phenomenon and expressive medium, and on the other hand, its use by art therapists in their clinical work with clients/patients. A hypothesis was that there is a correlation between personal involvement in photography in art therapists' lives and their tendency to use it in clinical work. Another presumption was that it is not only personal involvement in photography on the part of art therapists and their artistic skills that contributes to art therapists' attitudes regarding clinical applications of photography, but also various contextual factors (such as systems of art therapy training, a degree of orthodoxy of the professional community, prevailing therapeutic approaches). One of the target groups of our study included state-registered art therapists from the UK. Since there is no such profession as art therapy in the Russian Federation, the second target group comprised psychologists and psychotherapists in this country who had completed specialised post-graduate diploma courses in art therapy and used artistic expressions of their clients to reach therapeutic goals.

Findings

As was expected, 100 per cent of the thirty-three British respondents had completed artistic training before coming to the profession of art therapy and many of them continued to practise visual arts after qualifying as an art therapist. There were twenty-nine females and four males, with experience of working as art therapists ranging from two to seventeen years.

As for the Russian part of the study, twenty-four members of RATA responded to the questionnaire. Since artistic education is not considered to be a strict requirement in order to be accepted for most post-graduate courses in art therapy in Russia and to become a member of RATA, only three persons among the twenty-four respondents, were artists or art teachers. Since most trainees in art therapy had little artistic experience, a considerable part of their post-graduate training in art therapy included developing their artistic skills. There were twenty-two females and two males, with experience of working in art therapy from two to nine years.

Age when respondents first become aware of photography and involved with photography creatively

Most British and Russian respondents indicated that they first became aware of photography and made their first photographs (of family members, friends, animals) between five and seven years of age (75 per cent of respondents). Some indicated that this happened either before five or after seven years. Many respondents became more actively involved with photography creatively in their adolescent years. Many got their first personal camera at this time. Some respondents emphasised the role of their parents in their involvement with photography. As one of them indicated:

> My father was very passionate about photography so it was an important part of my life from a young age. Our kitchen was frequently converted into a darkroom, much to my mom's dismay . . . My father used to allow me to hand-paint his black-and-white photographs, hence my introduction to art (family photograph album contains lots of lucid photographs: I gave everyone rosy cheeks and lips and blue eye shadow, males and females!).

For some respondents the source of their inspiration was not only making photographs, but their perception as well. One of the art therapists responded by stating she first become aware of photography when she was about three:

> I was probably influenced by the traditional Victorian/Edwardian photographic portraits that hung in my grandmother's house. I used to wonder about those

pictures and the people captured in them who seemed to still be overlooking the household and all that went on within it. During my early childhood, the camera was used for special occasions – weddings, Christmas, family gatherings and rare summer holidays. The photos only recorded 'the good things'.

The use of photography while being at art school(s): art therapy training and artistic activities of respondents

Many British respondents frequently used photography as a supplementary or even main instrument of their artistic work while being at art school(s) before coming to the profession of art therapy. One of the respondents, who practised art therapy for seventeen years and graduated from Winchester School of Art and Design in the 1970s indicated that while at the school she 'used photos for her own sake, planning and experimenting with painting, photo etchings using either new or old photos'.

One of the art therapists, who also undertook her artistic training in the1970s, wrote that while at art school she made recordings of performances, treating them as moving images that could be frozen in a particular environment. Another respondent indicated that while at the London College of Printing in 1982 she began to use photography more creatively, making photomontages. For her final project she illustrated a fairly short story using images of children, animals and photographs she had taken in India with this in mind.

The British respondents' answers are indicative of their applications of photography as a significant instrument in their artistic work. The ways of creative use of photography and photographic images are very different and include using photography to record artworks, performances and interesting forms such as objects and colours, and making installations with photographic images. Photographic images are also often used as a stimulus for the personal artistic endeavours of art therapists. Some of the respondents indicated that they used mobile phone cameras in their artistic endeavours, valuing this new tool; as one respondent said:

> The restrictions of this tiny camera along with the immediacy of its accessibility have shaped my imagery as an artist. I didn't expect this and am beginning to really appreciate the unique visual perspective that it has enabled me to create – and to reflect upon.

Unlike their British counterparts only three of twenty-four Russian respondents had artistic training, but many of them developed their artistic skills while taking art therapy training. Though most respondents had no formal artistic education they used photography creatively – at least, from time to time making photographs of those objects and situations that are interesting for them. Only a few respondents use photography creatively on a regular basis.

It can be concluded, however, that the ways of using photography and photographic images in personal artistic activities of the Russian respondents did not seem to be as varied and sophisticated as those of their British counterparts, a factor that could be linked to the lack of artistic education.

The use of photography in art therapy practice

While answering the question, in what ways they have used photography or photographic images in their work with clients/patients, thirty of thirty-three British respondents claimed that they used it in one way or another. However, the absolute majority of them (thirty-one) used photography mostly for recording clients'/patients' art. Some of the respondents indicated that they made photographs of their clients' art during the whole art therapy process and put photographs in clients' personal portfolios, in order to make changes more observable, 'a metaphor for personal change and growth', as one therapist explains.

A considerable number of respondents (33 per cent) indicated that they often use photographs in their art therapy work with clients/patients as a material for making collages. Two of them also wrote that they sometimes let their clients bring photographs from their homes and then use these photographs in order to find significant images and themes for discussion in a session or as a stimulus for their artwork. However, they do this only when clients bring photographs on their own initiative.

Six of the thirty-three British respondents indicated that they used clients' personal photographs to stimulate memories and reflection of past and current situations. One of the art therapists wrote about how she invites her clients to draw an imaginary family photographic portrait. Another respondent indicated that he used photographic images in his work in an NHS community service with children and adolescents with learning difficulties, most often, as part of the ending:

> I ask my clients to take photos of each other, their art pieces and the art therapy setting, which I/we then make into a book, sometimes with words documenting the art therapy process. This was particularly helpful with children, especially those I had worked with for some time, but this also felt appropriate and helpful for some adults. I also took photographs of children during their therapy, which allowed us to keep a visual record of their process and progress. These regular photography sessions were easily anticipated and were particularly helpful for children with very low self-esteem. I now work in a studio setting (Studio Upstairs) where photography is used to record exhibitions . . . Photographs are also used as subject for art work, either photos that have a particular appeal or relate to past personal experience. I consider all the above uses of photography to have clinical value, but perhaps particularly, those with children and people with learning difficulties, for whom 'being seen' is a complex, often negative experience. Photography also provides a concrete correlate to the therapy process, and may act as a transitional object(s) binding the gap between the presence and absence of the therapist.

What was interesting was that only one respondent invited his clients to use photography as an artistic medium. He presented an example of this way of using photography with depressive clients, where he suggested photographing clouds. He claims:

> It was effective, as the resulting images stun people with their beauty. Reminds people that the world is very beautiful if you keep your eyes open, and that seeing and responding are part of what keeps us real and functioning!

In addition to using photography for recording artworks and the clients' artistic process, one of the respondents also used it as a valuable source of information in her clinical research and when teaching art therapy. One other respondent also wrote that working as a supervisor she often invites supervisees to bring photographs with them representing various situations in the art therapy process.

As their British counterparts, the Russian respondents use photography mostly for recording their clients'/patients' artwork (twenty persons, 83 per cent of respondents). A considerable number of them use photographic images for collage making (eighteen persons, 75 per cent of respondents). Fourteen respondents (58 per cent) also used photographic images for reflection on and discussion of various life situations of their clients/patients. Other applications of photography included the use of photographic images as a stimulus for their client's artistic expression, and creating narratives were indicated by four persons (33 per cent of respondents). As some of the ways of using photography with her clients (children and adolescents), one respondent indicated coming out of the art therapy studio and walking around the therapeutic centre with autistic children in order to let them take photographs, recording artistic activities of behaviourally disturbed adolescents in order to discuss photographs with them later, making photo-collages and photographs while working with young people, as well as discussing photographs that reflect changes throughout the course of therapy.

One respondent wrote:

> At present I use photography seldom in my art therapy work though I understand its rich possibilities. I presume that it is because I run interactive art therapy groups at the psychotherapy department of the hospital of war veterans, where clients' stay is very limited. Clients bring personal photographs to the department only on rare occasions and most of them are uncomfortable when someone takes pictures of them while they are in the hospital. I noticed that most of them also dislike video recording during sessions and when I ask for their permission to record their activities many of them are suspicious and refuse to be photographed. Though such negative attitude towards photographic and video recording in sessions slowly diminishes throughout the course of group work such negative reactions together with the limited stay in the hospital are main reasons why I don't make photographs of groups often. Clients mostly use photographic images from magazines for collage making.

Making photographs of various objects and situations by clients/patients in Russian art therapists' work appears to take place more often than in their British counterparts' work. Also, collage making and using photographs for reflection and discussion appear to be more popular among Russian clients/patients than among British clients, according to respondents' answers.

Plans for the future

While answering the question whether they consider making use of photography or photographic images in clinical work in the future, most of the British respondents (thirty-one) indicated that they are interested in using photography and searching for new ways of clinical application. However, some of them wrote that they are unsure how this could be done.

One art therapist indicated that she didn't use photography in her clinical work at all. However, she wrote that she would be interested in conducting a study in art psychotherapy and possibly using photography together with other media. Another art therapist wrote that she had been trying to establish a digital studio for a number of years. One other respondent wrote that 'photography is a creative process that adds another media/dimension to the scope of image making in art therapy. I also find myself wishing for a creative computer package as part of an art therapy room provision.'

One Russian respondent mentioned that she is interested in making photographs with therapeutic purposes; in particular, making photographic portraits and self-portraits of her clients using make-up and costumes. Another respondent indicated the following:

> In my individual work with clients I'm going to use their personal photographs for discussion and possibly implement other ways of using photographs. I'm unsure how I could use photography in my work with groups, but going to consider its possibilities, in particular, after this questionnaire. I understand the rich potential of photography with regard to art therapy and that it is still underestimated by many art therapists.

Conclusion

Intercultural differences

The study confirmed that photography does not play a significant role as an expressive medium in current art therapy practice, either in the UK or the Russian Federation. At the same time it is quite often used as a means of documentation that reflects therapeutic process and makes changes in clients'/patients' artistic expression more observable. Taking into account the limited number of specialists in both countries who responded to the questionnaire, it is interesting that the scope of practices involving photography in one or other form appears to be wide. Some of them demonstrate that art therapists and those with whom they work can indeed be very innovative and produce interesting expressive forms, satisfying various clients' needs.

The findings showed certain differences between British and Russian art therapists with regard to their artistic experience and familiarity with various professional artistic media. Comparing the answers of the British and Russian respondents, it can be observed that the Russian specialists use relatively simple ways of using photography in their own creative activities and the scope of these ways is not wide as in the artistic activities of their British counterparts. At the same time, the Russian respondents' answers are indicative of a variety of ways of using photography and photographic images therapeutically. The Russian respondents allow their clients/patients to take photographs of different objects and use collage making and photos for discussion and as a stimulus for clients'/patients' artwork quite often.

Different ways of practising art therapy and psychotherapy in general in the UK and Russian Federation should also be taken into account. While British art therapy and psychotherapy in general is more rooted in psychoanalysis, Russian art therapy and psychotherapy demonstrate variability of theoretical backgrounds and ways of practice, and often strong affiliation with cognitive-behavioural and clinical-psychiatric approaches.

Our impression is that British art therapists are more non-directive in their work with clients than their Russian counterparts and rely more on their clients' choice of artistic media. Another difference between the ways of therapeutic application of photography in art therapists' work in both countries is that Russian specialists are more inclined to use integrative art forms. Their responses indicate that they more often combine visual media and photography, in particular, with dramatic enactments, storytelling and a narrative approach than their British colleagues.

Obstacles for using photography in art therapy practice

Three respondents in our study indicated that they do not use photography often in their clinical work owing to ethical considerations and that making photographs of clients while they are involved in art work seems to be violating their personal boundaries and interfering with the creative process. As another significant obstacle to using photography as a creative medium with their clients, five British respondents indicated the need for certain technical competence and self-control on the part of clients. They believe that traditional art media provide more spontaneity and tactile stimulation for clients.

One art therapist wrote that she uses photography only to record clients' images and had never considered using photography for the people she worked with simply because it is not a medium she is comfortable with herself. As another respondent claimed he would readily work with photographic material brought or suggested by the client, but would be unlikely to suggest it himself, because 'too much technical stuff gets in the way'; he does not have facilities or computer hard/software for digital photography; and he is 'personally ambivalent towards the medium'. Three British respondents indicated the limited financial resources of the NHS in which they currently work to be one of the main obstacles to using photography more often in their clinical practice, because they cannot provide an art therapy studio with the technical media needed.

A certain discrepancy between the active use of photography in their own artistic activities and the comparatively limited scope of its applications in clinical practice by the British respondents can be noticed. The majority of them use photography and photographic images mostly for recording artworks and the clients' artistic process. Our impression is that the vast possibilities of photography, which art therapists use when involved in their own creative activities, are underestimated by them when they work with their clients/patients.

Only on rare occasions did respondents invite some of their clients to use photography as one form of expression. Perhaps most art therapists believe that those ways of working with photography and photographic images, which they practise as artists, can be too sophisticated for their clients/patients and require special skills and knowledge of modern art.

Another obstacle to the use of photography and photographic images in clinical practice can be the absence or insufficiency of relevant information and instructions in the ways of their clinical application in current art therapy education and literature. Art therapy training and publications concentrate on 'traditional' artistic media such as painting, clay work, etc., and various art media and practices including computers, video-art, etc. as ways of working with clients are discussed only on rare occasions. It is obvious that such innovative art media and practices, which most British art therapists are quite familiar with as they have attended art schools, cannot be mechanically brought from the postmodern art milieu into clinical situations, and need sufficient theoretical and experimental support from art therapists before they can become routine practice.

References

Andreyeva, T. (2007). The use of visual–narrative approach with ex-offenders. *The Healing Art: International Journal of Art Therapy*, 10(1), 4–29 (in Russian).

Andreyeva, T. (2008). The use of visual–narrative approach in rehabilitation of ex-offenders. In: A. Kopytin (ed.), *Practical Art Therapy: Treatment, rehabilitation, training* (pp. 133–160). Moscow: Cogito-Center (in Russian).

Ashastina, E. (2006). Working with an image of a house. In: A. Kopytin (ed.), *Phototherapy: The use of photography in psychological practice* (pp. 132–161). Moscow: Cogito-Center (in Russian).

Barbee, M. (2002). A visual-narrative approach to understanding transsexual identity. *Art Therapy: Journal of the American Art Therapy Association*, 19(2), 53–62.

Bogachov, O. (2008). The use of photographs in art therapy with the drug addicted. Paper presented at the 10th Annual Conference of Russian Art Therapy Association, 17–18 May 2008, St Petersburg.

Flusser, V. (2008). *In Favor of Philosophy of Photography*. St Petersburg: St Petersburg University.

Fryrear, J.L. and Corbit, I.E. (1992). *Photo Art Therapy: A Jungian perspective*. Springfield, IL: Charles C. Thomas.

Henley, D.R. (1992). Therapeutic and aesthetic application of video with the developmentally disabled. *The Arts in Psychotherapy*, 18, 441–447.

Kopytin, A. and Svistovskaya, E. (2006). *Art Therapy with Children and Adolescents*. Moscow: Cogito-Center (in Russian).

Landgarten, H. (1994). Magazine photo collage as a multicultural treatment and assessment technique. *Art Therapy: Journal of the American Art Therapy Association*, 11(3), 218–219.

Liebmann, M. (1986). *Art Therapy for Groups: A handbook of themes, games and exercises*. London: Croom Helm.

McNiff, S. (2004). *Art Heals: How creativity cures the soul*. Boston, MA: Shambhala.

Sventsitskaya, V. (2006). Experience of the use of elements of photography in the work with psychiatric patients. In: Kopytin, A. (ed.), *Phototherapy: The use of photography in psychological practice* (pp. 113–131). Moscow: Cogito-Center (in Russian).

Svistovskaya, E. (2008). A case of art therapy treatment of an anorectic adolescent girl. In: Kopytin, A. (ed.), *Practical Art Therapy: Treatment, rehabilitation, training* (pp. 74–86). Moscow: Cogito-Center (in Russian).

Thorn, B. (1998). Picture this: Phototherapy with chronic mentally ill adults. Unpublished Master's thesis, University of Illinois at Chicago.

Wadeson, H. (2002). Confronting polarization in art therapy. *Art Therapy: Journal of the American Art Therapy Association*, 19(2), 77–84.

Weiner, D. (1999). *Beyond Talk Therapy: Using movement and expressive techniques in clinical practice*. Washington, DC: American Psychological Association.

Part III

Research and the future

Chapter 13

Phototherapy and neuroscience
Marriage, cohabitation or divorce?

Hasse Karlsson

Abstract

The outcome of psychotherapy and the mechanisms of change that are related to its effects have traditionally been investigated on the psychological and social levels; for example, by measuring change in symptoms, psychological abilities, personality or social functioning, or in the experiential domain in single case studies. During the past few decades, however, it has become clear that all mental processes derive from operations of the brain (Kandel, 1998). This means that changes in our psychological processes are reflected by changes in the functions or structures of the brain. Although it would be plausible to study the neurobiological effects of phototherapy, because of its use of visual material and sometimes also meaningful motor activity in the therapy process, no studies on this have been published so far. In this chapter I will review the field, exploring the effects of psychotherapy on the brain, and then discuss its possibilities in phototherapy.

Introduction

A relatively new finding is that the brain is more plastic than has been acknowledged before. Changes in the brain in relation to experience have been detected at the cellular and molecular levels in animals using different experimental approaches. These plastic changes, however, in the human brain have been difficult to study. The advent of functional neuroimaging, including SPECT, PET and fMRI has made it possible to study changes at the brain systems level (e.g. by measuring changes in brain blood flow or metabolism), but increasingly also on the molecular level, using SPECT and PET in the living human brain and probing, for example, changes in the receptor systems. This has opened the field up to the innovative study of the effects of different psychotherapies on a biological level. The idea behind this approach is that psychotherapy engages processes that can be studied biologically; for instance, by using brain imaging technologies, such as emotional expression and regulation, learning, memory and self-experience. There is also increasing knowledge of the neurobiology of these functions in the human brain. However, phototherapy occupies additional functions in visual and motor systems, making its comparison with other forms of psychotherapy especially interesting.

Interestingly, the visual and emotional systems are extensively interconnected (Tamietto and de Gelder, 2010), making psychotherapies that make use of visual material especially interesting, because emotion processing usually has been considered to be one of the main vehicles for change in psychotherapy. One could argue that the use of emotionally meaningful visual material could enhance emotion processing. For the same reasons, these therapies would be good candidates for neuroimaging, where the neural bases of emotion and emotion processing are current focuses of interest. Unfortunately, there has been very little interest in neuroimaging in the field of psychotherapy, and in the field of phototherapy especially.

This probably reflects the traditional distinction between biological and humanistic research areas, and the somewhat outdated idea that their methods are different, answer different questions and should be kept distinct. However, new integrative concepts and approaches are emerging, one example of this being the emergence of Integrative Neuroscience, an area of research that attempts to bring together biological, psychological and clinical models of the human brain (Gordon, 2000). In these new approaches efforts have been made to break down the boundaries of different disciplines, and to foster free and innovative exchange of information between them. So far, there are more than 100 published papers on the neurobiology of emotion. Currently, it seems that it is possible to make a distinction between the basic emotions (anger, fear, sadness, happiness, disgust) on the brain level (for a recent meta-analysis about this, see Vytal and Hamann, 2010). This means that the different emotion states are associated with characteristic patterns of brain activity. An even newer research area is 'social neuroscience', which aims to map the neural underpinnings of human interaction. This area, however, poses additional methodological and conceptual challenges that owing to constraints will not be discussed in this chapter (see for example, Adolphs, 2010).

Why, then, should we study the brain in relation to psychotherapy? One reason is that this approach will in the future give us a more refined understanding of how different psychotherapies work. It is of course possible to study the mechanisms of different treatments on different 'levels' (biological, psychological, social). However, the human organ that has so far been completely lacking in psychotherapy research is the brain. And by this I mean the study of the biological functions of the brain that are relevant for psychotherapy.

These studies could in the future lead to the possibility of targeting treatments more accurately; for example, in relation to the patient's prevailing mood state that causes suffering. In addition, neurobiological research will help refine and verify or falsify psychological theories about the change processes. For example, a psychological theory could make claims about functions of the mind that are biologically impossible. In this way biology can restrict the possibilities of psychological reasoning; but also, the other way around, neuroimaging can verify traditional psychological concepts relating, for example, to traumatic experiences (Sherin and Nemeroff, 2011).

How does psychotherapy change the brain?

So far, about twenty studies on brain changes after psychotherapy for depression, anxiety disorders and borderline personality disorder have been published since 1992. In the first study, the researchers treated patients suffering from obsessive-compulsive disorder with SSRI-medication or behaviour therapy. The two interventions demonstrated similar changes, especially in the caudate. Published studies suggest that cognitive-behaviour therapy (CBT), dialectic behaviour therapy (DBT), psychodynamic psychotherapy and interpersonal psychotherapy (IPT) alter brain function in patients suffering from major depressive disorder (MDD) (Brody *et al.*, 2001; Martin *et al.*, 2001; Goldapple *et al.*, 2004), obsessive–compulsive disorder (OCD) (Baxter *et al.*, 1992; Schwartz *et al.*, 1996; Nakatani *et al.*, 2003), panic disorder (PD) (Praško *et al.*, 2004; Beutel *et al.*, 2010), social anxiety disorder (Furmark *et al.*, 2002), specific phobia (Paquette *et al.*, 2003; Straube *et al.*, 2006), post-traumatic stress disorder (PTSD) (Felmingham *et al.*, 2007) and borderline personality disorder (BPD) (Schnell and Herpetz, 2007; Lai *et al.*, 2007). Interestingly, these psychotherapies are mainly talking therapies. However, an important question is, in what ways do psychotherapies that use visual material and action differ in their effects on the brain compared with traditional talking therapies?

The majority of studies have reported similar brain changes after psychotherapy and medication. This finding could be interpreted to reflect the idea that the brain recovers in a similar way regardless of the treatment modality. However, recent studies have shown clear differences between different treatment modalities. In the study by Goldapple *et al.* (2004), treatment response for CBT among patients with MDD was associated with increases in metabolism in the hippocampus and dorsal cingulate, and decreases in the dorsal, ventral and medial frontal cortex. This pattern was clearly distinct from the pattern caused by paroxetine, which included increases in metabolism in prefrontal areas and decrease in hippocampus and subgenual cingulate. Also, a recent study from my group (Karlsson *et al.*, 2010) found clear differences on the molecular level between short-term psychodynamic psychotherapy (STPP) and fluoxetine medication.

Currently, however, we know little about the differences between different forms of psychotherapies. To date, the studies comparing active treatments have investigated the differences between psychotherapy and drug treatment. Further, some studies have looked at differences between treated patients and patients put on a waiting list.

Do these studies help us to understand the mechanisms of psychotherapy?

The basic aim of neuroimaging in the area of psychotherapy, one would think, should be to better understand the mechanisms that lead to changes in psychotherapy. The mechanisms can be studied on different levels (biological, psychological, social) and neuroimaging could provide us with additional understanding of these processes. In addition, just in reporting brain changes in relation to psychotherapies, these recent studies have made it possible to construct models that at least partly explain the mechanisms of change that the different treatments cause. These models can then be compared with the traditional psychological theories of these psychotherapies.

One possibility is to investigate through mapping the underlying phenomena that are the targets of change in psychotherapy. Thus, many psychotherapies attempt to enhance the patients' problem-solving capacities, self-representation and regulation of emotion. Something is known about the brain areas that play a role in these functions; they include the dorsolateral prefrontal cortex, ventral anterior cingulate cortex, dorsal anterior cingulate cortex, ventral and dorsal subregions of the medial prefrontal cortex, the posterior cingulate cortex, the precuneus, the insular cortex, the amygdala and ventrolateral prefrontal cortex (for a review, see Frewen *et al.*, 2008). More specifically, the effectiveness of, for example, cognitive therapy among patients suffering from depression could operate by bolstering prefrontal function involved in cognitive control of emotion, while antidepressant medication operates more directly on the amygdala, which has to do with the generation of negative emotion (DeRubeis *et al.*, 2008).

As one of the major hypotheses on the effect of CBT on brain functioning concerns a more effective, 'top-down' regulation of hyperexcitable limbic structures by prefrontal control systems, it seems that psychodynamic psychotherapy may also function at least partly via these mechanisms. The results of Beutel *et al.* (2010) are in line with this hypothesis, demonstrating both a frontal deactivation and an amygdala/hippocampal hyperactivation in symptomatic patients suffering from panic disorder, which were normalised when panic symptoms and anxiety levels were reduced following treatment.

Affective hyperarousal is the hallmark of borderline personality disorder (BPD) and the main target for dialectic-behavioural-therapy (DBT). This should mean that this treatment should lead to a decrease in the activity in relation to emotional stimuli in the brain areas that serve these functions. This was indeed found in the study by Schnell and Herpertz (2007), where a decreased hemodynamic response after DBT to negative stimuli in the right-sided anterior cingulate, temporal and posterior cingulate cortices, as well as in the left insula was found among patients suffering from BPD.

Molecular level studies

The previously referred studies have investigated the brain changes on the whole brain systems level, measuring either changes in blood flow or in brain metabolism. In order to understand the more basic mechanisms related to psychotherapy, possible molecular and cellular changes should also be studied. So far, only two Finnish studies have measured molecular level changes after psychotherapy, and in this way directly tested the hypothesis put forth by Eric Kandel. Kandel (1998) hypothesised that psychotherapy leads to changes in gene expression through learning, by altering the strength of synaptic connections between nerve cells and inducing morphological changes in neurons (Kandel, 1998). Interestingly, in both studies, the psychotherapy used was psychodynamic. In the study by Lehto *et al.* (2008), nineteen depressive outpatients received psychodynamic psychotherapy for twelve months. Of the subjects, eight were classified as having atypical depression. Midbrain serotonin transporter (SERT) and striatum dopamine transporter (DAT) densities were recorded using single photon emission computed tomography (SPECT) brain imaging with the [123I]nor-ß-CIT radioligand before and after psychotherapy. The researchers showed that midbrain SERT density significantly increased during psychotherapy in patients suffering from atypical depression, but not among non atypicals. There were no changes in the levels of DAT. Owing to the subgroup finding, these results are difficult to interpret, and one of the shortcomings of this study is the lack of a control group. In the other Finnish study, patients with MDD were randomised to receive either short-term psychodynamic psychotherapy or fluoxetine medication and scanned with PET using [carbonyl-11C] WAY-100635 (measures the density of 5-HT1A receptors) and [11C]raclopride (measures density of D2/3 receptors) before and after a four-month treatment. In the two published papers (Karlsson *et al.*, 2010; Hirvonen *et al.*, 2011), the researchers show that although the clinical outcome in both treatment groups was similar in terms of standard symptom ratings (59 per cent of the subjects reaching remission and 77 per cent of the subjects meeting the criteria for response), analysis of the change in the 5-HT1A receptor density in the treatment groups revealed a significant increase in the psychotherapy group compared to the medication group where no change was detected. However fluoxetine but not psychotherapy increased [11C]raclopride binding in lateral thalamus, in comparison to no change in the psychotherapy group.

Several previous studies have found changes in 5-HT1A receptor binding in MDD (Drevets *et al.*, 1999; Sargent *et al.*, 2000; Bhagwagar *et al.*, 2004; Parsey *et al.*, 2006) that is not reversed by SSRI treatment (Sargent *et al.*, 2000; Bhagwagar *et al.*, 2004; Moses-Kolko *et al.*, 2007). The most common finding has been that the density of these receptors is lowered among patients; however, studies reporting higher densities have been published. This could mean that the recovery process in MDD after psychotherapy is different from recovery after medication. Currently, the clinical implications of these findings are unknown, but they could be related to the finding that the relapse rate in MDD patients may be lower in those treated with psychotherapy compared to those treated with antidepressant medication (Hollon *et al.*, 2006).

Discussion

Although our subjective psychological life is reflected in on-going brain functions, any straightforward reductionistic stance aiming to reduce our psychological life to a predetermined dance of molecules is unfounded, as there is clear evidence that our subjective experiences affect the brain (Gabbard, 2000). This means that in addition to our genetic makeup, individual experiences also change our brains and makes us uniquely individual.

Although still preliminary, the studies using neuroimaging in measuring change caused by psychotherapy will in the long run lead to a more fine-grained understanding of how different forms of psychotherapy work. This may lead to a development in which, in the future, specific modes of psychotherapy can be designed to target specific brain circuits (Gabbard, 2000) and related symptoms or patterns of behaviour. Additionally, neurobiological research may help to refine psychological theories about the change processes.

Phototherapy would be an ideal candidate for neurobiological research because it probably affects larger brain areas than traditional psychotherapies by using visual input and activity doing as parts of the therapy process. It is also probable that there are differences in the intensity or nature of the process by which the use of personal photos induces emotional experiences. It would be interesting to study the neurobiological mechanisms behind this.

One could argue that it is difficult to grasp the uniquely individual experiences and process that are on-going in different psychotherapies. This is probably true and it may be that this part of the story is unavailable to this approach. At the same time, it is also likely, that there are common mechanisms between different individual psychotherapy processes – and these are, in principle, also open for neurobiological research.

In conclusion, opportunities seem to exist for a serious relationship between neuroscience and phototherapy. Currently, however, they are not even dating.

References

Adolphs, R. (2010). Conceptual challenges and directions for social neuroscience. *Neuron*, 65, 752–767.

Baxter, L.R., Schwartz, J.M., Bergman, K.S., Szuba, M.P., Guze, B.H., Mazziotta, J.C. *et al.* (1992). Caudate glucose metabolic rate changes with both drug and behavior therapy for obsessive–compulsive disorder. *Archives of General Psychiatry*, 49, 681–689.

Beutel, M.E., Stark, R., Pan, H., Silbersweig, D. and Dietrich, S. (2010). Changes of brain activation pre-post short-term psychodynamic inpatient psychotherapy: An fMRI study of panic disorder patients. *Psychiatry Research: Neuroimaging*, 184, 96–104.

Bhagwagar, Z., Cowen, P.J., Goodwin, G.M. and Harmer, C.J. (2004). Normalization of enhanced fear recognition by acute SSRI treatment in subjects with a previous history of depression. *American Journal of Psychiatry*, 161, 166–168.

Brody, A.L., Saxena, S., Stoessel, P., Gillies, L.A., Fairbanks, L.A., Alborzian, S. *et al.* (2001). Regional brain metabolic changes in patients with major depression treated with either paroxetine or interpersonal therapy: Preliminary findings. *Archives of General Psychiatry*, 58, 631–640.

DeRubeis, R.J., Siegle, G.J. and Hollon, S.D. (2008). Cognitive therapy versus medication for depression: Treatment outcomes and neural mechanisms. *Nature Reviews Neuroscience*, 9, 788–796.

Drevets, W.C., Price, J.C., Kupfer, D.J., Kinahan, P., Lopresti, B., Holt, D. *et al.* (1999). PET measures of amphetamine-induced dopamine release in ventral versus dorsal striatum. *Neuropsychopharmacology*, 21, 694–709.

Felmingham, K., Kemp, A., Williams, L., Das, P., Hughes, G., Peduto, A. *et al.* (2007). Changes in anterior cingulate and amygdala after cognitive behavior therapy of post-traumatic stress. *Psychological Science*, 18, 127–129.

Frewen, P.A., Dozois, D.J.A. and Lanius, R.A. (2008). Neuroimaging studies of psychological interventions for mood and anxiety disorders: Empirical and methodological review. *Clinical Psychology Review*, 28, 228–246.

Furmark, T., Tillfors, M., Marteinsdottir, I., Fischer, H., Pissiota, A., Langstrom, B. *et al.* (2002). Common changes in cerebral blood flow in patients with social phobia treated with citalopram or cognitive-behavioral therapy. *Archives of General Psychiatry*, 59, 425–433.

Gabbard, G. (2000). A neurobiologically informed perspective on psychotherapy. *BJP*, 177, 117–122.

Goldapple, K., Segal, Z., Garson, C., Lau, M., Bieling, P., Kennedy, S. *et al.* (2004). Modulation of cortical-limbic pathways in major depression: Treatment-specific effects of cognitive behavior therapy. *Archives of General Psychiatry*, 61, 34_41.

Gordon, E. (ed.) (2000). *Integrative Neuroscience*. Newark, NJ: Harwood Academic Publishers.

Hirvonen, J., Hietala, J., Kajander, J., Markkula, J., Rasi-Hakala, H., Salminen, J. *et al.* (2011). Effects of antidepressant drug treatment and psychotherapy on striatal and thalamic dopamine D2/3 receptors in major depressive disorder studied with [11C]raclopride PET. *Journal of Psychopharmacology*, 25(10), 1329–1336.

Hollon, S.D, Shelton, R.C., Wisniewski, S., Warden, D., Biggs, M.M., Friedman, E.S. *et al.* (2006). Presenting characteristics of depressed outpatients as a function of recurrence: Preliminary findings from the STAR*D clinical trial. *Journal of Psychiatric Research*, 40(1), 59–69.

Kandel, E. (1998). A new intellectual framework for psychiatry. *American Journal of Psychiatry*, 155, 457–469.

Karlsson, H., Hirvonen, J., Kajander, J., Lepola, A., Markkula, J., Rasi-Hakala, H. *et al.* (2010). Psychotherapy induces proliferation of 5-HT-1A receptors in human brain. *Psychological Medicine* 40(3), 523–528.

Lai, C., Daini, S., Calcagni, M.L., Bruno, I. and DeRisio, S. (2007). Neural correlates of psycho-dynamic psychotherapy in borderline disorders: A pilot investigation. *Psychotherapy and Psychosomatics*, 76, 403–405.

Lehto, S.M., Tolmunen, T., Joensuu, M., Saarinen, P.I., Valkonen-Korhonen, M., Vanninen, R. *et al.* (2008). Changes in midbrain serotonin transporter availability in atypically depressed subjects after one year of psychotherapy. *Progress in Neuro-Psychopharmacology & Biological Psychiatry*, 31, 229–237.

Martin, S.D., Martin, E., Rai, S.S., Richardson, M.A. and Royall, R. (2001). Brain blood flow changes in depressed patients treated with interpersonal psychotherapy or venlafaxine hydrochoride: Preliminary findings. *Archives of General Psychiatry*, 58, 641–648.

Moses-Kolko, E.L., Price, J.C., Thase, M.E., Meltzer, C.C., Kupfer, D.J., Mathis, C.A. *et al.* (2007). Measurement of 5-HT1A receptor binding in depressed adults before and after antidepressant drug treatment using positron emission tomography and [11C]WAY-100635. *Synpase*, 61(7), 523–530.

Nakatani, E., Nakgawa, A., Ohara, Y., Goto, S., Uozumi, N., Iwakiri, M. *et al.* (2003). Effects of behavior therapy on regional cerebral blood flow in obsessive–compulsive disorder. *Psychiatry Research: Neuroimaging*, 124, 113–120.

Paquette, V., Lévesque, J., Mensour, B., Leroux, J.-M., Beaudoin, G., Bourgouin, P. *et al.* (2003). 'Change the mind and you change the brain': Effects of cognitive-behavioral therapy on the neural correlates of spider phobia. *Neuroimage*, 18, 401–409.

Parsey, R.V., Olvet, D.M., Oquendo, M.A., Huang, Y.Y., Ogden, R.T. and Mann, J.J. (2006). Higher 5-HT1A receptor binding potential during a major depressive episode predicts poor treatment response: Preliminary data from a naturalistic study. *Neuropsychopharmacology*, 31, 1745–1749.

Praško, J., Horácek, J., Zálesky, R., Kopecek, M., Novák, T., Pašková, B. *et al.* (2004). The change of regional brain metabolism (18FDG PET) in panic disorder during the treatment with cognitive behavioral therapy or antidepressants. *Neuroendocrinology Letters*, 5(3), 340–348.

Sargent, P.A., Husted, K.K., Bench, C.J., Rabiner, E.A., Messa, C., Meyer, J. *et al.* (2000). Brain serotonin1A receptor binding measured by positron emission tomography with [11C]WAY-100635. *Archives of General Psychiatry* 57(2), 174–180.

Schnell, K. and Herpertz, S.C. (2007). Effects of dialectical-behavior therapy on the neural correlates of affective hyperarousal in borderline personality disorder. *Journal of Psychiatric Research*, 41, 837–847.

Schwartz, J.M., Stoessel, P.W., Baxter, L.R., Martin, K.M. and Phelps, M.E. (1996). Systematic changes in cerebral glucose metabolic rate after successful behavior modification treatment of obsessive–compulsive disorder. *Archives of General Psychiatry*, 53, 109–113.

Sherin, J.E. and Nemeroff, C.B. (2011). Post-traumatic stress disorder: The neurobiological impact of psychological trauma. *Dialogues in Clinical Neuroscience*, 13(3), 263–278.

Straube, T., Glauer, M., Dilger, S., Mentzel, H.-J. and Miltner,W.H.R. (2006). Effects of cognitive-behavioral therapy on brain activation in specific phobia. *Neuroimage*, 29, 125–135.

Tamietto, M. and de Gelder, B. (2010). Neural bases of the non-conscious perception of emotional signals. *Nature Reviews Neuroscience*, 11, 697–709.

Vytal, K. and Hamann, S. (2010). Neuroimaging support for discrete neural correlates of basic emotions: A voxel-based meta-analysis. *Journal of Cognitive Neuroscience*, 22(12), 2864–2885.

Chapter 14

Research and the future of phototherapy and therapeutic photography

Del Loewenthal

This book is largely about developments in the therapeutic use of photographs. Photography and therapeutic photography, having initially established themselves in Europe and subsequently developed more in North America, have now seen a European resurgence. These recent, mainly European developments can be seen to have been coupled with the explosion of digital photography that has enabled the digital image to be accessible to the majority. The particular focus of this final chapter is on research where different methods are examined and illustrated. However, before considering research into phototherapy and therapeutic photography, and concluding with thoughts on the future, this chapter starts with a review of the preceding chapters.

Part I of this book has described various theoretical developments: after first in Chapter 1 introducing phototherapy and therapeutic photography in a digital age (Loewenthal), Ulla Halkola in Chapter 2 explored from a unique Finnish context a photograph as a therapeutic experience. Here, the author, who has done so much to galvanise phototherapy in Europe, puts the case for the role of photographs in psychotherapy being functional, where the actual therapy is based on the professional skills of the psychotherapist, acquired within his/her specific frame of reference.

This was followed in Chapter 3 by Terry Dennett's excellent account of some of the approaches of the pioneering phototherapist Jo Spence's camera therapy, developed as part of her solo cancer survival programme under what Terry describes as 'the isolated, poverty stricken and difficult conditions she found herself in after her cancer diagnosis and treatment'.

Next, in Chapter 4, Mark Wheeler provides a central chapter that focuses on development in our photographic cultural practices as a result of our digital age offering insight into the psychological dimensions of making and viewing smartphone and online gallery images and how these affect therapeutic processes, whether explicitly acknowledged or not.

In Chapter 5 Mike Simmonds explores with us his original approaches to interpretation and healing through the creative practices of photography. The term 'a creative photographic approach' is used here to describe a method whereby individuals formerly engage in the process of reflection, interpretation and expression of personal experience, through the creation of original photographic artwork.

The second part of the book detailed different practices starting, in Chapter 6, with Rosy Martin (who is one of the original innovators and whose current work is one of the strongest European influences) describing how she evolved re-enactment photography. The therapeutic gaze, the performativity within the re-enactment phototherapy session, the importance of embodiment and transformation and the notion of the process as a form of creative adult play are explored in this chapter.

Then, in Chapter 7, Del Loewenthal shows how he uses photographs within more traditional counselling and psychotherapy, illustrating this with four young people he was asked to work with in a school. The chapter also outlines some advantages and disadvantages of using photographs in this way. This collaborative case study is returned to below when examining research tools for evaluating phototherapy.

In Chapter 8 Cristina Nuñez explains how she has developed her internationally recognised self-portrait approach. Cristina suggests that, by objectifying our 'dark side' in a photograph, we can separate ourselves from what we dislike and open up a space for catharsis and renewal. In this chapter Cristina argues that the self-portrait empowers us through forcing us into the now; it can help us perceive and express our essential humanity in a photograph.

Chapter 9 arises from conversations between Carmine Parella and Del Loewenthal regarding Carmine's pioneering work in creating community phototherapy, which can contribute to improved mental health and promote a better integration of the person who is the psychiatric patient. Drawing from a wide range of influences, Carmine shows how phototherapy is a medium to activate the healing process of both the individuals and the community of which they are a part.

Next, in Chapter 10, also from Italy, Rodolfo de Bernart shares his considerable experience in working with photographs in family therapy. Drawing from a systemic relational approach, the author explains how he uses the photographic genogram in practice.

This is followed in Chapter 11 with Julia Winckler who provides a stimulating account of how she has been able to witness students on a BA degree in Photography use photography in ways that have been cathartic and sometimes therapeutic for them.

Then, in Chapter 12, Alexander Kopytin examines the use of photographs as part of art therapy and describes research on this undertaken in Russia and the UK, which sheds light on why art therapy has yet to take more advantage of the digital age.

Finally, Hasse Karlsson in Chapter 13 expertly argues, given so much has been claimed about neurosciences, that, although it would be plausible to study the neurobiological effects of phototherapy, because of the use of visual material and potential meaningful motor activity in the therapy process, the research into this area is currently lacking.

It is hoped, therefore, that this book will provide the basis for various professions to develop their practices in therapeutically using digital photography. However, before concluding, the place of research needs to be considered (this aspect of this chapter has been developed from http://phototherapyeurope.utu.fi/photoeurope_handbook.pdf). In particular, it would appear not only that the digital use of photographs needs to catch up with other psychotherapeutic research now being conducted, but also that digital photography can provide a new form of research as a cultural practice.

Research

While Part I of this book was entitled 'Introduction: theories and approaches' and Part II 'The use of photographs in various practices', most of the theory chapters had elements of practice in them and vice versa. The same is true with the research that is in the title of this book's concluding Part III. Developments in research have already been mentioned and indeed in this final part of the book the preceding Chapter13 by Hasse Karlsson has importantly reviewed existing research in terms of phototherapy and neuroscience, where much is expected although too much may be claimed for currently.

What may now be required is that phototherapy and therapeutic phototherapy is subjected to randomised control trials (RCTs) although the use of RCTs is increasingly questionable for exploring the effectiveness of psychological therapies in general (Guy *et al.*, 2012). They are, however, still regarded as the main legitimising instruments in our current dominant culture.

An interesting important development is in the field of visual research (e.g. Banks, 2001) although currently it is still primarily seen as an adjunct to existing more traditional research methods. There is a particular need for qualitative research on the therapeutic use of photographs in a similar way to that now being conducted in counselling and psychotherapy, where approaches are used to aggregate primarily qualitative data from interviews using such methods as grounded theory, phenomenological research, discourse analysis, heuristic research, case study methods, etc. (see, e.g. Loewenthal, 2007; Loewenthal and Winter, 2007).

What is research?

Research can be considered as a cultural practice (fashioning and fashioned). Currently, it can be understood variously as an original investigation undertaken in order to gain knowledge and understanding (RAE, 2008), or an attempt to find out information in a systemic manner (Princeton, Wordnet Web, 2006).

In the broadest sense of the word, research is taken to be any gathering of data, information and facts for the advancement of knowledge. There again, scientific research can be seen as performing a methodical study in order to form a hypothesis or answer a specific question (www.experiment-resources.com) and be reproducible.

What is psychotherapeutic research?

Psychotherapeutic research has, as of late, been involved in examining processes and outcomes with an increasing interest from government and the profession in so-called 'evidence-based practice'. There exists an abundance of qualitative and quantitative approaches to psychotherapeutic research, though all have their limitations as well as strengths as it could be argued that the practice itself is the research (Lees and Freshwater, 2008).

Qualitative and quantitative research

Quantitative research is more associated with 'positivism' and is concerned with counting and measuring things, producing in particular estimates of averages and differences between groups, whereas qualitative research has its roots in social science and is more concerned with understanding why people behave as they do: their knowledge, attitudes, beliefs, fears, etc.

One of the aims of positivistic research is to discover natural and general laws and to enable people to predict and control events. This type of research generally assumes that reality is objectively given and can be described by measurable properties that are independent of the researcher. Conversely, interpretative research methods are designed to help researchers understand people and the social/cultural contexts within which they live by describing meaningful interactions.

Phototherapy, however, provides the opportunity to consider not only these traditional research approaches but also the growing field of visual research.

What is visual research?

Visual research uses both researcher-created data and respondent-created data, which could be compared with phototherapy and therapeutic photography, respectively. A prominent visual method is the use of photo elicitation, which would appear similar to projective techniques of phototherapy. However visual research is still considered a rather dispersed and ill-defined domain (Prosser, 2006).

Strands of visual research

There are two main strands to visual research in the social sciences (Banks, 2001):

- the creation of images by the social researcher to document or subsequently analyse aspects of social life and social interaction;
- the collection and study of images produced or consumed.

Using visual methods

Banks (2001) considers visual research methodologies should only be used as part of a more general package of research methodologies and the need for them should be indicated by the research itself. While psychotherapeutic researchers try and identify the research questions that lie behind the specific investigation, visual research methodologies are often used in an exploratory way (to discover what the researcher has not initially considered).

It is also important to note that the meaning of images changes over time as they are viewed by different audiences. Similarly, the meaning intended by the photo-therapeutic researcher when creating the image may not be the meaning that is read by the viewer. (Photographs are also used differently by phototherapeutic researchers who adopt either a positivistic or interpretative approach.)

Questions for the researcher carrying out research into phototherapy or therapeutic photography

Here are some further questions the phototherapeutic researcher might find useful to hold in mind:

- Who is the researcher?
- Is the client the researcher?
- Is the phototherapist the researcher?
- Is it collaborative research?
- Should the phototherapist be a practitioner researcher?

- Should the researcher be independent of all of the above roles?
- What is the reason for the research?
- Is the researcher interested in a positivistic or interpretative approach to research?

It would appear vital therefore that phototherapeutic researchers need both to make clear their position and to have thought about the above questions, before the research is carried out.

Examples of possible small-scale research projects within phototherapy and therapeutic photography

There is now an urgent need for research to be carried out on phototherapy and therapeutic photography, not only in terms of neuroscience (as described in the previous chapter) and if the funding is available in terms of RCTs (despite their limitations), but also in terms of the considerable practice-based research on professional postgraduate psychological therapies training programmes. Examples of the potential infinite number of research project areas could include:

- the representation of experience in phototherapy, with particular reference to mothers of children with a significant language delay;
- questioning the phototherapist as practitioner–researcher: asking questions in the therapeutic hour;
- the phototherapist's experience of working with despair in a UK prison setting;
- exploring the experience of trainee phototherapists working in organisations offering a time limited service;
- exploring phototherapists' experience of medical model thinking when working in both primary care and private practice.

In considering the relative merits of quantitative, qualitative and visual research, an example is now provided of research carried out to evaluate phototherapy as part of counselling and psychotherapy, previously given in Chapter 7. (Accounts of this work can be found in Uncertain States, www.uncertainstates.com/#11-essay-del-loewenthal.)

Phototherapy research in action

I would now like to present one example of a comparison of quantitative, qualitative and visual research where photographs have been used as part of counselling and psychotherapy. What follows should also be read in conjunction with Chapter 7, which describes four young people with whom the author was asked to work in a particular school.

The purpose of this 'collective case study' was to explore and, in turn, evaluate *talking pictures therapy*, which is the name the author has given to the use of photographs within psychotherapy and counselling, here as a form of counselling in a UK school setting with four children. The therapeutic work, which forms the data of this study, was carried out in a UK school. The children (Key Stage 3 to Key Stage 4), were informed that *talking pictures therapy* normally involved up to six sessions of one-to-one therapy with the purpose of enabling them to express and explore, in the therapy and potentially through photographs, aspects of their lives they would like to talk about.

Participants

The four children attended a school on the south coast of England in an area of relative deprivation, and ranged between twelve and fourteen years in age. The local community and in turn, the school was made up of a large proportion of white, working-class children with some children from Eastern Europe and Southeast Asia. The school is a secondary school with attached sixth form. This school, through the Special Needs Co-ordinators (SENCO), prioritised four children for the *talking pictures therapy*. These children, with the permission of their parents/guardians agreed to have the therapy and for it to be used for this research.

Method

Qualitative and quantitative methods, alongside using the children's choice of photographs in terms of visual research, were used. With regard to qualitative research, a case study method was utilised as the research approach based on Greenwood and Loewenthal (2005, 2007), where Husserlian bracketing is combined with hermeneutics, strongly influenced by Bleicher's (1980) work on the phenomenology of Heidegger and Gadamer. We, in turn, developed this further from Yin's (1984) consideration of case study method as a means of generalisation. A collective case study sample, including four children was chosen on Yin's (2003) recommendation that conclusions are often considered stronger in multiple case analyses in comparison to single case study analysis.

The case study method sought to reveal multiple meanings by a process of searching and then re-searching the therapist's account of the therapy. This research followed the four stages of a phenomenological-hermeneutic case study method (Greenwood and Loewenthal, 2005), both where the number of stages depends on the amount of 're-searching' for meanings that takes place and where there is no limit to this part of the process.

The case study emerges as a consequence of following the stages outlined in Figure 14.1 and represents the final stage of the method. Chapter 7 actually provides the four individual case studies and initial analysis along with the photographs chosen by the children.

A suitable quantitative assessment set: PHQ-9 (for depression), GAD-7 (for anxiety) and the Improving Access to Psychological Therapies (IAPT) Phobia Scale (IAPT minimum data set) and the popular overall measure CORE-10 were assumed to be the most common methods currently used to evaluate therapeutic effectiveness in the UK. The author also wished to consider the 'progress' of the therapy through client's choice of photographs and the individual meanings projected onto them (described more in Chapter 7).

With regard to evaluating the effectiveness of *talking pictures therapy*, alongside the descriptions from the clients of their chosen photographs (given in Chapter 7), the quantitative measures were recorded at the beginning and end of each client's course of therapy.

Stage 1

Begin with the therapy that forms the basis of the observation.

Stage 2

A therapist makes a written account of what took place in a session soon after the meeting (preferably directly afterwards).

Stage 3

These early reflections are subject to the considerable influence of the therapist's pre-understandings, perhaps in terms of their cultural background and gender that are inherent in any account of human observation. The therapist's supervisor can exert a potential influence by being involved in a process of reflection on the data from the sessions. At this stage the initial data will have been subject to a re-interpretation so allowing for additional meanings to emerge out from the influence of the pre-understandings.

Stage 4

The researcher will subject this therapeutic account to further scrutiny when writing up these findings in the form of a report providing a further opportunity for meanings to emerge and the possibilities to be explored.

Figure 14.1 The four stages of a phenomenological-hermeneutic case study method.

Results

Each of the four individual cases will be described, outlining the use of photographs as process and outcome alongside the pre and post therapy assessment set: PHQ-9, GAD-7 and CORE-10 data.

Below is an exploration of this quantitative data, which should be combined with the qualitative data/analysis of Charlotte, Winston, Linda and Amanda (the names have been changed) as presented in Chapter 7.

Charlotte

I repeated the PHQ-9, GAD-7 and CORE-10 measures that I had undertaken at the start of the sessions (Figure 14.2). The PHQ-9 showed the greatest movement with a score of 13 at the start (indicating moderate depression) and a score of 8 in the last one (indicating mild depression). Within this, there was a significant shift with regard to whether over the previous two weeks she had 'little pleasure or interest in doing anything'. This had moved from the previous 'nearly every day' to 'not at all'. Charlotte said 'I can be bothered to do things and I have been getting out a bit more.' There was also a change regarding 'poor appetite or overeating', which had moved from 'more than half the day' to 'not at all'. She said, 'I no longer need to keep eating and, look, my clothes no longer fit!' (showing me the belt now gathering up her skirt and the looseness of her buttoned blazer). She also saw herself as not being 'fidgety at all', whereas she had previously said she found this 'more than half the day'.

The GAD-7 score remained at 9, both at the start and end of therapy (where 5 and 10 are the cut-off points for mild and moderate anxiety). Regarding the CORE-10 measure, she scored 11 at the commencement of therapy and 9 at the end. Here, a score

Evaluative Measurement Tool	Scores	Charlotte	Winston	Linda	Amanda
GAD-7 (Anxiety)	Pre	9	0	2	4.5
	Post	9	0	0	4
PHQ-9 (Depression)	Pre	13	5	2	5
	Post	8	7	0	4
CORE-10	Pre	11	8	8	12
	Post	9	14	4	6

Figure 14.2 GAD-7, PHQ-9 and CORE-10 pre and post scores.

Note: The names of the children and other content have been changed for reasons of confidentiality.

of 11 or above is regarded as being in the clinical range, and the lower boundary of the 'mild clinical' level. One particular change here was that, over the past week, 'unwanted images and memories' had been distressing her 'only occasionally', whereas, at the start of therapy, she had seen them as 'occurring often'. She did, however, report difficulty in getting to sleep from previously only 'occasionally' to 'constant', which she put this down to having to sleep in the chair in the living room where her Gran did the same, with her Aunt sleeping in the bedroom – all this she spoke of for the first time in this last session. Charlotte did say that it looked like they were going to move to a larger place, so, for the first time she was going to have her own bedroom – though she was told they would not be able to initially afford a bed for her.

Winston

When it came to the evaluation questions (Figure 14.2), Winston had scored 5 on the PHQ-9 scale measuring depression at the start of the therapy, and 7 at the end of his last session, the main change being that he now felt he had trouble concentrating on things. This would indicate mild to moderate depression. On the GAD-7 scores, which attempt to measure anxiety and severity, he scored 0 pre and post therapy. Regarding CORE-10, his initial score was 8, and his final score was 14. Changes here were an increase in 'feeling depressed or unhappy', though he did now feel that he had 'someone to turn to for support'. Winston very happily accepted the gift of the game 'Connect 4' to play with his sisters.

Linda

The PHQ-9 score was initially 2, and in the final session, 0, which would indicate no depression. With the GAD-7, regarding anxiety (Figure 14.2), Linda again scored 2, and subsequently 0. With regard to CORE-10, Linda initially scored 8, and in the last session scored 4. Here the two changes were that over the week prior to the last session Linda felt she had 'someone to turn to for support when needed' 'most or all of the time' rather than 'sometimes'. Linda also felt 'able to cope when things go wrong' 'sometimes' rather than 'not at all'.

However, in the final session, I explained to Linda that I would like to ask her some questions as we had done when we first met. Linda responded to them but in a very automated way, as if she was experienced in evading any questions: replying 'not at all' to most questions. I said 'I might as well not ask you these questions?' 'Yes,' Linda replied with one of her smiles.

Amanda

With regard to the before and after evaluations, the PHQ-9 gave a score of 5 at the start of the first session and a 4 at the last session, which indicated a small reduction in mild depression (Figure 14.2). With regard to the GAD-7 representing anxiety, her initial score was 4.5, which reduced to 4, again suggesting slightly reduced mild anxiety. Of particular interest here was the IAPT Phobia Scale where regarding the extent to which she would now avoid 'certain situations because of a fear of particular objects or activities', this changed from 'always avoided' to between 'would not avoid' and 'slightly avoid'.

With regard to CORE-10, her score on commencement of therapy was 12 and in the final session, 6. This is where 11 or above is regarded as 'the lower boundary of the lower clinical range'. Changes here included that she now felt that she 'often' rather than 'sometimes' felt she had someone to turn to for support when she needed it. Also, Amanda reported that she had both less difficulty getting to sleep from 'most to all of the time' to 'sometimes' and less 'unwanted images or memories distressing her', which moved from 'sometimes' to 'not at all'.

Discussion

With regard to the evaluative data measures (see Figure 14.2), three clients (Charlotte, Amanda and Linda) saw a decrease in the PHQ-9 score between pre and post evaluation, alongside a decrease in CORE-10 score. Further, both Amanda and Linda scored higher on GAD-7 at pre than post evaluation. With regard to Winston, both PHQ-9 and CORE-10 scores increased between pre and post therapy. The evaluation tools PHQ-9, CORE-10, GAD-7 and the IAPT Phobia Scale were used as they are the main culturally accepted approaches to evaluation in the UK. It was found that they can, however, work against more phenomenological approaches to therapy. For example, the asking of questions can produce an expectation that the therapist is then going to solve the problem, as in, for example, a medical model, which therefore only suits a particular type of therapy. There again it was found that having such a framework that starts with asking questions can be a way for both clients and therapists of temporarily reducing the anxiety of 'two frightened people in a room' (Bion, 1990: 5).

Again, if the evaluation is done by someone other than the therapist (which can be seen to have potentially a less damaging effect on the therapeutic relationship), there is the further concern as to the client's experience of having to speak, possibly for the first time, with one person and then another. Further, in that all four clients appeared to respond more thoughtfully to CORE-10 than PHQ-9 or GAD-7, perhaps as CORE-10 was the last questionnaire, it was possible that they had gained more practice.

Using photographs as a potential evaluation of therapeutic change may, as I have tried to describe here and in Chapter 7, be a beneficial and complementary if not alternative approach to evaluation approaches such as GAD-7, PHQ-9 and CORE-10. Such approaches that allow the photograph of the disembodied client to come to mind have the advantage of, phenomenologically or post-phenomenologically, allowing something to emerge that is not predefined by, for example, a medicalised model of diagnosis and treatment, and hence, starting with a predetermined notion of, for example, clinical success. This change in language through digital photography changes culturally what, and how, we experience, in terms of not only being able to look back on such websites as Facebook, at what photos we and others posted of ourselves, but also the very nature of our experiences. Perhaps this change in our way of perceiving and thinking will be even greater than when photography, at the start of the twentieth century, changed the perception and thinking of so many people including Sigmund Freud (Bergstein, 2010).

The future

We might therefore expect to see in our twenty-first century both the increasing use of photographs in counselling and psychotherapy, and art therapy (and other arts therapies) using photographs more creatively, rather than just recording various stages of development of another art medium that appears to be more of what has previously happened. Photographs are already increasingly used in education and particularly in reminiscence therapy with older people and those with Alzheimer's disease (Krauss, 2009). It is also expected that there will be further growth of new forms of therapy using photography where the traditional position taken up by therapists becomes fundamentally different as in, for example, working alongside each other with a computer. I am also working in prisons, using photographs in a set of photocards I call 'Talking Pictures' as a way of enabling storytelling. It is further expected there will be rapid developments in video. It is also predicted that there will be a growing use of photographs in organisational and individual development, including management development. For example, I am working with a large pharmaceutical company exploring how photographs can help senior engineers envision how production facilities need to be developed; in another case how a team describes what it has become and what it would like to be; and in another organisation how managers describe their current level of a particular skill. . . . The possibilities are endless but the idea that a digital photograph can describe what is otherwise difficult to put into words remains the same.

We might also expect that there will be a growing use of group phototherapy. A recent meta-analysis of the effectiveness of creative arts therapies (Stamp *et al.*, 2009) suggest that what is therapeutically important is for clients to carry out a creative act and share it in a group. Digital images lend themselves particularly well to this and it is predicted that this will be a popular, cost-effective, therapeutic development.

Overall, we would expect that digital photographs will be used more extensively, not only in terms of, for example, digital storytelling, which is becoming available to many schoolchildren, but also in a wide range of professional practices and cultural activities including developments in social media. This will lead to new theories that will both be increasingly researched and lead in themselves to new research methodologies using digital photography.

What is clear is that the therapeutic power of the photograph to evoke powerful past emotions will continue and be creatively available digitally on an unprecedented scale.

Examples of this in terms of digital photography theory, practice and research have been provided throughout the book and more classical examples are provided in the Prologue by British pioneer Keith Kennedy and now in the Epilogue by the Israeli phototherapist, Brigitte Anor.

It is also expected that the therapeutic use of photographs will increasingly be used as an agent for social change (see for example www.photovoice.org) and in programmes for the psychological therapies (as I and others are currently providing in counselling, psychotherapy and art psychotherapy) both for trainees and existing practitioners – helping them to get up to date with what their prospective clients are often already familiar!

References

Banks, M. (2001). *Visual Methods in Social Research*. London: Sage.

Bergstein, M. (2010). *Mirrors of Memory: Freud, photography and the history of art*. London: Cornell University Press.

Bion, W.R. (1990). *Brazilian Lectures*. London: Karnac.

Bleicher, J. (1980). *Contemporary Hermeneutics*. London: Routledge & Kegan Paul.

Greenwood, D. and Loewenthal, D. (2005). Case study as a means of researching social work and improving practitioner education. *Journal of Social Work Practice*, 19(2) 181–193.

Greenwood, D. and Loewenthal, D. (2007). A case of case study method: The possibility of psychotherapy with a person diagnosed with dementia. In: Loewenthal, D. (ed.), *Case Studies in Relational Research* (pp. 88–113). Basingstoke: Palgrave Macmillan.

Guy, A., Loewenthal, D., Thomas, R. and Stephenson, S. (2012). Scrutinising NICE: The impact of the National Institute for Health and Clinical Excellence Guidelines on the provision of counselling and psychotherapy in primary care in the UK. *Psychodynamic Practice*, 18(1), 25–50.

Krauss, D.A. (2009). Phototherapy and reminiscence with the elderly: Photo-reminiscence. Unpublished paper given at the 2009 International Symposium on PhotoTherapy and Therapeutic Photography, Turku, Finland, 11 June.

Lees, J. and Freshwater, D. (2008). *Practitioner-Based Research: Power, discourse, and transformation*. London: Karnac Books.

Loewenthal, D. (2007). *Case Studies in Relational Research*. Basingstoke: Palgrave Macmillan.

Loewenthal, D. and Winter, D. (eds) (2007). *What is Psychotherapeutic Research?* London: Karnac Books.

Princeton, Wordnet Web (2006). Available from: http://wordnet.princeton.edu/perl/webwn?s= word-you-want (University of Oxford, Frascati definition) (accessed April 2011).

Prosser, J. (2006). The darker side of visual research. In: Hamilton, P. (ed.), *Visual Research Methods*. London: Sage.

RAE (2008). Research Assessment Exercise. Available from: www.rae.ac.uk (accessed April 2011).

Stamp, R., Stephenson, S. and Loewenthal, D. (2009). *Report on the Evidence Base for Creative Therapies: A systematic review*. London: UKCP.

Yin, R.K. (1984). *Case Study Research: Design and methods* (1st edn). Beverly Hills, CA: Sage.

Yin, R.K. (2003). *Case Study Research: Design and methods* (3rd edn). London: Sage.

Epilogue
Hands up – surrender to subjectivity

Brigitte Anor

I was recently startled by the graphic similarity of two famous photographs. Two young men – almost in the same pose – show us the palms of their hands, exposing a very intimate, vulnerable part of their body.

When I write 'I was startled', I am describing a potent, visceral jolt, and I am reminded of the phenomenon that Roland Barthes[1] refers to as *punctum*, similar to a 'knife blow', causing us to freeze in front of certain pictures. In this instant, we become emotionally immobilised.

While, on the one hand, I was fascinated by the graphic similarity of the two figures, I was also disturbed by the sharp difference in their historical context. I was also aware of the powerful emotions each picture evoked in me. I was then driven by the desire to render these figures into their most simple graphic form, into a schematic shadow, to search for their contours (see Photo 15.1).

In order to trace these lines, I needed to photocopy the photographs. I usually photocopy documents at the neighbourhood store and carried the photographs there in my hand in order to get started on this project. To my astonishment, the storekeeper categorically refused to serve me.

Before I had the opportunity to offer any explanation, he called to his wife who had been chatting with a passer-by on the sidewalk and they broke into lively discussion. 'Who dares to even place these two photographs side by side?' they asked, furious and blameful. I left the shop silently, thinking I understood the reason for their anger.

Only later, while relating this incident to a friend I had to provide a verbal description as I did not have the photographs with me. I then realised that these few words were needed to provide a narrative of the pictures; however, in doing so, my description had also offered an interpretation.

The first image is the famous photograph of a child from the Warsaw ghetto in 1942. He raises his arms, surrendering to the gun of a Nazi soldier (see Photo 15.2). For many people, this photograph depicts the vulnerability of the Jewish people and represents the six million victims of the 'Shoah'. This photograph was selected by the Italian newspaper *Corriere della Sera* as the most powerful picture of the twentieth century.

The second photograph is more recent. It is the photograph of a young Palestinian proudly showing his bloodied red hands to the crowd, after the lynching of two Israeli soldiers who lost their way and accidentally ended up in the Palestinian territory where they were beaten to death. This photograph (not shown here) appeared on the first page of Israeli newspapers and even made the cover of *Time* magazine in October 2000.[2]

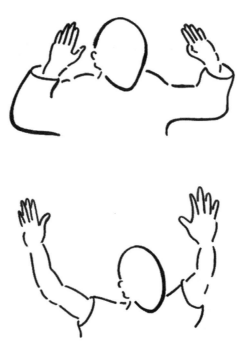

Photo 15.1 Hands up! (Anor).

At first, I quite naively believed that the act of looking at a photograph was a passive process, where each image could be read objectively. What I had not realised was that, in the role of viewer, I had taken on an active role and had in fact become the bearer or creator of meaning. An interpreter.

While looking at these photographs separately, something reached down and touched my personal storehouse of memories – like an invitation to dance a duet with the image to the rhythm of my own connection to the photographed event. My belonging to both of these pages of history was the music that was accompanying me. In fact, I was not even aware of who had been leading this eternal dance. Was it me who was constructing the image or was it the image that had constructed me?

However, by deliberately choosing to put these two pictures side by side, my role had become active: I had become the choreographer. I had created a more complex dance, a macabre and tragic ballet. In the process of placing these two pictures side by side, I had somehow become the storyteller. Still, there is a great deal of ambiguity in viewing these two photographs together. There will always be an open space for interpretation. My story might not be the one you might tell.

This scene depicts two young boys raising their hands up.

Is there a similarity between the two antagonists? Are we contrasting them?
Victim and executioner? Or maybe two victims?
Who has a monopoly over suffering?
What is strength? What is weakness?

Photo 15.2 Jewish boy in the Warsaw Ghetto (courtesy of the United States Holocaust Memorial Museum Photo Archives).

My questions are endless . . .

I took a closer look at these two characters: during the Holocaust my father was the same age as the little boy in the photo. He was Jewish just like him. My son is now more or less the same age as the young Palestinian. Despite the fact that he is serving in the Israeli Army and carries a gun, in my eyes, he is a victim as well.

Is it me as the daughter and the mother who pays the price? More than half a century separates these two photographic events but I am the link in the chain that connects them. How can I know anything about my own life story and the part that these two photographed images have already played in its construction?

Everything seems confused. Yet it has now become clear to me that it was not by chance that I chose these two images. In outlining the contours of these pictures, I had encountered the shadow of my past, the shadow of my life.

Notes

1 Barthes, R. (1990) *La chambre claire*. Paris: Gallimard-Seuil.
2 See www.crownheights/info/media/30/20111016/ramallah%203.png.

Index

Page locators for photographs and diagrams are in *italic*.

ethics 154
EU funding 82, 107
events, perceptions of 28
experience 26
'Experimental archaeology: within and
    beyond the archive' (course) 128–141
'Exploring and developing the personal and
    the professional as the practice of ethics
    through photography' (Loewenthal) 7
external world, perception of 50

Facebook 69, 79, 175; *see also* social
    networking
facial expressions 23–24
facilitators, art-therapists as 99
Fadiga, L. 23
families: death 59–60, 136–137; separation
    95, 134–135; *see also* significant others
family albums 7; as archives 58, 129–130;
    as diaries 24–25, 70–71, 79; informing
    relationships 45; and letters 134–135;
    mutilated 138–139; re-photographed
    133–134; *see also* memories
family histories 53–54, 125
family mementoes 136–137
'Family photos and movies' (Friedman)
    123
family therapy 120–121, 123–124
'family wounds' 125
fantasies 41
Fantômes (Calle) 129
Farge, Arlette 135
fathers 84, 90, 139–140
Ferrari, Stefano 96, 99, 104
Feuerbach, L. 100
films 32
financial resources 154
Finland 5, 7, 8, 162
First International Phototherapy Symposium
    5
Fisher, Helen 48
5-HT1A receptors 162–163
Flickr 69; *see also* social networking
fluoxetine medication 161, 162–163
Flusser, Vilem 144
Fogassi, L. 23
fones 40
fotos 40
Foucault, Michel 72, 130–131
found images 70
Fredrickson, B. L. 57

Freire, Paulo 114, 117
Freud, Sigmund 5, 22, 100, 175
Friedman, J. 123
Fryrear, J. L. 145
functional classifications 22
functional magnetic resonance imaging
    (fMRI) 23, 159

GAD-7 scores *84*, 92, 171–175, *173*
Gadamer, H-G. 171
Gallese, V. 23
Garson, C. 161
gazing 72–73, 95
Gell, A. 99
'gender stories' 145
genealogy approaches 131
genograms 123–124, 126–127
geographical settings 56
geometric relationships 50
gestalts 46–47, 73, 78
Gipsy communities 111
God 100
Godard, Jean-Luc 129
Goldapple, K. 161
grandmothers 135–136
Graphic elaborations of a photographic
    technique (Kopytin) *146*, *147*
'graphic elaboration' technique 145
Greenwood, D. 171
grief *see* bereavement; death
'Group Camera' 31
group phototherapy 175
guts, source of creativity 97–99

Hafner, Katie 132
Halkola, Ulla x–xi, xiv, xv, 13, 16, 19,
    21–30, *28*, 87, *88*, *91*, 166
Hands up! (Anor) *178*
Happich, Carl 34
hara (stomach) 97
Hart, D. A. 57
healing 109, 114; *see also* self-healing
heart, symbolizing memory 55
Heidegger, M. 171
Hemingway, E. 101
Henderson Psychiatric Hospital 31
Henley, David 147
hermeneutics 171
heroes/heroic 101–102
Hesse, Hermann 97
'higher self' 99–100, 103